To Harvard Yenching Institute
Library

Sociology and Social Change in Korea

by

Man-Gap Lee

Seoul National University Press

Sociology and
Social Change in Korea

Copyright © 1982 by Man-Gap Lee
Published and Printed
by Seoul National University Press
  (1963. 6. 15 Reg. No. 1-256).

———————————————————————

  This publication is made possible by the grant from the Seoul National University Academic Research Foundation, as part of its program for promotion of research publictions.
———————————————————— —Seoul National University Press

Preface

When one reaches old age, he is likely to look back the long way he walked and hopes to record special experiences or events he had. Koreans have a traditional custom to do it upon their sixtieth birthday. Last year, when I was inventorying my papers upon that occasion, I found a considerable number I had written in English, enough to compile them and to make a book. Fortunately, the Academic Research Foundation of Seoul National University has subsidized publication of the book.

All papers in this book, except "Social Change in Korea," were presented in international conferences, though all papers in English are not necessarily included herein. The subjects I have discussed in English can be classified into three major areas; modernization of Korean society, rural community development, and sociology in Korea or sociology in Asian perspectives.

When I decided to publish the book, I wondered how to organize it. It is evident that some contents of the articles are irrelevant or outdated, and therefore, I was afraid that they would mislead foreign readers in understanding contemporary Korean society. For example, "Politics in a Korean Village" was written on the basis of the situation in the middle 1960s which is considerably different from the present situation. But I decided to include it since I thought that it might be useful in historical perspective. In order to avoid misleading readers, I have indicated when and on what occasion I wrote the respective papers at the beginning of each paper in a footnote.

One embarrassing problem in publishing an English book about Korean society or culture is how to Romanize Korean. There are two systems of Romanization: one is the system standardized by the Ministry of Education of the Korean Government, while the other is the McCune-Reischauer system. I have had some difficulty in choosing between the two, because both suffer from some disadvantages. Before I could make my decision on the matter, however, the publisher adopted a new system which is said to have been tentatively standardized as a substitute for the MOE system. Since the publisher had already proceeded with the new system and it did not appear so bad, I decided to leave it as it is.

Whenever I finalized my papers, I always asked someone, usually an American friend, to edit the manuscripts for clarification. But I see there are still some mistakes or inadequate expressions in the papers, in spite of the fact that they were once published or presented publicly. Therefore, I had to have another proof-reading by one who is familiar with English language, since the Seoul National University Press does not have a native English editor. However, there may be still some misprints or awkward expressions.

Before closing the preface, I have to express my deep appreciation to those who corrected the manuscripts of the articles and proof read them. Particularly, I owe much to Dr. Glenn D. Paige in completing my first paper, "Trend of Social Sciences in Korea after World War II," which was written in 1960. Dr. Herbert R. Barringer and Dr. Vincent S.R. Brandt frequently gave me useful advice and suggestions on my various papers. Dr. John E. Sloboda, Mr. Richard B. Samuelson and Miss Susan Turnquist were of great help in completing "Social Change in Korea," which required great effort. I cannot forget the warm-hearted assistance of professor Shigeo Nohara, who carefully checked two articles, "The Structural Change in Korean Society and Its Modernization" and "Politics in a Korean Village," both of which I wrote when I was a visiting professor at the University of Delaware in 1966-67. Miss Marilyn Held must also be mentioned. While she was working with me, she assisted me greatly, particularly for "Cooperation among Sociologists in Asia." Finally I would like to express many thanks to Dr. Earnest Schusky and Mr. Edward W. Romary who advised me or did the proof reading for most of the book in the final stages of its printing.

May 1982

Man-Gap Lee

Contents

Preface iii

I. Modernization

The Structural Change in Korean Society and
    Its Modernization 3
Social Change in Korea 29
Socio-cultural Factors Bearing on Economic Development ... 94

II. Changes in Rural and Urban Communities

Consanguineous Group and Its Function in the Korean
    Community 119
Politics in a Korean Village 134
Rural People and Their Modernization 173
Some Problems Democracy Faces in Korean Rural Areas 193
Pushing or Pulling? 205
Socio-cultural Aspects of the Community Development
    Movement in Korea 219
Urbanization and Rural Development 237
Participation in the Saemaŭl Movement 246

III. Sociology in Korea: Asian Perspectives

Trend of Social Sciences in Korea after World War II 261
Development of Sociology in Korea 268
Problems of Research in the Korean Rural Society 281
Cooperation among Sociologists in Asia 295
Forum for Asian Sociologists 303
Problems and Needs of Communication Education in Asia ... 317

Index 324

I

MODERNIZATION

The Structural Change in Korean Society and Its Modernization

Introduction

This work[1] is primarily concerned with the general sociological factors which seem to be involved positively or negatively in the modernization of Korea. This does not mean, however, that political and economic factors will be completely excluded from this discussion.

The difinition of modernization may be controversial. It is widely understood, however, that modernization means the process of transformation of the traditional society into one in which economic development can be continuously accelerated. Under this general difinition, two different types of modernization would be observed: one is the change from the feudalistic society to the capitalistic, self-generated by the matured internal socio-economic conditions in the Western countries; and the other is one in which these conditions are not necessary.

To explain further, the countries which belong to the latter category were mostly colonial, have been modernized more or less by the encroachment of the capitalistic countries from outside, and obtained political independence recently without sufficient social and economic basis to operate the modern state. In those countries, the pre-modern stage was not feudalistic, but rather quasi-feudalistic or non-feudalistic, and the forthcoming society would be possibly capitalistic, quasi-capitalistic, or non-capitalistic. Korea apparently is one of these countries, although she has been in a situation different from other developing countries.

Sometimes the modernization of developing countries is confused with westernization. There is no doubt that some countries have already introduced, and will further introduce and imitate modern ideas, technology and social institutions from Western countries so that the change in these areas will take somewhat the appearance of westernization. Strictly speaking, however, the concept of modernization does not imply westernization.

Someone may wonder about the relation between modernization and democratization. This subject would require considerable and extensive discussion. For the time being, the writer hopes that the readers may be content with his tentative opinion that modernization of the developing countries does not necessarily imply democratization.

Another question could be raised about whether or not the major content of modernization is industrialization by which is usually meant the development of secondary industry. There is an opinion that it is a fallacy[2] to overemphasize the significance of industrialization for the continuous economic development in developing countries, or that it may be improper for those which are mostly agricultural to attempt an economic development only through industrialization without considerable effort at improving agriculture. Nevertheless, there are few countries which attempt to achieve an economic development without industrialization. It must be noted that this particular article is based on the tentative assumption that the modernization in Korea is largely a matter of industrialization.

In the organization of this work, the writer will begin with a brief review of the structural change of the Korean society during the past century which will be the basis of further discussion. Next, he would like to discuss the sociological factors which seem to be conducive or obstructive to subsequent industrialization. This will be done with a special reference to the scheme provided by Wilbert E. Moore, relating to the conditions of the industrialization.[3] Moore listed the following items as the sociological conditions of industrialization: value, social institution, social organization. Finally, the writer will try to reinforce his discussion with a brief consideration of some other aspects of the Korean society that appear to be essentially related to her modernization.

Structural Change of the Korean Society[4]

1. Social Stratification and Mobility

It would be very illuminating for understanding modernization in Korea if one could provide a clear picture of how the Korean people have been achieving social mobility from the latter stages of the Yi-dynasty to the present. Unfortunately, the findings of empirical research are very much limited in the area of social stratification during this period of time. Therefore, the writer is afraid that his view of this particular topic may be somewhat distorted.

It is understood that the social status system of the Yi-dynasty was composed of seven major status groups: the royal family, *yangban*(兩班), *hyangban*(鄕班) and *toban*(土班), *jung-in*(中人), *sŏ-ŏl* (庶孼), *sangmin*(常民), and *chŏnmin*(賤民).[5] This status system was not necessarily parallel with the economic ladder, though the people of high status could usually enjoy high economic standing. The status system became somewhat chaotic in the latter period of the Yi-dynasty, since some people could obtain the status of *yangban* through bribery or other means. But status discrimination was very rigid and there was little social mobility among the different status group.

The economic stagnation in traditional Korea is frequently attributed to the tight social structure. Particularly the role of the *yangban*, and their ideology of Confucianism. The *yangban*, the ruling class, was mainly concerned with the acquisition and maintenance of official positions which were the only sources of social status. They were rarely interested in production and community welfare. The power structure of the *yangban* was seemingly solid on the surface, and yet it was in fact ready to fall to pieces through the factional struggle of many years and the status chaos caused by the increase of the quasi-*yangban* in the later period of the dynasty. It was still strong enough to resist the struggles of the lower classes, a great majority of whom were just on the margin of starvation, and yet, was not strong enough to survive the militant threat from Japan.

After the Annexation in 1910, almost all key positions in the administrative organization and the modern civilian organizations were occupied by the Japanese. The Land Survey Project was implemented immediately after the Annexation to establish a modern private land owning system. During the Yi-dynasty, the farm land ownership was not legally permitted to the people, but many could own some land. After the Project was completed, a lot of land came to belong to the Japanese government, and the big Japanese land corporations as well as other Japanese citizens could take advantage in possessing the farm land. At the same time a good many *yangban* could remain at the top of the Korean society as land owners and willingly or unwillingly cooperate with the Japanese authority.

Urbanization was taking place to some extent during the Japanese rule. The Korean city dwellers could engage in the various fields of occupation. Some of them with relatively good education might find white collar jobs in the administrative and other modern social organizations, or some others could operate their own stores or shops, if they had some money. They probably came from the former *yangban* or the status groups next to the *yangban*. There were also many others who came mainly from the *sangmin*, that is the commoners, or from the lowest status group and were engaged as manual or service workers, or servants in the various fields.

Drastic changes in the social structure were occurring in Korea after World War II. First, the positions which the Japanese had held were taken by the Koreans with high levels of education or with some experience in operating modern social organizations. Many Japanese properties also came to belong to public agencies or private Koreans. Second, additional organizations including the army were established and they obviously absorbed many people. Third, the peasants could become land owning farmers directly or indirectly due to the land reform, which was carried out without any serious resistance from the former land owners.[6] On the other hand, those who had kept high social positions, and also a large number of the former land owners lost their power.

Moreover, the Korean War reshuffled the social positions of the people. The people who were traditionally oriented, concerned with "face-saving," and lacked the experience of modern social life could hardly adjust to the changing society. One of the distinctive features of the social stratification during and after the War may be the formation of the new upper class. This class secured

I. Pattern of social stratification

Yi-dynasty	Japanese period	After World War II.
royal family yangban hyangban & toban jung-in sŏ-ŏl sangmin chŏnmin	Japanese Korean upper class Korean middle class Korean lower class	upper class middle class lower class

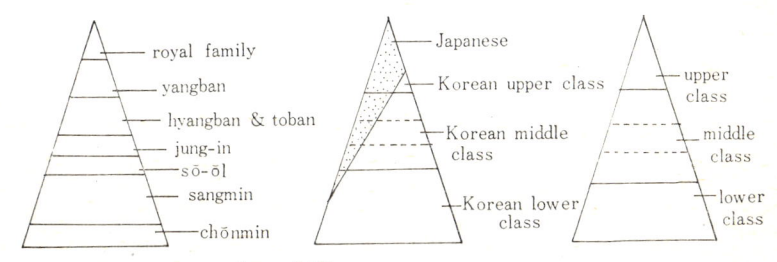

II. Means to upward mobility

a. position in the government	a. land	a. education
b. family background	b. education	b. skill
c. Confucian scholarship	c. skill	c. money

Note: The space of each class indicated in the triangles does not necessarily represent its proportion to the entire population.

relatively sound footing before the Korean War, but has risen up very rapidly since the War. The class is composed mainly of high ranking governmental officials and officers, and businessmen who probably made a deal with the persons in power so as to acquire economic favors.

The illustration shows the patterns of social stratification in the three different periods since the later period of the Yi-dynasty until now, and the major means to upward mobility in each period.

2. Whence the Driving Force for Social Change?

It can be hypothesized that the people with the strongest aspirations for bringing about social change in any society, and from whom the greatest force to that end arises, may be those of the stratum immediately below the ruling class.[7] They are not satisfied with their social position and have some confidence in competing with the ruling class; they attempt to identify themselves with the lower class and to seek support from them; and they attempt to create by themselves or introduce an ideology from available sources in order to justify their claim.

In the latest period of the Yi-dynasty, we can observe two distinctive groups which attempted to make a change: one is *"Donghag-dang"* or the East Learning Party, and the other *"Dognibhyŏb-hoe"* or the Association of the Independence. It may not be unreasonable to assume that the core members of the two groups were largely from the middle class in the traditional society, namely weak *hyangban* and *toban*, *jung-in*, and *sŏ-ŏl*, though the evidence for this statement may not be sufficient. The major differences between the two groups might be the following: the core members of the former, *"jŏbju,"* namely the local leaders of the Party, were more conservative, desperate, oriented to traditional ideas, and hostile to Western civilization; while those of the latter were more progressive and eager to introduce Western civilization including the democratic political system. The two groups were different from each other in their approaches, but they were alike in their dissatisfaction with the existing situation and in their aspiration to seek change.

During the period of Japanese control, almost all Koreans were resistant to the Japanese rule. This general trend was represented in the Independence Movement of 1919. Here again, we feel the lack of empirical evidence to define clearly which status background the active members of the movement came from; but we can assume that most of them, mainly from the old middle class, had modern education to some extent, and could hardly have a very hopeful perspective of their career. After the movement, some of them remained as conservative nationalists, some became sympathetic to Western democracy, and some turned socialist.

As mentioned above, the period of about one decade after the liberation was the most dynamic and dramatic in terms of social mobility. It may be true that those from the middle class would have become sympathetic to communism, if many colonial elements were retained and the former upper class could remain at the top of the society.

Upward social mobility, however, stopped after the Korean War. The better positions in the society were already filled. The young people, who had been absorbed into and were ready to be discharged from the army, or who were coming out from the higher educational institutions, could hardly find satisfactory jobs any more. Consequently, they were becoming discontented with the existing social situation and started to oppose Syngman Rhee's regime, provoked directly by the election interference with all kinds of unlawful means and indirectly by the prevailing corruption.

After the students' April Uprising of 1960, they expressed strong aspiration for a rapid economic development along with an establishment of the sense of national dignity. They loudly criticized the older generation, denied their competency, and complained about the unjust economic benefits of the upper class.

It may be necessary to provide additional explanation concerning the characteristics of the new middle class. The class which is meant in this work is defined primarily in terms of economic standing. There is no distinctive line to be drawn between the upper class and the middle class along this scale. It could be roughly said, however, that the upper class includes the people who can provide sufficient economic support to their family, have no economic difficulty in educating their children, and possess houses with modern facilities and other luxurious material properties.

The middle class may range from the people who can possess much of what the upper class has with careful allocation of the family budget to those who have serious economic difficulty in providing college education for their children. Let us take the population in Seoul as an example. Roughly speaking, the writer estimates that about 5 per cent of the population of the capital city belong to the upper class and 25 or 30 per cent may fall in the middle class. The distinction between the middle class and the lower class is clearer. The lower class comprises about 60 to 70 per cent of Seoul's population; they are usually exempt from income tax and cannot subscribe to a newspaper.[8]

By occupation, the middle class is composed mainly of some professionals, salaried men, and proprietors of stores and shops. The workers would not be included in this category. A great majority of the upper class and middle class seem to have come from the old middle class, although the descendents of the *yangban* may be found in both classes, and sometimes even in the lower class. The components of the middle class are heterogeneous in their social standing and value-orientation. They seem hardly to have a common organizational activity for promoting their economic interests because of the nature of their occupations. Their dissatisfaction with the existing social situation is chiefly reflected in newspapers and expressed in student demonstrations.

Sociological Factors of Korean Modernization

1. Value[9]

Confucianism was the dominant value system during the Yi-dynasty. It valued the five cardinal relationships of the human being, three of which were concerned with intra-family relations; and filial piety was of particularly great significance. According to Confucianism, everybody was supposed to be obedient to his parents, to take care of them with full warm heart, and to revere them through ancestor worship.

Confucianism is not a religion in a strict sense. It is a system of philosophical ideas rather than a religion, but it has been functioning as a religion because of the nature of ancestor worship. Ancestor worship was extremely important to everybody, particularly to *yangban*, for two reasons: one is that a person's soul could be consoled by his family after his death through ancestor worship, and the other is that his social status largely depended upon the achivements of his ancestors. Therefore, with the practice of ancestor worship, he could expect his offspring to take care of him not only while he was alive but after death, and demonstrate his dignified family status.

Though loyalty was also greatly emphasized during the Yi-dynasty, it was oriented merely to the king and not applied to the super-ordinate in the administrative or other social organizations as in Japan. Koreans might be faithful to their super-ordinate while he has authority in his position, but the attitude is not strong enough to continue to be maintained persistently after his retirement.

Confucianism was strongly held by the *yangban*; but the *yangban* were attached to it not because of its philosophical value *per se*, but because it was required of them to take a position in the government which was the exclusive means to attain the status of *yangban*. Unless one could hold the status of *yangban*, he could hardly avoid cruel corporal punishment, forced labor, confiscation or other unjust oppression.

The status-oriented *yangban* competed with each other for power, and blood-shedding factional struggles were repeated in the later period of the Yi-dynasty. The *yangban* would pretend strictly to follow Confucian norms in the social life of their family, kinship group, and the *yangban* status group, but many of them were not benevolent to the people of lower status. The increased number of the *yangban* population caused them to become corrupt. Therefore, it is not unreasonable to assume that a *yangban* could give up Confucianism if he could be given a good position by doing so.

Confucianism was still a useful political instrument for keeping the social order during the period of Japanese control. However, the rising force from the former middle class, who had been resistant to the *yangban* class and were more resistant to Japanese colonialism, became perceptive about the disastrous effects of Confucianism. They recognized that Confucianism discouraged productivity, practical improvement, creativity and dynamic social mobility. The major reason why Christianity has spread so rapidly in Korean society is that it appears to be attractive to those of the old middle class who were unhappy with the existing social situation.

It was generally taken for granted that all Koreans were Confucianistic in the period of the Yi-dynasty. It is important to note, however, that the *yangban* class was likely to monopolize the learning and practice of Confucianism. We can easily imagine that Confucianism would permeate even the lower class, but it does not seem to have been internalized deeply in their personality. The Koreans may still be Confucianistic, more so in the rural area, and mainly in the family life of the city dwellers. However, the active members of the society readily discard the Confucian attitude and in fact have already thrown off many of its elements. It appears that Confucianism is no longer a serious obstacle to the industrialization of Korea.

The same comment is applicable to Buddhism. There are many Buddhists, probably more than Christians, but there is no significant evidence that it is strong and has any negative effect on Korean modernization. The fact that Buddhism was rejected without much resistance during the Yi-dynasty shows how weak it was. The indigenous beliefs such as shamanism or animism and "naturalistic" ideas from China seem to have remained more persistently in the mentality of many Koreans than Confucianism. However, they also do not appear to prevent the Koreans from introducing modern scientific devices, but rather seem to be supplementary.

A serious defect in the action orientation of the Korean people which hinders industrialization more seriously than anything else may be a lack of devotion to the community. There was "*hyang-yag*"——a kind of community development organization——led by some local *yangban*, and it is said that the *sangmin* maintained mutual assistance among themselves. In spite of these facts, Koreans in general could not develop the sense of devotion to the community as a whole. This might be another distinctive social character of the Korean people which is different from that of the Japanese. This trait is assumed to be the outcome of the particularistic culture of Korea, and more concretely, the result of familism on the one hand and of status orientation on the other.

The Koreans have a strong sense of obligation to the family and seek high prestige status for the glory of the family at any cost. If they once obtain a high position, they can enjoy the same prestige even after resignation. They are not evaluated according to what they have contributed to community life but in terms of what they are. Since the sense of devotion to the community was weak, the leaders of any social organization were unlikely to be regulated and criticized by the consensus of the people in the community. Sometimes, they did not feel shame for their illegitimate conduct. This particular defect of the lack of conformity to the law had been formed during the Yi-dynasty when ideal and formal types of legal and normative systems introduced from China did not fit the existing conditions. Even now, we can observe the same trend in this respect.

2. Nationalism

It will be proper to say something about nationalism as related to Korean values. Nationalism is regarded as one of the basic conditions necessary for a rapid economic development in developing countries. Nationalism in Korea has unique features because she has been under peculiar circumstances. Firstly, Korea was ruled by the Japanese who are ethnically very similar and are geographically only a short distance from her. Secondly, the independence of Korea was not earned by the Koreans, but was recovered through the victory of the Allied Nations over Japan. Thirdly, the Western missionaries, mainly the Americans, have been sympathetic to the Koreans' efforts for independence and friendly to them. Fourthly, Korea has been divided into two different territories and the Communist group in the North invaded the South.

Consequently, Korean nationalism involves strong feelings of anti-Japanese and anti-communism, an antagonistic attitude toward totalitarianism, and a friendly attitude toward Western democracy. These feelings and attitudes urge the Koreans to take precautions aganist any possible aggression by the North Korean Communists and to be superior to them on the one hand, and to cope with the Japanese and their possible attempt at invisible encroachment on the other. At the same time, they are generous enough not to regard Western influence with a great deal of suspicion.

Anti-American feelings were rarely expressed in Korea except for the agitations which were led by the leftists during the period of the American military occupation. The friendly attitude of the Korean people toward the United States was well shown in their warm welcome during visits of the American presidents to Korea. This does not mean, however, that there has been no criticism of the United States. For the time being, the images or opinions about the United States which seem to prevail among some Koreans, particularly the young intellectuals, are the following: that she may have "ugly" intentions as a capitalistic country; that she is likely to give more favors to the Korean capitalists of the people in power; that she has pressed the Koreans to adopt "the American democracy" some of which might not fit the Korean situation, and sometimes cause social disintegration or stimulate excessive aspiration for consumption; and that she has given more benefits to Japan.

In addition to these opinions, no matter how valid they are, there seems to be a trend among the intellectuals to express criticisms motivated by xenophobia which exists ironically with xenophilia. If there are really those feelings in Korea, it may not be difficult to predict that even some casual events may result in increased criticism. It is noteworthy that one of the opposition parties expressed complaints to the United States several times, though it was thought to be more friendly to the United States than the present leading party once was in the past.

3. Education

Needless to say, education is one of the essential means to modernization. The Korean pioneers of the modernization movement recognized this necessity in its early stage. For example the "*Dognib Sinmun*" (Independence Press), which was related to the Association of Independence mentioned earlier, emhasized repeatedly the significance of education as the means of first priority to the goal of national independence for Korea.[10] Other innovators also have paid a great deal of attention towards educating the illiterates. On the other hand, from the individual's point of view, education has been regarded as the most useful means for securing high social status.

In the very beginning of the independence of Korea, the government established the compulsory education system. Accordingly, the illiteracy rate has been tremendously decreased. Now, the aspiration for high education is so intense among the people above the middle class that "the national ruin by education" has been voiced sometimes.

Then, two serious social problems are arising ralative to education. One is that high educational aspiration is intensifying social unrest, because it is hard for the graduates of higher educational institutions to secure a satisfactory job and the material comfort for which they might study hard.[11] This drives the government to promote rapid economic growth. Another is that the government is tremendously overloaded in supporting even the elementary schools, which will reduce the amount of capital to be invested in economic development.

On the whole, education is no longer a serious obstacle for the industrializatlon of Korea. There are many educated people who can work for it. The only weak point is that there are insufficient numbers of professionals, experts, and skilled technicians of high quality.

4. Journalism and Mass Communication

One should not fail to refer to the role of journalism and mass communication in the discussion of modernization in Korea.[12] They have been functioning as the essential tools for introducing the modern ideas, stimulating the Koreans to transform their traditional values, and promoting social justice. The Korean innovators were aware of these functions from the beginning of the modernization process. Therefore, various newspapers appeared since 1896, despite the fact that the number of subscribers was very small.

Since the liberation, Korean journalism has enjoyed freedom to some extent, although it was interfered with and oppressed by the government occasionally. The government could not control as it wished, partly because the journalists strongly resisted any attempt at control, and partly because the government was afraid to lose the support of the free nations.

At the same time, journalism has some significant defects. Criticisms have often been made that Korean journalism is not financially independent enough; that distorted, agitative and untrue news and editorials are frequently found; that some newspapermen are corrupt; and that the press stimulates excessive aspiration for consumption and accelerates social disintegration by introducing the various ideas and values inconsistently.

In spite of these criticisms, Korean journalism has made a great effort to indoctrinate the people and to encourage them to be independent, rational, and competent in every field of the social life. Specifically, it has interacted with the active elements of the population, mainly the middle class who are a majority of the subscribers to the newspapers. The April Uprising is generally understood to have been carried out by the students, but it is very doubtful that it could have happened without the newspaper. It is interesting to note that the majority of the newspapermen have been replaced by young, competent college graduates since the Uprising.

The newspapers are not widely available for the lower class and the rural people as yet. Recently, however, radio is rapidly diffusing among these people and is playing a major role as a substitute for the newspaper, though it has some disadvantages in disseminating political and economic matters.

In summary, then, we may conclude that the traditional ideas functioned to impede social development to a great extent before World War II, but it is no longer the case with present Korea. It can hardly be denied that many traditional ideas and practices still remain, but they do not appear to be strong enough to prevent Koreans from accepting new ideas for economic development.

5. Social Institutions and Social Organizations

The social institutions and social organizations are also very important conditions for modernization. Most of the essential institutions for industrialization had been established in Korea prior to the end of World War II. Subsequently, other social institutions, mainly political, have been developed in accordance with democratic principles.

There are some problems, however, that do not derive from the lack of social institutions required for industrialization, but from the fact that some of them are not realistically organized. For example, the general election system extended the voting privilege even to people who were scarcely prepared to appreciate and assume such a responsibility. It is of course very desirable to provide the democratic right to everybody, but the unrealistic institution may produce disfunctional effects, and sometimes give rise to disillusionment about the appropriate institution.[13]

Within the last decade, social organizations in Korea have operated with relative adequacy. However, they have some serious weaknesses that should be noted. First, the economic feasibility is too weak to maintain these social organizations. The modern social organizations in Korea have been established mainly by the government or with its sponsorship. Since the amount of the revenue of the government is insufficient, some social organizations of low priority do not function as expected. Corruption is also caused partially by the inadequate salary system.

Another weakness is that the number of highly qualified experts and specialists is very much limited as mentioned before. The best organized social groups in Korea might be the military and police organizations, but recently other administrative organizations have started to carry out programs to improve the quality of their officials.

Finally, the particularistic pattern of behavior impedes the establishment of a merit system in personnel administration and the efficient functioning of the modern bureaucracy. Particularism in Korea is partly related to familism, and partly to the affective orientation. In addition, personal anxiety about the security of position seems to be another significant factor contributing to the particularistic orientation.

6. Family and Kinship

Even before World War II, it was loudly claimed that early marriage had to be stopped and the low status of women had to be improved, but no voice is heard about it anymore. In spite of widespread opinion that the extended family type was popular in Korea, empirical studies have shown that it had not been the prevailing type, though it had probably been maintained among and appreciated by the wealthy *yangban*.[14]

It is often said that patriarchal control is very rigid. It was true and still is in the rural area to some extent. The authoritarian relationship between a father and his children may be the most persistent among the traditional norms of the Korean society. Nevertheless, the parents above the middle class, particularly the well educated people, are becoming far less authoritarian than before. Those of the lower class are likewise becoming so, since they do not have economic capability enough to support their family and the knowledge by which they can guide their children. Now, the parents are losing their influences over children in both mate selection and occupational choice. One of the drastic changes in family relations[15] is the considerable rise in women's status and the freer contact between the sexes. In 1960 the Korean government legislated the new civil law, which was intended to raise women's status considerably. This was carried out without any serious opposition except for the case where the circle of local Confucians protested against the lifting of the prohibition of marriage between those who are related to each other by the same family name with common origin.

In the rural area, the kinship group has been preserving its traditional functions to some degree. Sometimes it is used as a political instrument for an election campaign. Yet, it greatly lost the economic basis after the land reform. There is little possibility that the kinship group can interfere in the private matters of its members.

7. Motivation

During the Yi-dynasty, the Koreans were strictly required to "keep their own proper positions." It was almost impossible for those of the lower class to rise to higher status through national examinations as in China.[16] They could hardly even have the freedom to be contented with making money as the merchants in traditional Japan. All they could do was to sigh at their misfortune. Still, it was possible for them to survive by attaching to somebody, no matter how miserable it was.

Today, however, there is nobody whom he can depend on. Everybody has to make a living by himself. There are some people who are on the margin of starvation, but probably most of them under the age of forty have had elementary education and military training. Moreover, they have observed that some people who had been in similar conditions have succeeded in changing society. It is not hard to imagine that this would motivate them to seek every possible means to the better life.

Another social stratum which has high aspirations for the better life is the middle class. Their economic conditions are much better than those of the lower class, but sometimes they may be even more dissatisfied with their standing than the latter. When they evaluate their own social status, they usually refer to the people who are in somewhat better condition than themselves. With this psychological mechanism of evaluation, they seem to be critical of the sources upon which the social standing of the current upper class is based and eager to compete with them.

They have also been status-oriented, but monetary success is becoming more appreciated, though this would be more so among the lower class. With the experiences in the past decade, the Korean people notice that the high positions in government or public organizations are unstable, being subject to criticism, and that wealth is more useful than other elements, namely power and prestige. Relating to this trend, it may be interesting to note that more of the competent graduates of high school are applying for the commercial or technological institutes than previously.

8. National Character

Some have argued that the social character of the people in a society is very important in achieving its modernization. As to the national character of the Koreans, the negative traits were more frequently indicated than the positive. Many foreigners who came to Korea in the latter period of the Yi-dynasty were very pessimistic about the Korean's social character, but others in the later period did find some admirable traits. In contrast to this, some of the Koreans, particularly the social leaders or intellectuals, sometimes held more pessimistic views than the foreigners. A recent example is found in the attempt of the military government to rebuild the national character of the Koreans. While it may be true that the Korean people did show some undesirable aspects of their personality in the latest period of the Yi-dynasty, we may be able to assume that these would be more the case with the *yangban*, on the one hand, and with the mass who were in extreme poverty and ignorance on the other, rather than the middle class. Interestingly, a report by the Russians around the end of the last century pointed out that one of the best armies in the world could be organized among the Koreans, if they were led by a smart commander.[17]

Observing the behavior of the present Koreans, we cannot find any great defect in their social character which would impede industrialization, when compared to those of other people who are making a successful modernization. If there is need to practice character-building, it will be more necessary among the social leaders who are required to be responsible, creative, austere, and cooperative in their unified action than the lay people. This does not mean that the present middle class is more moral and better disciplined than the upper class, for both belonged largely to the same class before World War II.

9. Democracy and Political Stability

Political stability of some degree seems to be an essential condition for economic development.[18] It is more so with the developing countries, in which a long-range plan for economic growth must necessarily be carried out. But, it may be a question of what kind of political stability and to what extent it is necessary for continuing economic development.

As far as Korea is concerned a regime may be able to keep power a long time, since the government possesses a great part of the available resources for political and economic manipulation. On the other hand, those in power seem to have some difficulties in maintaining their authority over long periods of time for the following reasons. First, the social structure itself is still unstable. Second, the economic poverty intensified by population problems imposes pressure on the leaders in power. Third, improper conduct, lack of discipline, and administrative incompetency are frequently observed among the people in power. Fourth, the democratic political system sometimes causes decentralization of power, social disintegration, and slow action. Fifth, the unification of a political party is based neither on a consistent system of political ideas, nor on the support of a certain populace, but rather on the dynamics of the particularistic personal relations in terms of power, so that various factional conflicts easily occur in the critical moments. Sixth, there is a prevailing opinion that more benefits have been provided to the wealthy people and the unfair burdens loaded on the middle class and the farmers.

This does not imply that these reasons are serious enough to cause immediate political instability, but rather that they are factors which cause some kind of social instability. Political stability may depend largely upon the extent to which the leading politicians can establish discipline to regulate themselves, identify with those who raise complaints, and achieve consistent economic growth. For the time being, the people who raise complaints are mainly of the middle class, and their dissatisfaction is expressed in newspapers and student demonstrations. Sometime in the future, however, there is the possibility that complaints might be increasingly raised by the working people.

Some Other Problems

So far, the writer has discussed the sociological conditions related to industrialization in Korea, ignoring the economic conditions. There could be an argument about the extent to which economic factors are related to modernization, but the discussion about it is beyond the scope of this work. Prior to ending up the presentation, however, the writer feels it necessary to comment on two other problems; one is the relation between the industrial economy and agriculture, and the other is the external situation.

1. Relation between Industrial Economy and Agriculture[19]

The above discussion was based on the assumption that modernization in Korea is industrialization. Now, it must be admitted that this assumption itself may hardly be free from criticism. The question about how much weight must be given to the urban industrial economy and rural agriculture respectively for the modernization of the nation as a whole can be answered through more extensive arguments. Anyway, the writer feels strongly that it would be very improper to ignore rural economic development in this discussion since Korea is still an agricultural country.

It is true that the rural people in Korea are very much traditional in many ways, but it may be untrue that they are not ready for social development. They may still be familistic and irrational, and yet these are not strong enough to prevent them from accepting modern devices for economic development. Many of them are more interested in other occupations including commerce than in farming. They are eager to introduce modern culture. Radio is rapidly spreading to the rural community. Buses run to almost every part of the rural area. But, they are still poor and slow to make a change.

In the writer's opinion, the stagnation of the rural economy is caused mainly by the following conditions:

(1) Industrialization in Korea has been implemented without much regard to agriculture. It is not carried out to promote the linkage with agriculture.

(2) Governmental policy has been more concerned with keeping the prices of agricultural products low in order to support the urban people and to maintain government employees, soldiers, and other salaried men at cheap cost.

(3) The administration of the government has been unrealistic and inefficient in programming, and strict in control.

One cannot deny that the farmers are backward in the application of technology and that their productivity is not high. One must note, however, that the farmers sometimes over-produced, through encouragement by the government, and eventually lost due to the lack of markets. If the above mentioned conditions are improved, and if the farmers find favorable markets with the aid of capital and other forms of assistance from the government, they will certainly make rapid economic development.

2. External Situation

It is surprising to learn that some scholars who have discussed modernization have not paid much attention to the effect of the external situation of a nation on her moderinization. Relationship with other countries and external conditions seem to be significant for the developing countries in the following aspects:

Firstly, they need to introduce technological devices and ideas from the outside. Secondly, they are economically not independent enough and are likely to be subject to the changing policies of the strong, wealthy, and advanced countries. Thirdly, it is necessary for them to squeeze into the foreign trade market to sell their manufactured products, though it is usually very difficult.

Korea has had some unfavorable conditions in her external situation. (1) The Koreans did not have much experience in contact with the advanced countries during the Japanese period. (2) Since World War II, she has been located on the extreme margin of the free world. Her main channels of contact with the outside were available mainly through Japan, with whom national relations have been only recently normalized, and with the United States which is at a remote distance from her. (3) National security is not safe because of the potential aggression from North Korea. (4) In the past she could hardly establish any close economic relations with neutral emerging nations.

Recently, some favorable conditions have appeared in the area of international relations of Korea. She is making more substantial contacts with various countries. Moreover, it is economically very significant that she has restored normal relations with Japan which is the most industrialized in Asia. The foreign trade in Korean labor such as mining workers, technicians, and even professionals has increased. This new trend may greatly stimulate the Koreans to look for better opportunities abroad and to seek new ideas.

Conclusion

In reviewing the major sociological factors involved in the modernization of Korea, we can conclude that there is no serious impediment. The only crucial point appears to be the competence and discipline of the people in power. If they can improve these matters and implement adequate economic policies to utilize the internal and external resources so that they may be able to meet with the expectations of the middle class, for the time being, and those of the working people, which will be gradually intensifying, then modernization in Korea will be steadily moving ahead. Recently a foreign economist commented that Korea was in a "take off" stage.[20] From the sociological point of view, there is no reason why Korea cannot do so.

[NOTES]

1) This article was originally presented at the annual conference of the Association of Asian Studies in 1967 with the subject, "Sociological Implications of Modernization in Korea." The present work is not different from the original version except changes of some words and more items in "Notes." The writer's ideas about the modernization process of Korea have not been basically changed from what was expressed in this work, even now, although they may have been developed further on the basis of it.
2) William Letwin, "Four Fallacies about Economic Development," *Daedalus; Journal of the American Academy of Arts and Sciences*, summer 1963, pp. 396-414.
3) Wilbert E. Moore, *Social Change*, (Englewood Cliffs, New Jersey: Prentice-Hall, Inc., 1963), Chap. 5.
4) Later the writer gave a more extensive discussion about this topic. See Man-gap Lee, "Kankoku shakai no kozotekihenka (The Structural Change of the Korean Society)," *Asian Cultural Studies* 9, International

Christian University Publications III-A, December 1977, pp. 45-82.
5) Tokutaro Tanaka, "Chosen no shakai kaikyu (Social Class in Korea)," *Chosen*, March 1921.
6) Man-gap Lee, *Hangug nongchon sahoe ŭi gujo wa byŏnhwa (The Social Structure of the Korean Village and Its change)*, (Seoul: Seoul National University Press, 1973), pp. 96-98.
7) Everett E. Hagen gives us an important suggestion about this. See his work, *On the Theory of Social Change*, (Homewoed, Ill.: The Dorsey Press, Inc., 1962), p. 30. Bert F. Hoselitz indicates the deviant behavior by marginal individuals in bringing social change. See Bert F. Hoselitz, *Sociological Aspects of Economic Growth*, (New York: the Free Press, 1960), Chap. 3.
8) No written evidence was found to support this but we found that about 70 per cent of the households in Seoul in 1962 were exempted from income tax. And also many empirical studies in Seoul show that about 70 per cent of the respondents, each of whom represented his household, said that they would belong to the lower class.
9) See Man-gap Lee, "Hangug sahoe ŭi gachi gujo (Value Structure of Korean Society)," *Sasang-gye*, monthly, May 1961, pp. 62-71.
10) The writer discussed it in the presentation of "Values Reflected on the Independence Press," which was based on the content analysis of its editorial, at the symposium of Oriental Studies organized by the Institute of East Asian Studies, College of Liberal Arts and Science, Seoul National University, in 1962.
11) Man-gap Lee, "The Problems of the Intelligentsia," *Atlas*, June 1961. (This is an English summary of the paper in *Sasang-gye*, monthly).
12) Kyu-whan Kim, "The Role of Intellectuals in the Process of Modernization through Mass Communication Activities," *International Conference on the Problems of Modernization in Asia*, pp. 679-686.
13) Later the writer discussed this topic in his article, "Social Organizations," *A City in Transition*, ed. by M.G. Lee and H.R. Barringer, (Seoul: Hollym, 1971), p. 374.
14) Hiroshi Shikata, "Richo jinko ni kansuru mibunkaikyubetsuteki kansatsu (Observations on the Population in the Yi-dynasty by Social Status)," *Studies of Korean Economy*, No. 3, Essay, Vol. 10, Law Science Study Group, Keijo Imperial University, (Tokyo: Iwanami Shoten, 1938).

15) Man-gap Lee, "Change of Korean Family after World War II," *Kazoku hendo no shakaigaku (Sociology of Family Change)* K. Aoi and K. Masuda ed., (Tokyo: Baifukan, 1973), pp. 166-177.
16) Yong-ho Choe argues that the way to be government officials through the national examinations was widely opened to the commoners during the early Yi-dynasty. See Yong-ho Choe, "Commoners in Early Yi-dynasty Civil Examinations." *The Journal of Asian Studies*, Vol. 33, No. 4, 1974, p. 631. But Yong-mo Kim says it was not so in the late Yi-dynasty. See his doctoral desertation, "Josŏn malgi jŏngchi jibae-chŭng ŭi sahoe-jŏg giwŏne gwanhan yŏngu (A Study of the Social Origins of Political Elites in the Late Yi-dynasty)," 1977.
17) *Ministry of Agriculture and Commerce* (Japan) tr., *Kankokushi*, (the original text was published by the Russian Finance Ministry in 1905), p. 296.
18) Political stability was not emphasized as an essential condition for modernization by Moore, but it has been often discussed by politicians in Korea.
19) Man-gap Lee, "Rural People and Their Modernization," *International Conference on the Problem of Modernization in Asia*, ed. by Asiatic Research Center, Korea University, 1965, pp. 665-675.
20) W.W. Rostow made a speech about "Economic Development in Asia" at Seoul National University in May 1965.

Social Change in Korea

The Social Structure of Traditional Korean Society

1. Environmental Background of the Korean Society

In the middle of the last century there was a theory that the biological character of a society was strongly related to the stagnation or development of the society.[1] This theory was frequently cited to justify colonial rule by capitalist countries. George Kennan, who came to Korea at the beginning of the 20th century, witnessed Koreans sleeping idly at the roadside, failing even to brush away the flies which clung to their eyes. As friend and advisor to the then President of the United States, he argued that Koreans didn't have the ability to take care of their own country; and it would, therefore, be better to let the Japanese establish colonial rule over Korea.[2]

Kennan's report didn't explicitly state that the Korean race suffered from an inherent biological defect, but it was likely to leave readers with such an impression. In contrast, however, the Russians who observed Korean society in the late Yi-dynasty reported that Koreans could become fine soldiers if trained well. Some foreigners in Korea during the early Japanese domination period also noted that Koreans had excellent learning abilities and mastered techniques quickly.[3]

Subsequent research studies have shown that, in general, it is erroneous to prejudge personal characteristics, including mental faculties on the basis of gross racial characteristics. When we see that the Japanese, whose biological characteristics are similar to those of Koreans, have succeeded in modernizing their society, it may be readily presumed that Koreans don't suffer any biological characteristics which would impede modernization.

Another important factor that may possibly affect economic development in Korea is its natural environment. For example, the temperate climate might be advantageous for Koreans in terms of promoting their capacity for adapting to natural changes. Toynbee has said that an adequate challenge is necessary to stimulate cultural development.[4] In ancient times when technology was primitive, the challenge from nature was possibly the main stimulus to cultural development. It has frequently been noted that most high civilizations in world history have developed and flourished in the temperate zone conceivably because it is there that the most appropriate degree of environmental challenge exists to stimulate cultural development.

Possibly the chief reason why the climate of the temperate zone is especially stimulating is its four seasons. Because of the four seasons food is not always at hand; it must be prepared and stored in advance for the winter, and people must make an effort to cultivate and gather foodstuffs from spring to fall. It is necessary to adapt to these seasonal changes not only to secure food, but also to obtain clothing and shelter. The changing of the seasons must be well understood, and a calendar must be developed to meet this necessity; people must know when the soil thaws, when plants sprout and bud, and seasonal periods of rainfall and drought. Great inventiveness therefore is needed to overcome difficulties and obstacles.

The region of the temperate zone where the economy developed most rapidly is of course Europe. East Asia, in spite of its early brilliant civilization, did not develop as rapidly as Europe. In this regard, many economists and historians have attempted various explanations; but personally I think the slower pace of Asian development can be attributed largely to the geographical and socioeconomic character of China, which historically has been the dominant force in Aisa.

The temperate zone area where economic development was

initially slowest is North and South America. It is very strange that this region, which suddenly began to develop after the Europeans arrived, was not developed by the original inhabitants. An important reason why the American Indians did not achieve great economic development may be that the various tribes of their small population which were scattered over such a large continent had little chance to compete or struggle with one another. Consequently, there was little cause for them to raise their productivity.

Korea is located in the temperate zone and has four seasons. She also accumulated considerable knowledge and technology before the onset of modernization. Ancient Korea, which was heavily influenced by Chinese culture, was formerly one of the most developed countries. Unlike the Western European countries which awakened from the dark middle ages in the 16th century and subsequently began to modernize, Korean civilization never fell behind and in some ways was superior to that of Europe. Korean printing typography is one example of this superiority.

It is obvious that Koreans are very adaptable people and have the potential to bring about change. But quite apart from Europe, where various discoveries and inventions and remarkable economic development took place during the transition from medieval feudal society to modern capitalism, Korea did not achieve comparable development and fell into stagnancy.

There are several important reasons why Korea did not develop economically. One of these can be found in the peculiarities of Korean geography. Korea is a small peninsula jutting out from the eastern part of the Asian continent. Its northern part borders on Manchuria, while its southern coast confronts Japan across a narrow strait. The sea surrounds the country on the east and west. In ancient times before long distance sea travel was possible, there was little contact with China. But beginning with the age of the three Kingdoms, Korea began to feel great influence from Chinese culture.

Small Korea had considerable contact with powerful China, and this had an important effect on the development of Korea. When Chinese culture was rich and its society highly developed, Korean culture was also likely to be rich and its society highly developed. But when Chinese society failed to cope with the strong European influence and military power, Korea, which was partially subject to China and had a strong tendency to follow Chinese thought and institutions, naturally came to the same fate.

Japan, on the other hand, is located near enough to China to have been influenced by Chinese culture, but far enough away to offer little incentive for military invasion or political control by China. Japan has never been successfully invaded by foreign countries throughout her long history, and therefore has had greater opportunity than Korea to develop her own culture.

The most important geo-political characteristic which distinguishes Japan from Korea is that Japan was sufficiently isolated to prevent foreign intervention in her internal development. In contrast to Japan, Korea is so near to China that there has long been a close relationship of mutual interest. China has often intervened in Korea, sometimes even at the request of the Korean court. This circumstance has necessarily restricted the independence of Korea's internal development. From the standpoint of Korea's rulers, if they were protected by powerful China their governing system could more easily be maintained; therefore they developed a disposition to follow China, that is, to "serve the great power." At the same time, because there were few serious threats or challenges from other countries, Korean rulers didn't feel the necessity to make ambitious military, political or economic efforts. And therefore, when there were invasions from the outside, it was very difficult for Korea to respond successfully.

Even though there were certain revolutionary movements that attempted to change incompetent and corrupt governments during the Yi-dynasty, it was almost impossible to bring about great political change in Korea. Once again, this was mainly because of Korea's political dependency on China. If large scale political changes occur too often, disorder becomes serious and the economy cannot develop. But it is generally accepted that moderate political change is often necessary to spark economic improvement and increased production.

2. Status System and Social Change

Korea has maintained a highly centralized political system since the unification of the peninsula under the Sinla Kingdom nearly one thousand years ago. We cannot be certain as to whether such centralization was because of the influence of China which has also maintained a centralized political system, because of the small size of the Korean territory, or because Korea is racially and culturally homogeneous.

It may be possible that if Korea were located farther from China, it would have been more difficult for China to intervene, and therefore Korea might have become divided into political spheres that either competed with or opposed each other. Reischauer emphasizes that this factor had great influence on Japanese modernization; Japan maintained a feudal system which had various political spheres similar to those found in western Europe.[5] In Japan's case this theory seems to have considerable validity.

From the standpoint of a feudal lord, what was most important was protecting himself from invasion and, if possible, expanding his power through the annexation of the adjoining territories, or at least defending himself successfully in the ensuing struggle. To do so, it was of course necessary for him to keep a strong army, to bolster his administrative organization, and to establish a proper legal system so that the people in his territory would be able to conduct their affairs safely and effectively. He also had to increase economic productivity, in order to maintain a strong army and survive in any struggle.

The economic productivity of feudal fiefs greatly increased during the Tokugawa dynasty; *Edo* (presently Tokyo), the governing center of the Shogunate, was very prosperous, and its population during the *Genroku* period (1688~1703) is reputed to have reached approximately one million. This would have made it the largest city in the world at that time.

Because Korea had a centralized government for about five hundred years during the Yi-dynasty, there were no separate territorial entities in conflict with each other. There was no persistent foreign threat either. Consequently, Korean rulers did not feel any great necessity to maintain strong military and economic power to insure the survival of their own country. Of course, it is not quite true that Korea faced no foreign threat or challenges whatsoever. There were two Japanese invasions, including the *Imjin* Korea-Japan war (1592~98), and the *Byŏngja* Korea-China war (1636~37). But these conflicts merely created social disorder without stimulating the economic productivity of the Korean people.

Historians and economists have usually divided the social status groups of the Yi-dynasty into four categories: *yangban* (ruling class), *jung-in* (technocrats or specialists), *sangmin* (commoners), and *chŏnmin* (lowly people). These four comprised the basic status system which persisted throughout the entire Yi-dynasty. This classification, however, does not necessarily lead one to a correct understanding of the dynamics behind the social changes that took place from the end of late Yi-dynasty to the present.

An alternative view[6] divides the Yi-dynasty status groups into seven categories instead of four. They are: (1) the royal family and their relatives, (2) *yangban*, (3) *hyangban* and *toban*, (4) *jung-in*, (5) *sŏ-ŏl* (6) *sangmin*, and (7) *chŏnmin*. In this case, there may be some objections to regarding the royal family and their relatives as one category of social status. It is very important, however, to recognize the two status groups of *hyangban* and *toban*, and *sŏ-ol*.

The status of the *yangban* is well known, but the definition of that status is not as clear as is often thought. *Yangban* originally meant both literary men and military officers occupying certain positions in the government, but the term was later extended to include their families in a broader sense. Since the word was not used as a legal term which could be clearly defined, but rather as a means of identifying prestigious persons in daily conversation, the extent to which the families of actual officials were included in this status group is ambiguous. But nevertheless it seems proper to define *yangban* as consisting of the persons who were four generations lineally ascendant and descendant of a particular official.[7] I say this because in Korea the boundary of the kinship group has traditionally been four generations descending directly from a particular ancestor, and consequently, ancestor worship has been performed by those of the same kinship group for ancestors of up to four generations.

Hyangban can be defined as the group consisting of persons whose ancestors had enjoyed formal *yangban* status and privileges, and who still behaved as *yangban* in the countryside, but were looked down upon by true *yangban*, because there had been no ranking government officials in their family for more than four generations. *Toban* were very similar to *hyangban*. The only difference between them is that *toban* were persons whose very distant ancestors had been in government service; therefore, the *toban* had even less prestige than the *hyangban*.

Sŏ-ŏl were the children of *yangban* by concubines. Although their fathers were *yangban*, they could not enjoy the privileges of the *yangban* and were strongly discriminated against by many simply because their mothers were concubines.

One may easily disagree with the definition I have given of these three status groups, particularly the *hyangban* and *toban*. But the important thing is not the definition of these groups, but the existence of such groups at the margin of the ruling class in the late Yi-dynasty. And the reason their existence is important is that they were the primary strata dissatisfied with the society and therefore were most anxious to change it.

It has often been observed that the strata which challenge the ruling class and attempt to bring about a new system are neither the ruling class nor the oppressed class, but rather those who had once been included in the ruling class but are now dispossessed of their former status and relegated to the margin of the upper class.[9] Everyone, when he evaluates his status, tends to use someone else as a referent. He is satisfied or dissatisfied with his own status by comparing himself with this reference. In most cases, the referent is in a similar or competitive situation with him.[10] One who is too superior or too inferior to him can hardly be his referent.

The *sŏ-ŏl* were apparently one of the groups who were most strongly discontent with the political system ruled by the *yangban* class. Most of them had grown up under the same economic educational conditions of their brothers who were the legitimate sons of the same father. It was only because their mothers were concubines that they were forced to endure contempt and discrimination. Therefore, revolts were often incited by them during the late Yi-dynasty.

The *hyangban* and *toban* were two other groups who were unhappy with the *yangban*. The status of their families had formerly been glorious, but that glory had faded. And even though they enjoyed prestige to some extent in their own communities there was little opportunity for them to acquire real power or material prosperity. Moreover, they continually suffered unreasonable treatment at the hands of the *yangban*. Therefore they became increasingly critical of the *yangban* and the established system.

If some particular values are cherished above all others but the institutional means to attain them are not widely accessible, men tend to seek their attainment through revolt.[11] The values that were most important during the Yi-dynasty were occupying a government post, winning the status of *yangban*, and maintaining a high family reputation. In principle, governmental posts could be obtained by passing *gwagŏ*, the national examination for government officials. Everyone could apply to take the *gwagŏ*, but in practice most higher governmental posts were monopolized by powerful *yangban* lineages. It was very difficult for poor common people to study and take the *gwagŏ*, and although there were a few common people who passed it, their positions were never very high.

In the later period of the Yi-dynasty, factional strife became wide spread. The disputes were mostly concerned with ritual etiquette, institutional procedures, and Confucian norms, but the deeper motivations for the strife probably involved a scrambling for power. As I already mentioned, occupying a governmental post was the only way to achieve high social status. The number of posts was limited but the number of persons who wanted to occupy them was continually on the increase. And of course, once one attained a certain position he would either retain it as long as possible or try to reach an even better one. And if he lost it, he would make every effort to regain it. Under such competitive circumstances the *yangban* class tended to fragment and lose sight of any common aim. This trait of factionalism among *yangban*, incidentally, was so strong that it has been mistakenly construed to be the social character of the whole nation.

There is a view that the *jung-in* had great influence on modernization in Korea. Since most *jung-in* were engaged in technical occupations, they were in a position both to pratice and introduce Western techniques. And since they were not among the higher classes, they did not have much to lose if there were changes in the power structure. For that reason we may presume that they contributed, at least in a technical sense, to the modernization of Korea.

I should hasten to add that *jung-in* were relatively well treated during the Yi-dynasty and therefore didn't have any reason to be discontent with their status. And moreover, they were not so restricted in their professional activities that they might regard the social system of the Yi-dynasty as a bottleneck in developing their skills. Therefore, there was no reason for them to feel a strong desire to destroy the old system and construct a new order at the risk of their lives.

3. Social Value

The system of ideas that the *yangban* espoused was Confucianism. In general, they were well acquainted with the Confucian scriptures and were supposed to master the doctrines of Confucius, Mencius, and other Confucian scholars. They especially appreciated *Chu Hsi's* doctrines, which emphasize ritual courtesy. They also respected the idea of benevolence, the supreme virtue of Confucianism, and cherished highly its three cardinal principles and five moral rules, all of which foster authoritarian human relationships.

Confucianism, of course, is useful for maintaining social order, but not for bringing about material progress. Under the ethics of Confucianism it is very difficult to introduce or create new ideas is opposition to traditional ones. Also, in Confucianism filial piety is regarded as supreme in human morality and respect for ancestors is practiced through ancestor worship. Descendants are commanded to adore the virtue of their ancestors and to cherish the traditions of the family. Ancestors within four generations are worshiped and strong kinship unity must be maintained. Consequently, a person may expect to encounter discouragement not only from his parents but also from his kinsmen, if he attempts to deviate from traditional ways.

Confucianism had little interest in labor and production; rather, it was concerned with the proper way of behavior in social life. It was the philosophy of the literati-officials who ruled the people, and therefore they disvalued manual labor, technical matters, and practical things. However, agriculture was highly appreciated. They said that agriculture was "the great foundation of the world" and took it for granted that poor *yangban* could be honorably engaged in farming. Of course, in every traditional society the people engaged in commerce and technical industry were lower in status than the ruling class people; but in traditional Korea this situat ion was especially severe. Accordingly, the organization of business and industry in pre-modern Korea was very limited and the technology primitive, compared to that found in capitalist countries just prior to their modernization.

Because of the philosophical and abstract content of the Confucian books along with their difficult Chinese composition, it was almost impossible for the common people to comprehend them. This surely served to make the gap between *yangban* and the commoners wider. Moreover, the *yangban* had no ideological element that would identify them with or ally their work with that of the common people. In village life there were few events that might unify the village beyond status differences. Consequently, all of the important decisions of the village were made by the government who favored the needs of the *yangban;* therefore cases decided in the interests of the whole village were very rare. In this respect, it may be said that the communal tie of the village as a whole was very weak, while status differences were very important.[12]

Since the commoners learned from and took after the behavioral patterns of *yangban*, they honored Confucian values to some extent. But this was not strongly demanded of them. More deeply rooted in their creed than Confucianism were ideas descending from certain primitive beliefs such as shamanism.

It can hardly be denied, of course, that *yangban*, particularly women, also retained certain of the ideas of shamanism. They were also greatly influenced by the idea of geomancy which is related to Chinese naturalism and which was widely practiced in selecting the site of a tomb. Beyond that, an aesthetic conception of nature related to Taoism was common among *yangban*, as were other indigenous beliefs, some involving prophecy. Nevertheless, Confucian ideology was still dominant among the *yangban*, at least in public, and all cultural elements that were contrary to Confucian principles were for them not worthy of consideration.

Contrastingly, most evidence suggests that Confucian ideology was not strong among the common people. For example, they were not required to perform the ancestor worship ceremony for ancestors up to four generations beyond their parents,[13] and the common women were more free and had more opportunities to act outside the home than *yangban* women. This fact suggests the possibility that the common people preserved more faithfully indigenous cultural elements of Korea which predated the advent of Confucianism. And because of this fact, the commoners were probably more pragmatic and had a greater disposition to expose natural human wants. In addition they probably harbored less psychological resistance toward new ideas than the *yangban*. These tendencies appeared most prominently in the people of *Pyŏngan* and *Hamgyŏng* provinces where *yangban* were rare.

4. Collapse of Traditional Society

During the late Yi-dynasty social disturbances became more wide spread. At that time the *yangban* population was increasing very rapidly in relation to the number of common people who were of course the actual labor force. This circumstance, when combined with the fact that the upper class *yangban* enjoyed far better economic conditions than commoners, was definitely one of the causes for the disturbances. But a more important factor was the severe exploitation of commoners by *yangban* and government officials. In order to cope with this exploitation, many commoners purchased government posts in order to protect their property and enjoy the privileges of the government officials. Other commoners fled into Manchuria or Russian territory, and still others fled to powerful *yangban* for protection.

Simultaneously, the *yangban* were deeply involved in a brutal struggle among themselves in order to secure political bases. They thus became eager to commit bribery, exploit the lay people, and embezzle government property. Under such tumultuous circumstances many commoners put themselves and their land under a *yangban*'s care. Therefore, the financial situation of the government worsened and the livelihood of the common people became more difficult.

Because the number of the government posts was restricted even though the *yangban* population was increasing, the number of *yangban* who were either ruined or excluded from power and prestige also increased. They naturally became strongly discontented with and critical of social institutions, actually sympathizing with the common people who were suffering from poverty and oppression. From the beginning of the 19th century there appeared posters illustrating the dissatisfaction of the common people. Likewise, songs criticizing social corruption were popularized, and riots frequently occurred all over the country.

The greatest revolt in the last period of the Yi-dynasty was attempted by the *Donghag* group in 1895. The name *Donghag* (Eastern Learning) was taken in opposition to Christianity which was regarded as Western Learning. It was a new religion mixing Confucianism, Buddhism, and *sŏngyo* (a mixture of Taoism, shamanism, and other indigeneous beliefs). Choe Je-wu, the founder of *Donghag*, was born the son of a Taoist scholar and a widow whose former husband had been a student of her new husband. Therefore, Choe's social status was not high. He began to learn Chinese composition during his childhood, but he lost his parents at an early age and was forced to wander throughout Korea as a peddler. Later he turned to religion, and finally developed the *Donghag* doctrine, which claimed that the human being was the embodiment of heaven (God) and that the human mind was the embodied mind of heaven. He advocated the ideal of establishing the kingdom of heaven on earth. It is not surprising, then, that his thought was very attractive to farmers who were extremely oppressed by both officials and *yangban*.

The *Donghag* rebellion began with the movement to apply for a petition to rehabilitate the status of Choe Je-wu, who had been executed. At that time the government, which had held a policy of seclusionism, failed to defend itself from pressures to open the country and from intrusions by foreign powers, thereby losing its authority. Moreover, the economic situation of farmers grew worse because of the intrusion of Japan, which by then was already a proto-capitalist country. Meanwhile, discontent among the common people had peaked, sharpened by taxes and oppression and exploitation at the hands of the *yangban*. At last the movement, which had originally only sought to rehabilitate the reputation of the founder of *Donghag*, turned to violent action, demanding the rejection of foreign powers, the abolition of unjust taxes, the removal of corrupt officials, and the reorganization of the social status system.

The *Donghag* rebellion flared up quickly due to the avid support and active participation of farmers, and in this sense it could be called a rebellion of farmers. But the central members of the *Donghag* rebellion were the *jŏbju*(subleaders) who commanded the celluar organization of *Donghag*. Many of them were actually ruined *yangban* who had received some degree of education and had a sharply critical attitude toward the current social problems. Jŏn Bong-jun, the chief commander of the rebel forces, belonged precisely to that status group. His father, a low-level local official, had attacked a local government office in retaliation for its poor administrative performance and was subsequently executed. He himself was an instructor in Chinese composition at a *sŏdang*(a small private Confucian academy).

Another attempt to change the traditional society during the late Yi-dynasty was the enlightenment movement of the Independence Association which was founded in 1896. The aims of the Independence Association were to achieve independence from the control of China and establish a modern state by preventing foreign armed intervention, the transfer of economic rights to foreigners, and other aggressive colonial actions. In order to achieve these aims, they sought to enlighten people through education, to encourage political participation on the part of the press and the people, and to advance industry. The Independence Association published the *Dognib Sinmun* (Independence Press), the first private newspaper; it was written in the Korean alphabet so that the common people would be able to read it easily. The most important leaders of the Independence Association were the progressive *yangban* intellectuals and officials who struggled against the entrenched conservatives.[14] They were generally diplomats or former students studying abroad who had the chance to make contact with either Japan or the Western civilizations and therefore had witnessed great worldly changes. For example, the editor of Independence Press, Seo Jai-pil, had earlier fled from Korea for political reasons, become a physician in the United States, and married an American woman. However, it is doubtful that the majority of those who agreed with the objectives of the Independence Association, became active members, and subscribed to the Independence Press, were *yangban* in the strict sense of the word. There is little empirical evidence in regard to this issue; however, I personally suspect that most of them were not of the pure *yangban* class, but rather the class just under the *yangban*, that is, *hyangban* or *toban*. One piece of evidence substantiating this notion is that the Independence Press was composed solely with the Korean alphabet and hence there was little in its content to attract members of the *yangban* class.[15]

In spite of considerable popular support, the *Donghag* rebellion was eventually suppressed as a result of Japanese intervention. Although the *Donghag* continued to influence the rural people to some extent even after the rebellion was suppressed, it failed to exert an important influence on the prevailing social-intellectual climate, since it lacked the elements necessary to propel Korea toward modernization.

The Independence Association, on the other hand, was comprised of progressive members and therefore had the necessary potential for exerting considerable influence on Korean modernization and democratization. But the members did not seem to have the strong will required to foment revolutionary action.

The most important structural characteristic of the late Yi-dynasty society is that there was no bourgeois class such as that in western Europe which would have been able to act as a vehicle for facilitating modernization. In general, modernization in Western nations involved a transformation from a feudal to a capitalist society. Sociologically, it was a change in the medium of social relations from status to contract; economically, a change from a system in which land was the major productive tool to a free enterprise system in which capitalists could invest in industrial production for the sake of profit; and politically, it was a change from autocracy to democracy. In the Korean society of the late Yi-dynasty, the movement which attempted to eliminate status restraints and to democratize society appeared to be relatively strong, but an industrializing bourgeois class had not yet been formed, and an economic situation which would allow modernization similar to that of the Western nations and Japan had not yet matured. An editorial of the Independence Press said that Korea fell behind Japan by only about 10 years in education. The implication, of course, is that if Koreans were educated properly, Korea could become like Japan. But this projection was too optimistic. It betrayed a misunderstanding of the nature of modern society and the socio-cultural and economic conditions that are necessary for achieving it.

Korean traditional society began to crumble mainly because of foreign political, economic, and cultural oppression. In coping with strong foreign powers, Korea, which had previously maintained a policy of strict seclusionism, was forced to make treaties of amity and commerce, and yield various concessions. Thus, the land-based traditional ruling system of the central government which had survived for so long began to crack under the strong wave of capitalism.

Around that time Japan, which had already evolved a capitalist system, made every possible attempt to penetrate Korea and control its economy and politics. She moved the Korean government to abolish the traditional status institutions by means of the *Gab-o* Reform. Through this, the Korean people became formally free from the restrictions of the former system, and at least theoretically would have the option of social mobility. The *Gab-o* Reform, however, was not initiated by a rising class, eager to break down the traditional society and build a modern social system. Such a class, in fact, had not yet appeared. As mentioned earlier, farmers and other oppressed people wanted to abolish or restructure the old status system. But they did not demand its replacement by a system which conducted modern human relations on the basis of contract.

Another event which hastened the destruction of the traditional society was the land survey. Japan, which was ready to colonize Korea after the Russo-Japanese war (1904-05), needed a system by which property, mainly land, could be sold and bought more conveniently. Otherwise, capitalist enterprise and colonial exploitation could not be efficiently carried out. The land survey, an investigation of the size, form, ownership and so on of all Korean land, started a year before the Japanese annexation of Korea, and proceeded rapidly after annexation.[16]

Social Structure during the Japanese Domination

1. Changes under Colonial Domination

The Japanese began implementing a colonial governing system in Korea at the time of annexation. The first thing that they began to change was the system of law and administration. They abolished or amended the old laws and made new ones conveniently suited for themselves. They also designed an administrative system that was planned and executed only by Japanese.

With few exceptions, their most important principle of colonial rule was the maximization of economic interest. Therefore, they made facilities to advance Japanese capital and to supply essential raw materials, and they expanded the market for their goods in Korea. In order to alleviate Japan's chronic food shortage they appropriated Korean agricultural products, including grain, and in order to solve the Japanese population problem they sponsored colonial settlement. A second principle was to restrain Korean resistance as much as possible. Initially, Japan instituted a military government in Korea. After the Independence Movement in 1919, however, this policy was modified to one with a native cultural emphasis which seemingly mitigated the oppressive policy. Yet the Japanese still maintained a strong police force with which to oppress Koreans. In order to assuage rebellious feelings among the Koreans, especially within the old *yangban* class, they preserved the royal family and arranged for the prince to marry a Japanese princess; they also allowed most *yangban* to remain in the upper stratum of Korean society as landowners.

A third principle was to use Korea as a base for expansion. Of course, at the beginning of Japanese colonial domination, Japan was busy in managing Korea itself and therefore made few efforts to advance into the Asian continent; but as the economy developed they expanded their policy, and Korea began to function as a logistic base for Japanese expansion. Accordingly, industrial and transportation facilities were extensively developed. All of this, of course, was carried out only to further Japanese interests. For example, the railroad from *Busan* to *Sinŭiju* was established not for well-balanced economic development in Korea but rather to facilitate Japanese economic and military expansion into Manchuria and China.

Outwardly, the Japanese upheld the principle that Koreans and Japanese should be treated equally, but in practice they discriminated against Koreans in many ways. Koreans, for example, didn't have the right to participate in the legislative body. Likewise, they were restricted in their appointment as officials, and were discriminated against in terms of receiving higher education, which was the only avenue through which one could hope to become a high ranking official.

Statistical figures show that rapid economic development took place in Korea during the Japanese domination. Of course, this does not at all mean that the development was planned for the welfare of the Korean people,[17] nor that its benefits were shared equally by Koreans and Japanese. But we will discuss this topic in detail later.

Instead, let us look at some of the main features of Korea's development during the period of Japanese rule. First of all, transportation developed greatly. By 1910 a 1,118.5km railroad had been laid, and by 1937 it was extended to 5,267.8km. Within a quarter of a century, railroad trackage increased 470 percent.[18] As the railroad system grew, the transportation of passengers and cargo increased, too. In 1910 the annual number of passengers was 2,020,000 while by 1937 it had increased to 36,000,000, almost 18 times the number of passengers in 1910. During the same period cargo increased from 900,000 to 11,370,000 tons which is about a 13-fold increase.[19] Not only internal but also external transportation was developed. Regular sea routes to Japan, China, and Russia (Vladivostok) were established. Modern ports including *Busan* and *Inchŏn* were developed. After 1929, when civil air flight to *Tokyo* became available, the network of air routes also increased.

The most developed economic sector was probably industry, especially the mining industry. There were 796 approved mine-lots in 1911, a number which increased to 7,454 by 1936, and to 11,735 by 1942.[20] Similarly, in 1926 there were 23,299 miners, and their number increased to 139,934 by 1936.[21] The value of mining industrial products produced in 1911 was 61,850,000 *yen*, but by 1936 this stood at 1,104,290,000 *yen*.[22] This is a tremendous increase, even if inflation is taken into consideration.

Similarly, the electrical industry developed greatly. In 1910 Korea's electric power generating capacity was only 190kw. By 1937, however, capacity had increased to 848,452kw.[23] The number of manufacturing factories increased as well, from 252 in 1911 to 6,952 in 1937; workers increased from 14,575 to 207,003 and the volume of industrial products in terms of product-value grew from 20,000,000 *yen* to 967,000,000 *yen* during the same period of time. After 1937, when Japan started to invade the Chinese mainland, she bolstered her Korean facilities as a logistic base for the military operations and further accelerated industrial development in Korea.

The most important industrial sector in terms of product value was the food industry, the output of which was valued at about 200,000,000 *yen* in 1936. The second most important sector was the chemical industry, with output valued at 195,000,000 *yen*, and third was the textile industry, with output valued at about 100,000,000 *yen*. Trailing these three were the gas, electric, metalworking, ceramics, machinery, printing and bookbinding industries.[24] From index levels of 100 in 1936, by 1939 the output of the metalworking industry had developed to an index level of 403, the machinery industry to 394, the chemical industry to 256, the lumber and wooden goods industry to 212, the textile industry to 202, the ceramics to 198, and the food industry to 164. Thus the heavy and chemical industries developed particularly rapidly.[25]

Agriculture was not as rapidly developed as industry, but it also grew considerably. The average yield for one *dan* (approximately 9,450 square meters or roughly 0.1 hectare,) of rice, the chief grain, was 0.8309 *sŏg* (one *sŏg* is approximately 5 bushels) on the average from 1910 to 1914, a figure which increased to 1.2937 *sŏg* during the period 1935 to 1937. This is about a 1.5 times increase. However, the productivity of other kinds of grain improved very little. From index levels of 100 at the beginning of the colonial period, barley yield levels reached only an index of 106 thirty years later, chestnut yields increased to 103, while wheat yields fell to 99, and soybeans to 90. Since the area of cultivated fields increased, the total volume of the annual harvest grew. The volume of the rice harvest averaged 11,815,000 *sŏg* from 1910 to 1914, and increased to 21,364,000 *sŏg* or by 1.8 times by 1935 to 1937. Total barley production increased 1.44 times, soybean production 1.22 times, chestnut production 1.35 times, and wheat production 1.23 times.[26]

Apart from the economy, advances were also achieved in education. Korean people by tradition have strong educational aspirations. In the year of the Japanese Annexation, the total number of students enrolled in elementary schools was 16,946, and there were 19 high schools.[27] During the Japanese colonial period, modern educational facilities were expanded greatly. According to the annual report by the Government-General in 1944, the number of Korean children in regular elementary schools was 1,710,948. In addition, schools with shorter curricula were attached to regular public elementary schools and enrolled 117,211 children. Private primary schools had 54,323 children enrolled. Almost all of the students in these schools were Koreans, making a total of 1,882,482. In the middle schools, the total number of students was 97,650, and in the governmental and public middle schools, 40,309. Private students numbered 11,422; those in various technical schools numbered 39,886; and those attending normal schools numbered 6,033.[28] The number of college and university students was 3,909. There were also many Koreans who studied in foreign countries, especially in Japan and Manchuria.

Another trend that accelerated during the Japanese period which must be pointed out is urbanization. Initially, urbanization did not proceed rapidly. In 1925, 15 years after Japanese Annexation, the urban share of the total population was no more than 5.04% and in 1935, only 7.01%, in spite of the fact that farm villages didn't have enough land and were filled with poor, starving farmers. This was because Korean cities were by and large dominated by Japanese. This prevented Koreans from finding occupations easily. But by 1942 the urban share of the population increased to 14%, twice that of 1935. During the same period of time, the Japanese population in Korea increased to 169,359, 0.64% of the entire population of Korea.[29] We may therefore infer that most of the increasing urban population during that time were Koreans.

But urbanizaion under Japanese domination was significant not because of the increase in urban population, but rather in the modern form of urban life which emerged. The modernization of Korean cities began in the late Yi-dynasty. At that time electricity, the telephone, and electric cars were introduced. But the majority of the Korean people did not experience urban life (in terms of such amenities as pavement, water-works, sewerage, urban gas, department stores, and movie theaters) until after the Japanese Annexation.

Such developmental changes during the Japanese domination were accompanied, of course, by the ruthless exploitation and oppression of the Korean people. There were many Western observers who took note of such outward development but failed to see the sacrifice of the Korean people; reports made by such men were used for propaganda by the Government-General.[30] But Koreans attempted to disclose the truth as well as they could despite the fact that criticism of Japanese colonial policies was strictly regulated. For example, the *Sidae-ilbo* of 10 March, 1925 reported, "In short, the livelihood and business opportunities for the Korean people have deteriorated every year. The number of persons who have been ruined financially has increased geometrically. This is mainly because the Government-General has imposed too much of a tax burden on the Korean people. Thus, while the means of livelihood and commercial prosperity of Koreans have deteriorated, the income of the Government-General has increased." Later the same paper on 12 May, 1925 reported, "To expand the railroad means to arrange transportation so that it seems superficially to civilize and modernize society; but because today's situation in Korea is unique, the more it is arranged, the more rapidly our life is ruined."

Concerning the plan for increasing rice production, the *Donga-ilbo* of 12 July, 1925 pointed out, "It changes ultimately the staple of Koreans from millet to the roots of grass, their shelter from houses to tents, and their clothing from worn clothes to nothing." The *Josŏn-ilbo* of 23 May, 1926 also emphasized that Koreans had become poorer and that the number of wanderers had increased because of the plan to increase rice production. As an example, the *Josŏn-ilbo* on 31 May, 1927 reported that Korean tenant farmers, merchants with small capital, and workers had become poorer because the great Japanese capitalist *Mitsubishi* had established a hydro-electric power station at *Hamhŭng*. In addition there were many articles that pointed out inhumane Japanese policies of oppression and exploitation, not only economically but also culturally, educationally, and politically.

But why do I mention these features of the Japanese modernization of Korea? Because I think that in spite of its compulsory and oppressive nature, Koreans were successful in adapting to the new ideas concerning modern life, and this directly influenced the development of Korea after the liberation.

2. Social Structural Change[31]

We have indicated that industry, education, and urbanization developed considerably during the period of Japanese rule but that it was done by the Japanese, ultimately for the Japanese, and at a great sacrifice to the Koreans. In the case of the land survey, land for which ownership was either not clear or not reported properly fell into the hands of the Government-General. A great deal of woodland also fell into the hands of the Government-General through the Forest Ordinance. Altogether, the total amount of land, both farmland and woodland, owned by the Government-General was 8,880,000 *jŏngbo* (one *jŏngbo* is approximately 2.4 acre or one hectare) which constituted about 40 % of all the farm and wood land in the whole country according to the statistics of 1930. Later the Government-General sold part of the land cheaply to companies managed by Japanese, including the Oriental Development Corporation, and owing to this, many Japanese became great landowners in Korea.[32]

Agriculture was the industry in which the majority of Koreans were engaged. According to the statistics of 1937, the total number of farmhouses was 3,060,000 in Korea and the proportion of the Japanese farmhouses to it was only 1.6%. But the great landowners, i.e. those persons who owned more than 100 *jŏngbo*, included 655 Koreans (67.4%) as compared to 317 Japanese (32.6 %). Among these great landowners, the total acreage owned by the Japanese was 156,340 *jŏngbo*, while that of Koreans was 166,042 *jŏngbo*. This obviously means that the average size of farmland per Korean landowner was smaller than that of his

Japanese counterpart.

Korean farmers under the Japanese domination became poorer. In 1918, tenancy was 38.1% of the total farming population, but by 1937 it had increased to 55.1%. E. de S. Brunner, who surveyed Korean farming villages probably in 1927, reported[33] that according to government statistics, over a two-year period the number of independently owned farm houses had decreased by 11,623, which translates to a decrease of 11% over 10 years, while the number of partly independent and partly tenant farmers' houses decreased by 41,584 or 22% over a 10 year period. On the other hand, pure tenancy among farm households increased by 43,482, or 20% over 10 years. And during the same period, the number of landless farmers, who were forced to engage in fire-field (swidden) cultivation, increased from 30,000 to 70,000. Also, the amount of farmland per farm house decreased from 163 *jŏngbo* to 145 *jŏngbo* during the period. This suggests that the average farmland per farmhouse was decreasing steadily year by year. In 1930, about 60 or 70 per cent of all tenants had no grain to carry them through the spring.[34] Therefore, most of them ran into debt on which they had to pay high interest, and consequently only survived by eating roots and bark. Others were forced to begin a wandering life.

The exact number of Korean emigrants to Manchuria, Japan and the other foreign countries during the Japanese domination is not known. According to the government's estimate, there were 460,000 Korean emigrants in Manchuria by 1920. This figure increased to about 810,000 persons by 1935, most of whom were engaged in agriculture. In Japan there were about 30,000 emigrants in 1920, and the number increased to about 530,000 persons by 1930.

Farmhouse debt steadily increased during the Japanese domination. In 1927, Brunner investigated 145 farmhouses in the northern area and found that two of every five of them had carried a debt of 60 *yen* at an average yearly interest rate of 30%. He also surveyed 110 houses near Seoul, and observed that four out of five families had an average debt of 100 *yen* which carried a yearly interest of 48%. And of the 130 families he studied in the southern area, 111 had a debt exceeding their yearly income and on which they paid an average yearly interest of 36 %.[35] All of these statistics vividly show what poor lives Korean farmers had.

It is true that industry developed during the Japanese domination, but as I mentioned, it was managed and its benefits were realized mostly by the Japanese. The number of manufacturing companies in Korea in 1938 was 5,414. And of these the number of companies which had Korean directors was 2,278 (42.1%) while the number with Japanese directors including a few other foreigners was 3,136 (57.9%). The total paid-up capital of the Japanese companies was 958,622,000 *yen* and that of the Korean companies was 122,660,000 *yen*. In other words, 87.7% of the total paid-up capital in Korea was in Japanese companies; the companies which had Korean directors were therefore very small in scale.

The types of industry in which Korean investments were highest were commerce (26.2%) and agriculture and forestry (20.7%); Japanese investments were highest in financial operations, industry, electricity, marine products industry, mining, transportation, and warehousing. Of these, electricity, marine products industry, mining, transportation, and warehousing were virtually monopolized by Japanese.

In spite of Japanese oppression the degree of Korean participation in the mining industry increased to some extent. In 1910 Koreans controlled not more than 4.8% of the entire mining industry, while Japanese controlled 22.7% and other foreigners 72.5%. By 1935, however, Koreans controlled 13.4%, Japanese 80.5%, and other foreigners only 6.1% of the entire industry. At the same time the number of Korean mine-lots increased to 47.2% of all mine-lots in 1935. But nevertheless the Korean mines produced only 13.4% of the total output. This means that the Korean mines were in general small and poor in yield.

The same tendency appeared in industry. Sixty-six factories were managed by Koreans in 1910 which was only 26.2 per cent of the total number of factories. By 1928, this figure increased to 2,751 factories (51.7 per cent of the total); by 1936 it had grown to 3,415 factories (57.6 per cent of the total number). However, the productivity of Korean-owned factories remained very low. In 1928, for example, their production share in value terms was only 26.6 per cent of the country's total. This may in part be attributed to the fact that there were few Korean factories which used modern equipment and technology. In 1933, among 54 factories with paid-up capital of between 300,000 *yen* and 1,000,000 *yen* 23 were owned by Japanese and 37 by other foreigners, while Koreans owned only 4 factories. There were twenty-three factories which had more than one million *yen* in paid-up capital, yet Koreans owned not even one of them.

Now let us look at the labor conditions of the Korean workers. According to the statistics of 1931, out of a total of 65,374 factory workers the number of Koreans was 55,991 (85.7%), the number of Japanese 6,169 (9.4%) and the number of Chinese 3,214 (4.9%). The kinds of industries in which Korean workers were most numerous were textiles (97.1%), food processing (96.7%), and printing and binding (93.6%); and those in which they were least numerous were the sawing and wooden goods industry (51.4%), chemical industry (66.6%), and metal working industry (68.4%). Japanese made up large shares of the workers engaged in the chemical industry (32.7%), gas and electric industry (25.9%), machine industry (23.2%), and metal working industry (13.3%).

The wages of Korean workers compared with those of their Japanese counterparts were very low. At the minimum wage level, this difference was most severe. Accoring to the statistics of 1937 which show wage levels in factories with more than 50 workers, the wages of Japanese male adult workers averaged 1.88 *yen* per day, but that of Koreans was only half that, or 0.95 *yen*. The wages of Japanese female adult workers averaged 0.98 *yen*, but that of Korean women was ony 0.48 *yen*.

About 80 per cent of all factory workers had to work more than 10 hours per day, and 50 per cent were forced to work more than 12 hours. Under such harsh circumstances, labor disputes were frequent. In 1930 and 1931 when the oppression was not so strong, there occurred 160 and 204 cases, respectively, involving labor unrest. More than 90 per cent of the workers involved in these disputes were Koreans. But later labor movements were oppressed strongly, and finally prohibited when the Japanese began to prepare for their continental invasion.

In the case of government officials,[36] most of the posts involving actual decision-making were, of course, occupied by Japanese. Though there were a few Koreans appointed to important posts, this was only because the Japanese wanted to give the impression of treating Koreans equally. In reality these posts were controlled by Japanese. According to the statistics of 1942, among 3,443 higher officials, the number of Koreans was not more than 490 (14.2%). Among 7,420 middle officials, there were 27,286 Koreans (36.9%). Only in the case of lower officials were there more Koreans than Japanese.

This discrimination against Koreans was even more severe in education. At the beginning of Japanese domination, the colonial rulers prepared educational establishments for Japanese children, but they neglected the elementary education of Koreans. In 1920, 10 years after the annexation, 91.5 per cent of the Japanese children of school age were students in elementary school, but the figure was only 3.7 per cent for Korean children.[37] The Japanese began to develop Korean elementary education only in order to obtain trainable low-wage nonskilled workers.

The discrimination against Koreans was even stronger at the middle school level.[38] As mentioned earlier, the total number of Korean students in middle schools in 1942 was 97,650 or 0.38 per cent of the whole population of Koreans. On the other hand, the number of Japanese middle school students in the same year was 37,183 which constituted 4.9 per cent of the total Japanese population in Korea.

In higher education, there were 3,909 college students in Korea. Grossly speaking the number of Korean students outnumbered that of Japanese students, but in the government-operated colleges the number of Japanese students was 2.5 times that of Korean students. The same tendency was found in the Keijo Imperial University, the only university in existence before 1945.[39] It means that a great number of Korean college students had to study at private colleges which had worse facilities than government colleges.

The Korean people were ruled by a handful of Japanese who numbered only about 3 per cent of the whole population. The main field in which the Japanese people in Korea were most active was government. The statistics of 1937 show that about 41 per cent of the 750 thousand Japanese in Korea were government employees or professionals, 28 per cent were engaged in commerce and transportation, 16 per cent in the manufacturing industry, 7 per cent in agriculture and forestry, and 8 per cent in others. Contrastingly, the great majority of Koreans (78% of the entire Korean population) were occupied in agriculture. Other fields where they were employed were commerce (7%), manufacturing industry (3%), government employees (3%), and others (9%). There were a few Koreans who were big land-owners, entrepreneurs, high-ranking officials, or professionals, but it is obvious that most Koreans were relegated to a life of poverty at the bottom of the society.

Many Koreans occupied in primary industries rapidly shifted to secondary or tertiary industries in the latter half of the 1930s. In 1930, 80.5 per cent of all Koreans were occupied in primary industry, but by 1938 this proportion had decreased to 75.7 per cent, and by 1942 to 68.2 per cent.[40]

This shift probably occurred because the Japanese augmented the secondary industries, especially the military-related industries, in preparation for their invasion of China. The expansion of the secondary industries required many Korean workers and low level employees. On the other hand, when Manchuria came under Japanese domination and Japanese power extended to the Chinese mainland, many Korean farmers and traders emigrated to these areas. This is another explanation for the shift of the farm population.

In this way, during the last decade of Japanese domination, a number of Koreans who left the agricultual sector and were engaged in modern industry increased rapidly. Most of them were probably simple workers who therefore did not require sophisticated skills. But it seems that a number of entrepreneurs, managers, professionals, or others, who were engaged in positions which could play an important role in managing a modern society, would more sharply increase during this period of time than ever before.

3. Thought under Colonial Control
⟨Development of Modern Thought⟩

Modern Korean thought was already forming during the late Yi-dynasty, and that thought was disseminated by certain newspapers such as the Independence Press.[41] It was further propagated by schools and Christian groups, and was popularized by statesmen and social leaders who had observed Western society, including the members of the Independence Association.[42]

Western ideas gained broader acceptance in Korea during the age of Japanese domination. Traditional Confucian thought lost its influence gradually, and conventional beliefs, customs, and other unscientific and unproductive ideas were criticized. During the period of Japanese rule, the reason that Western thought was so successful in spreading its influence was that it had been developed in powerful and rich nations and seemed, therefore, to promise prosperity. Moreover, China, the sovereign state of Confucianism, had become semi-colonized by these Western nations.

One of the Western ideas that had the greatest influence during this period was Christianity. The Western people who infiltrated Korea most persistently were not merchants but rather Christian missionaries. They established schools and hospitals as well as churches and actively proselytized. In this way they provided Koreans with many cultural benefits. Their work also continued through the period of Japanese domination. Christianity, however, was not attractive to *yangban*. They were familiar with the tradition of the Chinese classics and schooled in difficult Chinese composition. Consequently, they were apt to regard simple preaching in *hangŭl* (the Korean alphabet) and the singing of psalms as a bad influence. Furthermore, they disliked Christianity's opposition to ancestor worship. Therefore, Christianity initially won support among the common people, who were alienated from power. Later it expanded broadly among both the urban and rural populations.[43]

Christianity as a religion was not related to modern thought directly. But Western missionaries brought Western civilization with them, and institutionalized it in the schools and hospitals they established. Also, they fostered democratic ideals and rational thinking, both openly and secretly. When the Japanese started imposing an inhumane colonial governing system and attempted to eradicate Korean culture, even going so far as to enforce worship at Japanese *Shinto* shrines, Christian missionaries encouraged the Korean movement toward independence. Christian groups thus functioned as important catalysts for Korean independence, while at the same time fostered modern development.

The other organizations which introduced new ideas to inspire the common people were the newspapers and schools. The newspapers managed by Koreans promoted both anti-Japanese sentiment and modern ideas, and were inspired by a mission to enlighten the common people and to help realize social justice. Since there were many Japanese teachers in Korean schools and the government could easily interfere there, values relating to politics were not openly emphasized in the public educational system. In the private schools, however, which had few Japanese teachers, anti-Japanese thought was emphasized strongly.

In the elementary schools where the Japanese government could interfere easily, there was an effort to instill pro-Japanese values in Korean students. The Japanese enforced the sanctification of the Japanese Emperor, devotion to Japan and worship at Japanese *Shinto* shrines. Since Japan was as yet an underdeveloped capitalist state, she needed to promote Confucian ideas in order to maintain authoritarian social order. But maintaining Confucian ideas had another important purpose in Korea. During the age of Japanese domination, the *yangban* landowners who still had great power believed in Confucianism strongly. Hence, the Japanese supported the *hyang-gyo* (community Confucian schools), allowed ancestor worship, and infused Confucian values into textbooks, all of which was done to get support from the *yangban*.

Later Japan invaded Manchuria and China and openly conspired with the Axis countries to oppose the Western democracies. Japan strengthened her totalitarian control over Korea, and tried to eliminate individualism, liberalism and democratic elements entirely. But ironically, this policy only served to make Koreans more sympathetic toward Western thought. This tendency was probably strongest among the urban intelligentsia, and those who were engaged in the occupations related to social concerns such as the press, religious groups, and cultural organizations.

⟨The Rise of Nationalism⟩

Another importans phenomenon that must be emphasized is the rise of nationalism.[44] The Independence Association developed into a national movement for independence, performing a vanguard role in inspiring nationalist ideas, and most especially stimulating the national consciousness of the people through the Independence Press. Some of the participants in the Independence Association had been exposed to the civilization of the advanced Western nations. These men felt that it was urgently necessary to promote a policy for maintaining independence and constructing a wealthy and powerful Korea, because they observed that the powerful Western countries were often able to use strong military and economic power in order to dominate weaker countries. Also, they realized that the influence of Japan and Russia on Korea had become too strong.

It was only after the Japanese Annexation that Koreans developed a distinct national consciousness, however. After Japanese annexation, volunteer guerrilla forces and secret associations appeared which attempted to oppose the Japanese conquerors with force. Many organizations were organized which aimed ultimately at independence while outwardly keeping a legal appearance. Since it became very difficult to spread such a movement for independence in Korea because of ruthless control by the Japanese army and police, many nationalists took refuge in China and America and conducted systematic activities there. Some attacked the Japanese conquerors with armed force from across the Manchurian border.

After President Wilson of America formulated principles of racial self-determination at the end of the First World War, patriotic leaders declared a manifesto of Korean independence on the 1st of March, 1919, and initiated a movement for independence on a nationwide scale. But it was soon repressed by force of Japanese arms.

After the Independence Movement, Japanese rulers changed their coercive military policy to a more moderate cultural policy. With the change of Japanese colonial policy, various cultural movements became popular among the Korean people.[45] They developed education, studies on Korean language and Korean history, and other pursuits related to the development of a national culture.

Along with this trend, there was a new feature in the Korean national movement and that was the rise of socialism as an ideology; it had already spread among intellectuals to some extent before 1920, but it was not strong enough to be characterized as a socialist movement. However, after 1920 there appeared several philosophies related to socialist thought, including anarchism and communism. Initially, the socialist movement was somewhat popular because Marxian theory attracted some young intellectuals with the idea that the national fate of Korea should be understood not solely from an emotional or political point of view but rather in terms of the nature of capitalism, the final stage of which was thought to be imperialism.

Secondly, the Russian Revolution, which succeeded in establishing communist rule over a nation for the first time, provided a new gospel to Koreans who were disappointed with the past performance of their independence movement and the idea of racial self-determination. Moreover, after World War I communist ideology became popular among the Japanese, and consequently Korean students who were studying in Japan were influenced by it too. Also, a Korean communist party was organized in Russia and subsequently spread to Korea.[46] Thirdly, Koreans became more strongly concerned with economic problems because of the prevailing world wide depression at that time, which aggravated the already miserable economic situation of the Korean people.

With the appearance of communist ideology, the world of Korean thought became separated into three divisions: (1) Confucianists, who represented the feudal power; (2) nationalists, who strove to restore national independence, while accepting the modern capitalist system; and (3) socialists, who attempted to liberate the nation through a class struggle approach. These three groups struggled against each other. Although the Confucianists exerted influence over lay people to some degree, they gradually began to decline and become isolated from the main current of Korean society. Communists, on the other hand, were not regarded as a legitimate group and were oppressed by the rulers of Japan, particularly during the last years of Japanese domination.

Social Structure after the Liberation

1. Social Confusion

Korea was liberated by the triumph of the Allied Powers over the Axis countries, and was promised independence by the declarations made at Cairo and Potsdam. Unfortunately, however, prior to achieving independence, Korean society was extremely disorganized.

The reason for this disorganization was, first, that after the Japanese defeat, no proper administration for maintaining social order was prepared. The Japanese army and administration remained in power until the army of the the Allied Powers advanced into Korea and took control. Therefore, Korean self-government was organized in an attempt tentatively to maintain social order; but as it turned out, they were unable to accomplish it effectively. The army of Soviet Russia moved into northern Korea very quickly, but the United States army advanced into the southern area much later. Accordingly, social disorder was more severe in South Korea than in the North.

The second reason for the disorganization was that the war-time structure of Korea was suddenly changed into a free open-door system. Even in a country where the administrative machine functions normally, the shift from a war-time situation to a peace-time one is likely to result in confusion. It is not surprising then that Korea, which shifted so drastically from a government of strict control to one with virtually no control, fell into chaos. And it must be noted that the economic and political confusion were particularly severe. Indeed, the price of goods went up precipitously, and, almost overnight, numerous political factions appeared.

The third reason for the disorganization may be attributed to the division of Korea. Korea, previously an integral part of the whole Japanese system, was separated from it suddenly, and more importantly, was divided at the 38th parallel. The two parts, of course, were occupied separately by America and Soviet Russia, states with fundamentally different and seemingly incompatible systems. We can easily imagine how seriously Korea was paralysed.

The fourth reason for the disorganization was that the American army of occupation did not have a distinct policy for Korea. They believed in the idea of democracy and adopted as their supreme principle that all decisions be made by the inhabitants themselves. Consequenty, they didn't seek to actively control the disorder.

The fifth reason for the disorganization was that during the colonial period, most social institutions were occupied by Japanese who wouldn't permit self-governing activities on the part of Koreans.

Nor, for that matter, did they permit organizations to exist which would actually reflect the opinion of the Korean majority. Moreover, the persons who were capable of managing these activities were by and large not residing in Korea. Therefore, the Korean people had to wait until the leaders of the anti-Japanese, independence movements in China, America, and the other countries returned to Korea. Finally, while North Korea was unified by a communist government under the control of Soviet Russia, South Korea was torn by the ideological struggle between the right and the left, in which no one faction could dominate. This conflict allowed communists to infiltrate into the administrative, legislative, and judicial systems, as well as the army, police, and even schools, both openly and secretly.

In 1948, South Korea became independent as a liberal democratic nation under the leadership of Syngman Rhee. He took strong action to destroy the communist party in South Korea. Nevertheless, the violent activities of the communist party continued unabated. Guerillas operated throughout *Jeju* province, and a revolt occurred in the army which had been dispatched there to suppress them. Later, party members who were secretly dispatched from North Korea secured positions and expanded their power.

Social disorder in South Korea peaked by the outbreak of the Korean War. Houses were destroyed, many men died or were separated from their families, and people eked out a precarious living under the communist system. When the Red Chinese army intervened and the UN Forces retreated south of the *Han* River, most of Seoul's inhabitants fled to *Busan*, *Daegu*, and other southern places and remained there until the restoration of the capital. The decade of disorder lasting from the liberation to the end of the Korean War had a great influence on Korean society. First, illegal and non-ethical behavior became more widespread, and was especially severe in public organizations because the standard laws which applied to these institutions didn't correspond with the disordered reality of society. Also, because the salary of those who worked in public institutions was very low, corruption was commonplace.

Second, the integration of values could not occur easily and accordingly social integration did not take place. In other words, the functions of the social organizations were not performed as desired by the people. This tendency appeared in all aspects of society, and was especially prominent in institutions like the family, which is managed by customs rather than codified rules. In Korean families of this period, the traditional authority of fathers became weak, and women and children became relatively free. Therefore ideas which previously had not been respected, and persons who had been badly treated began to act more freely.

Third, social and geographical mobility became possible with the destruction of the established system. As mentioned above, many people moved down to South Korea both before and during the Korean War, and the inhabitants of South Korea also migrated in search of refuge. They included not only city dwellers, but also farmers who had never left their land before. Most male adults who could fight served their military duty in the army or one or another of the various defense organizations, including the National Guard, which were organized during the Korean War.

This necessarily caused Koreans to cast away traditional elements which did not have practical survival value and cling to those new ideas which would allow them to successfully adjust to changes and difficulties. In many ways, Koreans were in a situation comparable to that of the early immigrants who settled on the American continent. Those early immigrants, imbued though they were with European values and ideas, no doubt had to discard those cultural elements that were not useful positions. Most of them had belonged to the middle class during the period of Japanese domination. This sudden and widespread upward mobility of the middle class after the liberation had an important influence on the development of an anti-communist attitude among Koreans.

History teaches us that the class which most often attempts to change a society is the class belonging to the margin of the ruling class and yet excluded from its privileges. The core of this class during the late Yi-dynasty, which attempted social change, were *hyangban, toban,* and *sŏ-ŏl*. Likewise, during the colonial period the persons who struggled against the Japanese for national independence were also from the middle classes and were frequently descended from *hyangban, toban* and *sŏ-ŏl*.

If the colonial governing power or the upper class which conspired with it could have maintained power after World War II, the middle class might well have adopted a communist ideology and attempted to change Korean society over to a communist system. Among the intellectuals who were highly educated during the Japanese domination, there were certainly some who either espoused communist ideology or favored it. After the liberation, however, there was no need to foment a communist revolution, since the colonial governing power and the upper class that conspired with it had already lost their power.

This characteristic of class structure after the liberation also had a special implication with regard to egalitarianism. Traditional Korean society had a strong tendency to emphasize status distinction rather than equality. But after the liberation most of the persons who performed the important roles were young men originating from the middle class. By and large they didn't have any distinct qualifications that would entitle them to these eminent positions, excluding the few who had demonstrated remarkable devotion to the anti-Japanese independence movement. To them all Koreans were victims of Japanese imperialism. In other words they were apt to identify with the farmers and workers who suffered the brunt of economic hardship and to recognize them as their brothers. This egalitarian notion was also consistent with the democratic ideals which Korea, as an emerging young state, was trying to cultivate. Thus an egalitarian social climate was formed in Korean society for the first time in her history.

The other important change in terms of social structure was found in rural society. In 1939, the percentage of tenant farmers in the total farm population was 52.3%, while that of partly independent and partly tenant farmers was 23.8%. Because most of the farmers were tenants, informed persons recognized that there was a need to enact some kind of land reform in order to create appropriate conditions in which democratization and modernization might take place. In March of 1946, a year after the liberation, land reform was enforced in North Korea. The government confiscated land from landowners without compensation and distributed it to tenant farmers at no cost, granting only the right of cultivation, not ownership.

In South Korea, however, land reform wasn't enforced until June of 1949. Nevertheless, even before that much of the landowners' land had been passed over to tenant farmers under relatively favourable conditions for their survival. Thus they developed a pragmatic way of thinking. This is one of the reasons that Koreans have become oriented toward a materialistic outlook as well as become more adaptable to change in their thinking.

2. Dynamics of Social Structure

The social structure of Korean society changed drastically after the liberation. As the Japanese withdrew, the important high positions they formerly occupied became available to Koreans. The few Koreans who did achieve high socio-economic status during the Japanese period could not take leading public roles because most of them had cooperated with the Japanese either intentionally or unintentionally. Landowners were largely ruined because after the liberation the U.S. military government protected tenant farmers from ruthless exploitation, and enforced a new system that decreased tenant rent levels from the former half-share of the output to a lower 30% share. Land reform was enacted in 1949 one year after the Korean government was established.

Koreans had to be recruited for the important posts in government, companies, and social organizations which had previously been occupied by Japanese. The political and military organizations essential for Korea as an emerging nation also had to be managed by Koreans. The persons who were recruited for these positions could not be old, uneducated, rural people who were tradition-oriented. Rather they had to come from the younger groups, who had a proper understanding of modern society and the required experience to act in a modern organization. As such even persons under 30 years of age frequently occupied important conditions. According to an academic report, farmers had already acquired just as much as that which was later distributed under the land reform law.[47] Because the situation in North Korea was widely known, landowners in South Korea no doubt judged that a reasonable transaction as soon as possible with their tenants would be advantageous in the long run. In any case, after the land reform about 80% of South Korea's farmers became independent.

Generally, Korean economists seem to be critical of the land reform of South Korea.[48] But from a sociological point of view, the fact that most farmers were able to own their own land had very positive effects, even though the average holding size per farmer was not more than 1 jŏngbo; farmers had not only the economic satisfaction that they would be entitled to the fruits of their labors, but also the psychological satisfaction that they had finally acquired precisely that asset which they had so long been anxious to have. Morover, it was very significant sociologically that the very landlords who had exploited them had suddenly disappeared, and that the farmers could discuss and solve their own problems themselves.

In spite of many defects, the land reform made it difficult for communist guerrillas to take root in South Korea. After World War II, there were many guerrillas in the rural areas of Asian countries, and that included South Korea. In South Korea, moreover, their strength was augmented by the support of North Korea. But farmers in South Korea, most of whom already had their own land, were generally not attracted to the communist slogans. And in fact, many farmers were greatly disappointed by the ruthlessness of the communists, and particularly by their burdensome tax policy during the Korean War.

Right after the liberation, upward mobility was hastened mostly through the distribution of Japanese property and positions, but also by recruitment to the newly formed government. After the Korean War, mobility was further stimulated by the expansion of the army, the increase of its influence, and the influx of foreign economic support for reconstruction. During this period, entrepreneurs in the *Gyŏngsang* Provinces generally found themselves in a very advantageous position.

Even before the outbreak of the Korean War there were many persons in North and South *Gyŏngsang* Provinces who had already gained experience in modern economic ativities. These two provinces, in fact, had greater potential for economic development than any in South Korea except Seoul. We may be able to suggest some reasons for this such as *Daegu*'s herb medicine market with its long history, *Busan*'s early opening as a modern port, and the movement of Japanese commerce and industry through these provinces. Moreover, many persons from the *Gyŏngsang* Provinces went to Japan as workers or on other business, and the pipe-line for Japanese colonial management and continental invasion began in *Busan* and passed through these areas.

Furthermore, during the retreat period of the Korean War, all the important institutions in Seoul moved to *Busan* or the surrounding areas, and every effort for development was made there. Therefore, it is quite natural that the people of the *Gyŏngsang* Provinces enjoyed better economic opportunities.

The social structure, unrecovered from the post-liberation period of chaos, was once again severely shaken by the Korean War. Until then, only persons who participated in the independence movement or had contributed to national development were allowed to occupy important positions; but many of these persons were found to lack the experience, knowledge and judgment necessary for managing a modern nation. Moreover, those who were disliked by Syngman Rhee for political reasons began to lose their power and or positions. The upper class during the Rhee government period was reconstructed to consist of important administration officials, high ranking military officers, and entrepreneurs who were strongly attached to his government.

The Rhee government collapsed after the student uprising in April, 1960, just after the election which took place on the 15th of March, 1960. The immediate reason for the collapse of the Rhee government was widespread corruption. But the more fundamental cause may be attributed to the discontent of the middle class with their status situation. The middle class was split into two goups during the process of social change after the liberation; a minority belonged to the new upper class, while the great majority remained in the same social position. The latter believed that the former were prospering through either unjust and corrupt behavior or by conspiracy with those in political power, and indeed there was much evidence to support this supposition. Moreover, this assumption was convenient for venting the frustration of the middle class.

The discontent of the middle class was highlighted by the media. The press, which by nature has a strong tendency to promote social justice and democratic values, especially freedom of speech, censured and exposed the wrongdoers. And since most of the reporters, editors, and readers of the press were middle class people, the content of the press tended to reflect the tastes and values of the middle class.

The discontent of the middle class was also manifested in the actions of university students. University students were prohibited from involvement in political activities, and originally showed little willingness to engage in such activities. But during the latter years of the Rhee regime, students developed strong discontent with the political situation. This was mainly because through their education they had become concerned with justice and shared the middle class mentality.

Also important was that the economic perspective for students was gloomy. University graduates were drafted into the army during the Korean War, but after the cease-fire the army had to discharge many of them. Consequently, the young people who had just completed military service as well as those who were not drafted by the army after graduation wandered within the society looking for jobs. But the society was critically short of jobs for them. Therefore, they became very critical of the current state of society. It was under these conditions of instability that the students' uprising of April 19 occurred. After the student uprising, the government could not retain effective political control. All kinds of social groups particpated in demonstrations concerning various issues. It may be an exaggeration to say that the society was paralyzed, but the situation seemed quite close to it. Many parts of the society were in disarray, and the government lost its ability to hold the social fabric together.

People were becoming extremely worried about the increasing economic difficulties and social unrest which followed upon the student uprising. The students shifted their focus from elimination of injustice and establishment of democracy to austerity and the unification of Korea. But later they began to raise the question, shall we have liberty or shall we have bread?

The military coup of 16 May 1961 happened under these circumstances. Little empirical evidence is available concerning the extent to which this military action was supported by the people. It may be said that many intellectuals, journalists, and students more or less disfavored it. It cannot be denied, however, that the coup was looked upon favorably by the middle class who at the time had a strong fear of social unrest and economic collapse.

One of the goals of the military government was to bring about the "miracle of the *Han* River," a term echoing the remarkable economic development along West Germany's Rhine River after World War II. The military government recognized that democracy is a very desirable ideal but that initially more emphasis should be given to economic development. And accordingly, it started to execute the First Five Year Economic Development Plan in 1962.

3. Family and Social Organization

In discussing the modernization of Korea, social organization is one of the important subjects; in this connection it may be said in a sense that the skillful organization and management of economic, political, eduational, cultural, and military systems determines the success or failure of modernization. Korean society has all of the important modern functional organizations, but these are not necessarily organized or managed rationally or efficiently.

Although public institutions in Korea are not significantly different from those of the modern Western nations when it comes to their principles of organization, the persons who work in them are, in general, more acutely status-oriented than their Western counterparts. Therefore, they tend to discount efficiency in favor of displaying status symbols. This is one of the main causes for the disfunction found in many of Korea's modern social organizations.

Also, the gap between the ideals of institutions and their actual functioning makes it difficult to execute laws and procedures properly. Usually in many of Korea's modern public organizations there are latent procedures or customs that are deviant from or somewhat against law or rule, and yet admitted conventionally as necessary vices. [49] For example, in most public organizations the salary scale is unreasonably low, and, consequently, illegal devices have been introduced in order to provide additional payment. Needless to say, this often promotes injustice and corruption.

Likewise, there are undesirable practices in private business organizations. For instance, the key personnel in a private enterprise often consist of the director's relatives, so that private considerations intervene in office work, which, therefore, cannot be conducted efficiently. This is not only because managers are obliged to help their poor relatives, but also because it is expected that any illegal behavior can easily be kept secret among those relatives.

When we look at social organizations with regard to the modernization of Korean society, the influence of family shouldn't be excluded from our discussion since it affects social development strongly. To wit, it is (1) the source of population growth; (2) the context of important economic activities; and (3) the means of transmitting basic social values through the socialization process.

The Korean family has a strict patriarchal system, in which the father has great authority. Koreans have traditionally respected filial piety, ancestor worship, and the preservation of family honor. For centuries the first duty of a married woman was to (1) respect her parents-in-law and then (2) to bear many children, especially sons, in order to continue the family line. It is known that the size of ordinary Korean families in the traditional period was not large, averaging about 5 persons; but the *yangban*, who were rich, maintained large families, and among them there existed strong kinship solidarity perpetuated through ancestor worship.

Under such a family system, there could be little innovation or progress, since it was essential to follow the practices that had been handed down by tradition. If anyone attempted to violate these, he would meet not only the opposition of his parents but also that of relatives. Koreans were required to act not as independent persons, but rather, as members of a particular family. Because families were expected to bear many children, the population increased. This was especially true after the introduction of modern medicine, which led to a decline in the death rate. As a result, the population increased rapidly during the Japanese colonial period. In 1910 the Korean population was 13 million, but by 1935 it had increased to 21 million. By 1960, the population of South Korea alone had reached about 30 million. This factor caused severe economic difficulty.

But the traditional family could not help but suffer change under the impact of modernization. Changes in the family began during the late Yi-dynasty with the abolition of the status system and the *Gab-o* Reform which permitted widows to remarry. Changes continued to take place during the Japanese domination, at which time Western family morals were introduced, and school attendance and employment for women were made possible. In the late Japanese period, women were needed for wartime labour requirements, and so the role of women became more important.

The Korean family was modernized even more rapidly after the liberation.[50] The first reason for this is that the economic base of the traditional patriarchal system was eroded by the land reform. This directly weakened the traditional patriarchy. The father could not demand so much of his children, because he no longer had land to bestow or withhold. Since the land reform also weakened the economic base of kinship organization, the change of family structure toward nuclearization inevitably followed.

The second reason for change in the family structure may be attributed to the various democratic institutions introduced in Korea. All men and women, for example, were granted suffrage and the right to run for public office. All were also educated under the same compulsory education system which considerably increased the opportunity for seeking better social positions among young men and women. Another institutional reform was the establishment of the New Civil Law enacted just before the collapse of the Syngman Rhee regime in 1960. This law somewhat democratized the legal foundations of the family.

The third reason may be found in the social disorder that prevailed after the liberation and during the Korean War. Because of communist control in North Korea, many persons took refuge in South Korea. At that time there were many cases in which men escaped secretly alone while their wives took charge of home affairs and children's care. During the Korean War there were also many cases where women managed home affairs alone, hiding their husbands and sons. As mentioned earlier, among refugees it was difficult to discriminate strictly between sexes, and between the old and young. Furthermore, circumstances made it difficult to have many children. Therefore, there were many people who opted for induced abortion and/or practiced family planning. The average age at marriage became quite high due to the economic distress. And in this connection, it is interesting to note that during the Japanese period, Korea newspaper editorials often highlighted the problems incurred by marrying at a young age.

The fourth reason is that there occurred various social changes which expanded the role of the housewife, allowing her to participate more widely in society. These changes were largely brought about by the conditions I have already mentioned. But in addition, because their husband's income was not sufficient, the wives had to help economically. Men who were engaged in modern organization could neither know much about nor manage household affairs. Therefore, these responsibilities, including the education of the children, fell to the wife.

The fifth reason is that modern Western values, which were introduced *en masse* through mass media, changed many of the old ideas about the family. The backward-looking, ancestor-centered attitude was changed to a future-oriented attitude, which was reflected strongly in the raising and teaching of children. The authoritarian family system gradually became a conjugal system that respected the emotional relationship between a husband and wife. The association of men and women became free, and the trend toward regarding marriage as a problem not of the family, but rather of the persons who contemplate it, began to grow.

The most distinct change in family structure with respect to the modernization of Korean society is the rise in the social position of women. The comfort of women was disregarded under the traditional institutions. But the rise of their social positions removed many of the obstacles which had hindered their free activities. Today they are increasingly interested in the growth and social success of their children and in achieving stable lives after retirement with support from their children.[51] In that sense, modern Korean women are prone to act more pragmatically than their husbands.

It cannot be said, however, that the Korean family is fully modernized, particularly in the case of rural people. In spite of the land reform, the economic basis for kinship solidarity has not been completely eliminated. Strong kinship solidarity has repressed the development of community as well as solidarity, and thus hampered the growth of democratic processes. Political leaders often tend to make use of kinship solidarity in order to win votes.

Moreover, no matter how women and youths strive to become free, certain traditional elements still survive in the Korean family. Generally speaking, for example, the Korean family displays strong "gemeinschaftliche" solidarity. It is therefore inclined to engender particularism rather than universalism, affective behavior rather than affective-neutrality, and ascriptively oriented actions rather than achievement-oriented actions in the context of modern social organizations. Yet, in all, it must be granted that these conservative characteristics have become much weaker in the modern Korean family.

4. Cultural Characteristics after the Liberation

After the liberation, the idea most strongly stressed in the Korean society was, for lack of a better term, "anti-Japanism." Later anti-communism also became an important idea. These two ideas may be called the two basic elements of Korean nationalism.

Intuitively it is not surprising that Koreans, oppressed as they were under Japanese domination, should have strong anti-Japanese sentiments. However, we must explain further the attitude of anti-communism.

Koreans developed strong anti-communist attitudes for several reasons. First, this occurred due to the social structural characteristics after the liberation which we discussed earlier. Second, after the land reform, farmers weren't attracted by communist propaganda. Third, the Korean communist party left a poor impression on the people because they approved of a plan to put Korea under the trusteeship of four major powers for several years, a decision agreed upon by U.S., British and Russian representatives at a meeting in Moscow in 1945. This was regarded as a betrayal of the nation. Moreover, the communist leadership didn't arise through the support of the people, nor share their suffering. From the beginning they acted as bureaucratic rulers under the protection of Soviet Russia, especially during the Korean War.

Fourth, for years Koreans have had a pro-Western attitude. Korea was colonized by Japan but later Western states assisted her independence movement. Western missionaries also established schools and hospitals in Korea. Therefore Koreans generally preferred Western democratic ideas to communism, and were even favorable toward the free enterprise system.

Besides anti-Japan sentiment and anti-communism, democracy has been strongly emphasized. This is because democracy is a value respected by many intellectuals throughout the world; in addition, Korea was colonized by totalitarian and militaristic Japan but liberated by democratic countries. From the time of liberation the value of democracy has been espoused zealously, and subsequently many democratic institutions similar to what we find in the West have been established in Korea.

This tendency prevailed because there was no strong conservative power to discourage or inhibit young intellectuals from establishing democratic institutions. Therefore, democratic institutions were easily introduced and established in Korea without many of the obstacles, sacrifices and long delays seen in the West. A democratic political system in which all people have the right to vote and be elected was introduced, a compulsory educational institution was established, licensed prostitution was abolished, and other modern democratic laws were enacted.

But since Korea is under military threat from North Korea, and since the private sector is still weak due to the generally low economic and educational level of the whole nation, democracy is respected in principle but its actual practice is sometimes reserved. Democratic practices are still only weakly embodied in day-to-day social and organizational behavior. It was also very important for modernization that Koreans have become more materialistic and pragmatic as a result of several factors.

Among these are that Koreans do not have a strong future-life orientation. Instead, they have a temporal orientation. Also, the *yangban* landowners, who despised material things and instead respected moral principles and courtesy, were ruined. Furthermore, social disorder after the liberation eroded many elements of the traditional values leaving only pragmatic things to be respected.

In the cultural sphere one of the most remarkable changes that has characterized Korean society is the extension of education. From the traditional period on, education was recognized as very important. As mentioned earlier, during the late Yi-dynasty those persons who made contact with Western civilization felt that education was the most important means for achieving modernization and constructing a wealthy, powerful nation. Therefore, they made special efforts to promote education. This tendency became stronger after the liberation. In 1950 compulsory education through elementary school was initiated. The number of elementary schools increased from 2,834 in 1945 to 4,602 in 1960. The number of teachers increased from 19,729 to 61,749 over the same 15 years, and students grew from 1,366,024 to 3,599,627. Most notably, the number of female students increased some 3 times.

During this period middle school education also developed greatly. The number of middle schools incrased from 97 to 1,053 (10.8 times), the number of teachers from 1,810 to 13,053 (7.2 times), and the number of students from 50,343 to 528,614 (10.5 times). This same tendency was also found in high school education. Likewise, the number of universities increased from 19 to 63 (3.3 times), and the number of university students from 7,819 to 97,819 (12.5 times).

Such educational development may be attributed in part to the extraordinary efforts of government and social leaders, but it is also due to the Korean people's strong aspiration for education. Education quickly became recognized as the most important means for achieving success and personal respect under the social conditions which existed after the liberation when all traditional status restraints were abolished. As a result, parents today tend to dedicate their efforts and property to their children's education rather than their inheritance.

It was unquestionably a heavy burden for the government to invest in education under the difficult economic conditions during and after the Korean War. Moreover, investment in education does not bring remarkable effects immediately. It takes time. On the other hand, those who are fortunate enough to become educated are often more strongly concerned with their own reward than the service they are expected to do for society. Instead, their discontent with existing conditions sometimes leads to social unrest.

In Korean society, the gap between an ideal educational system and reality has brought about many undesirable results. For example, the Parent-Teacher Association in Korea lost its original aims by becoming an organization through which schools tried to squeeze money from parents in order to supplement budget shortages. The differences among schools in terms of quality has also been a big problem. Students' eagerness to enter good schools has given rise to various problems including teacher favoritism, over-competition in entrance examinations, and over-concentration of the student population in Seoul where many good schools are located.

All of these could easily have had negative effects on the economic and social develpment of Korea. However, the educational system seems to have improved greatly, keeping pace with Korea's recent economic development. And now, education in Korea has begun to demonstrate what had always been claimed by the social leaders of this country since the late Yi-dynasty. That is, that education is the most important means for achieving independence and prosperity in Korea.

Mass communication should not be ignored in the disussion of modernization in Korea. As mentioned earlier, the Independence Press, founded in 1896, repeatedly highlighted the need for education as a prerequisite for national independence. During the Japanese domination, the newspapers functioned as the mouthpiece for Korean nationalism. Many newspapers appeared under the democratic system after the liberation. In principle, a newspaper exists for the people in general, but in fact, the great majority of the subscribers are from the middle class who are strongly interested in public issues and can afford the subscription. Moreover, the majority of writers for newspapers are educated young intellectualls who are also of a middle class background. Therefore, it may be argued that they have a middle class bias.

The newspapers in Korea have made tremendous contributions toward the advancement of modernization and democracy. It is true that the main force which toppled Syngman Rhee's regime were the students, but it could not have been successful without the strong support of the newspapers. I hasten to add, however, that newspapers may also cause certain dysfunctions. For example, newspapers are apt to introduce various ideas and values without upholding consistent principles. This can ultimately lead to social confusion. They have also been known to be too idealistic and hasty, ignoring limitations and/or existing conditions.

Radio was not popular amongst the lower class until the later 1950s. But the Syngman Rhee government began to develop a special communication system in rural areas, as a result of which every household in many villages was given a speaker connected to a village broadcasting center. Later, in the 1960s transistor radios were produced in Korea, and spread rapidly among the lower urban classes and rural dwellers. Since then Koreans have had ready access to news and commentary. Through radio they have also gained knowledge about social issues and solutions to problems.

Conclusion: Socio-cultural Factors Bearing on Modernization in Korea

In the late 19th century traditional Korean society was challenged by the capitalist powers. This shook the small kingdom which was barely able to sustain itself, depending as it had for so long on China. Actually, however, Korea was doomed to ruin in any event because of internal corruption, factional strife, economic stagnation, and ever increasing discontent on the part of the people. Since then, the modernization process of Korea has followed its unique course. Initially, the Korean economy was not mature enough for Koreans to modernize by themselves, nor was there any strong class that could carry out revolutionary action. Such a class simply had not emerged. The core people most eager to change the traditional society were chiefly from the alienated middle class comprised of *hyangban*, *toban*, and *sŏ-ŏl*. But they were not a capitalist class capable of making a bourgeois revolution.

Those who promoted social change during the Japanese period had the same social status background as the persons who sought social change during the late Yi-dynasty. Their ultimate goal was to thwart Japanese imperialism and obtain national independence, and their means for achieving this goal was through enlightening the people. After the *Gab-o* it bacame possible in principle for people to move geographically according to their own will, and to move up the social ladder according to their capabilities. But in reality the great majority of Koreans suffered from political oppression and economic exploitation at the hands of the Japanese.

Those with an intellectual conscience in other developing countries once colonized by Western capitalist powers might think it unjustifiable for a nation which suffered from capitalist imperialism to pursue economic and social development under the capitalist free enterprise system.

However, Korea's experience was unique. First of all, she was colonized by an oriental neighbor who was capitalist but also totalitarian. She was emancipated by the Western democratic countries, the United States in particular. The Americans, who have been in Korea since the last years of the Yi-dynasty, contributed to medical, educational, and other cultural development. Moreover, the United States has never imposed any imperialist policy on Korea since her liberation. All these have intensified Korea's friendly attitude toward the United States and the Western democratic countries in general.

Secondly, the ruling colonial authorities withdrew from Korea immediately after the liberation, and the social structure of Korea underwent a fundamental change. The former Korean upper class who were mostly tradition-bound landowners lost their source of power, which allowed the middle class better opportunities for upward mobility. Therefore, they did not need to resort to radical ideology. Moreover, farmers, the majority of the Korean population, were content with the system after the liberation because land reform was implemented. Moreover, the communists made many tactical mistakes, which made the Korean people strongly anti-communist and subsequently more favorably oriented toward the free enterprise system.

It is often said that some degree of political stability is necessary for eonomic development. Korean people do not have a national religion which might encourage social integration and promote communal activity for common goals. But Korean nationalism, based on anti-Japanese sentiment, and intensified by anti-communist sentiment, seems to have been greatly conducive to Korea's national integration.

There was a possibility in Korea that conflict and destruction rather than unity and construction would become stronger because of social corruption, population pressure, economic difficulty intensified by inflation, and a widening economic gap between the new upper class and middle class. As a matter of fact, the dissatisfaction of the middle class has been a persistent theme of intellectuals, journalists, and religious people, and has frequently led university students to radical action in the name of social justice. The student movement as such might easily come to have a socialist flavor as it has in other developing countries. But because of the strong anti-communist social climate in Korea, the movement can hardly go to extremes for fear on the part of the people that it might be taken advantage of by the North Korean communists.

It is widely held that successful economic development requires a motivated populace capable of rational economic behavior. As argued at the very beginning of this paper, the Korean people have always had to work hard in order to meet such basic needs as food, clothing, and shelter in their changeable climate with its four distinct seasons.

During the late Yi-dynasty, however, institutional constraints impeded the active participation of Korean people in economic production. Since the *yangban* could enjoy a pleasant life at the expense of people of lower status, and since there was no particular challenge from other countries, they did not strongly feel any neccessity to bring about economic development. On the other hand, the common people did not have the freedom to make an effort toward the betterment of their own economic life, particularly since all that they earned could be easily taken away from them by either *yangban* or other powerful persons. Women and young people were particularly regulated in their social activities.

After the liberation, however, the social institutions that restricted individuals disappeared. The traditional status system was abolished much earlier. Paternal authority became weak and exploitation by absentee landowners became illegal due to the land reform. Thus economic opportunity was opened to everybody, allowing those who worked hard to prosper. In other words, the average Korean was put in a situation of ceaseless competition and had to adapt to it. Otherwise he could not survive. Koreans therefore could no longer ascribe their low status to others.

At the national level, Korean nationalism based on anti-Japanese and anticommunist sentiment seems to be tremendously important. Anxiety will probably always exist if Korea's national leaders believe that Japan will eventually rearm and invade Korea again sometime in the future. They may think that even though there is little possibility for Japan to govern Korea, she may be able to exert undesirable political and economic influence on Korea. In any case, Japan provides a reference group with which Korea will always compete in many ways.

In this respect, North Korea may be called a negative reference group. It is regarded with fear by South Koreans, and for that reason it is also a source of national vitality. All public welfare policies originating from either the government or civilian sectors, including economic development, development of democracy, and strong social control for national security can be easily justified with reference to the threat from North Korea.

The United States is very frequently referred to as a model of democracy, economic prosperity, and cultural development. Of course, other Western nations are occasionally referred to, but far less frequently than the United States. She is not, however, the source of Koreans' enthusiasm for modernization. Generally speaking we may say that the United States has been a useful model for modernization. What has been successfully achieved in the United States has been easily introduced in Korea without much criticism. Today this is still true although the trend is declining slowly as the uniqueness of the Korean situation is increasingly emphasized.

Many sociologists believe that social values are one of the most important factors that influence economic development. During the Yi-dynasty, the value which was most strongly appreciated among the *yangban* class was to have a high position in the government and to maintain the glory of their family. They respected Confucianism, particularly the teaching of *Chu Hsi*, which encouraged people to be more strongly concerned with empty morality and formal courtesy rather than with work and production. On the other hand, those who were alienated from power, mainly the *hyangban*, *toban* and *sŏ-ŏl* were not as attracted to Confucianism as the *yangban*, and were ready to cast it aside in order to bring changes to the traditional system in which *yangban* dominated.

During the period of Japanese rule, the pre-modern value system was fading but was still very influential, particularly in the rural areas. The Japanese government made it their policy to maintain it to a large extent, and the people who supported it, mostly the landowners of *yangban* background, had strong economic power.

After the liberation, however, the landowners were ruined rapidly, mainly because of the land reform, and the rise of young, educated persons, most of whom were of an urban middle class background. Modern Western values such as democracy, freedom, equality, science and technology, rationality, practicality and efficiency were emphasized widely. To be sure, most of these Western values have been conducive to economic development in Korea, but it must also be noted that the uncontrolled influx of Western values might have served to intensify social unrest.

In adapting to the drastic social changes after the liberation, the Korean people became more realistic. That is, Koreans did not develop ideas about life after death in their historical process. Instead, they were strongly concerned with happiness in the temporal life. Buddhism flourished prior to the Yi-dynasty, and Christianity is now popular in urban areas. But Koreans in general do not appear to be strongly attached to any religion. This kind of mentality may have made it possible for them to adjust successfully to modernization.

It is now often said that Koreans are very materialistic and pragmatic, and value monetary success excessively, and no Korean seems to deny it. In the traditional society, *yangban* people were strongly oriented toward status, prestige, and formal courtesy rather than toward material prosperity, at least on the surface. This status orientation seems still to be quite strong among Koreans. Therefore they are inclined to buy something not because of its practicality or because of the material comfort it provides, but rather, because of its appeal as a status symbol. This materially oriented attitude is far stronger than ever before. Indeed, some contemporary Koreans seem to think that they can achieve everything, even status and honor, with money.

As recently as a decade ago, some people might have regarded laziness as part of the national character. But no one would now say that Koreans are idle. On the contrary, it is widely said that Koreans are diligent, perhaps even too aggressive in their pursuit of money. They were idle in the past because industry was not properly rewarded, and now they have become diligent because they expect that they would be rewarded in proportion to how much they work.

It is generally agreed that education is one of the most important factors that have direct bearing on economic development. Social leaders in Korea made special efforts to develop modern education beginning in the later period of the Yi-dynasty, and in fact, education later progressed to the extent that the illiteracy rate was only about 20 per cent in 1960. But it should be noted that education in Korea has had two negative effects; one is that it required so much investment that Korean economic growth was perhaps delayed, and two, that over production of educated people has induced social unrest, because jobs were not available for many of them. But there is no question that education in general has contributed very positively.

There is another thing that should be emphasized with regard to education; and that is the training of Koreans in foreign countries. After the liberation, many Koreans were sent to foreign countries, especially to the United States under a variety of assistance programs. They were not only young students but also soldiers, professors, officials, and technicians. Perhaps it is safe to say that almost all Koreans who have been in key positions of modern social organizations have had some experience with foreign life. This is particularly important because they have been the essential driving force of modernization from the start.

Along with education, the role of mass communication should not be ignored. The newspaper was the most useful instrument for modernization of Korea from its very beginning. Until the end of Syngman Rhee's period, newspaper and radio were restricted almost exclusively to the upper and middle class. But early in the 1960s radio became very popular, and everybody had access to what was happening outside, as well as the solutions for problems related to their own lives. Through mass communication, even the people in deep rural areas could have information about important events, and about the nature of proplems they would encounter, along with suggestions to solve them.

Many traditional elements of Korea may still be observed in modern family life. The strong sense of family-orientation, which puts more value on the unity of the family rather than on the unity of community or social organization where a man works, may prevent him from devoting himself to the development of public society. It also encourages him to be particularistic, affectional, and ascriptive in his behavior, which may cause problems in modern social organizations. In spite of these disadvantages the Korean family has at least been democratized enough to allow both youth and women to study and work as they want without serious restriction.

The role of women, incidentally, has a particularly important meaning with regard to modernization. They are often more pragmatic than their husbands and more likely to oppose anything that may hinder the happiness of their immediate family members, namely, their husbands and children. Consequently, they are often very willing to sacrifice immediate gratification to these ends.

It would be wrong to insist that traditional elements can or should be entirely eliminated from a society and the people in it. Indeed, we may observe that many traditional elements are retained and sometimes even intentionally preserved in the developed Western countries. We can hardly deny that there are many traditional elements in many parts of the Korean society; some are undesirable, but some others may be desirable even in this modern age.

After reviewing all the important factors that are usually considered to have a close relationship with modernization, we may conclude that there are some serious items worth mentioning which may impede economic development in Korean society from a sociological point of view. The people of Korea are highly motivated to achieve material progress; many traditional values have been replaced by modern social values; there are many modern social organizations that are functioning well; and the social institutions necessary for managing modern society have been developed.

However, the modernization process of the Korean society still faces certain obstacles. One obstacle is the possibility of internal conflict between the new upper class and the middle class, and— perhaps less immediate— between these groups and the working class. But if such potential conflict can be properly channeled with an appropriate interplay between tolerance for social protest and maintenance of social order, it may very well function positively rather than negatively in terms of spurring the trend toward modernization. Another possible obstacle is the international environment within which Korea must function. Korea is still weak. If she encounters overwhelming agression or shock from outside that impairs her capacity for recovery, she may suffer destruction very easily. Therefore, it is important for the continued success of Korean modernization that such internal and external challenges be anticipated and adequately planned for.

[NOTES]

1) Joseph Arthur de Gobineau is one of the theoreticians.
2) Andrew J. Grajdanzev, *Modern Korea*, (New York: Institute of Pacific Relations, 1944), pp. 34-39.
3) Ministry of Agriculture and Commerce (Japan), *Kankokushi* (translated version in Japanese, originally published by the Ministry of Finance, Russia in 1905), p. 296. See also Arthur J. Brown, *The Mastery of the Far East*, (New York: Charles Scriber's Sons, 1921, rev. ed.,), Chap. III.
4) Arnold J. Toynbee, *A Study of History*, Vols. I-VI, abridged by D.C. Somervell, (New York: Oxford University Press, 1946), pp. 187-208.
5) Edwin O. Reischauer, "Special Features in the History of Japan," a special article at the end of *Japan-American Forum*, Vol. 10., No. 10, Nov. 1964, pp. 12-19.

6) Tokutaro Tanaka, "Chosen-no shakai kaikyu (Social Class in Korea)," *Chosen*, March 1921.

7) Seong-mu Lee, *Josŏn chogi yangban yŏngu* (*A Study on Yangban in Early Period of Yi-dynasty*), (Seoul: Iljogag, 1980), p. 40.

8) Man-gap Lee, "Jŏntong-jŏg hyŏbdonggwa chonragsahoe ŭi baljŏn (Traditional Cooperation and Development of Rural Society)," *Hangug sahoe wa munhwa*, Vol. III, (Seoul: Academy of Korean Studies, 1980), p. 17.

9) This idea first appeared in the author's article, "Sociological Implication of Modernization in Korea," which was presented at the annual conference of the Association of the Asian Studies in 1967. This article is included in this book with a minor revision as "Structural Change and Modernization in Korean Society" (See pp. 3∼28 More discussion was done in the same author's article, "Kankoku shakaino kozoteki henka (The Structural Change of the Korean Society)," *Asian Cultural Studies* No. 9, (Tokyo: International Christian University, Dec. 1977), pp. 45-82.

10) Leon Festinger, "A Theory of Social Comparison Processes," *Human Relation*, 7, pp. 117-140.

11) Robert K. Merton, "Social Structure and Anomie," in *Social Theory and Social Structure*, (Glencoe, New York: The Free Press, Inc., 1957), Chap. IV.

12) See "Politics in a Korean Village," in this book (pp. 134∼172). As to the historical background of politics in the traditional Korean village, see the following book; Man-gap Lee, "Jŏntong-jŏg hyŏbdong-gwa chonrag sahoe ŭi baljŏn)," *Hangug sahoe wa munhwa* (*Korean Society and Culture*), Vol. III, (Seoul: The Academy of Korean Studies, 1980), pp. 5-42.

13) It is indicated in the legal code, *Gyŏng-gug daejŏn*. See Bongsa-jo, Ye-jŏn in the book.

14) Yong-ha Shin, *Dognib hyŏbhoe yŏngu* (*Studies on Independence Association*), (Seoul: Iljogag, 1976).

15) Man-gap Lee, "Dognib Sinmune pyosi-doen gachigwan (Values Expressed in the Independence Press)," in *Sahag Nonchong* (*Historical Essays*) for memorizing the retirement of Dr. Han, (Seoul: Jisig sanŏb-sa, 1981), pp. 593-623.

16) Yong-ha Shin, *Josŏn toji josa saŏb yŏngu* (*A Study on Korean Land*

Survey Project), (Seoul: Hangug yŏngu-won, 1979).
17) E. de S. Brunner, "Rural Korea," in *The Christian Mission in Relation to Rural Problems*, Vol. VI, (New York: International Missionary Council, 1928) Chap. IV, pp. 116-118.
18) Minoru Himeno (ed.), *Chosen keizai zuhyo (Economic Figures and Tables of Korea)*, (Seoul: Chosen Tokei Kyokai, 1940), p. 65, table 27.
19) M. Himeno, ibid., p. 69, table 29.
20) Korean Government-General, *1940 Statistical Yearbook*, 1942, pp. 113-115, table 91.
21) Minoru Himeno, ibid., p. 256, table 101.
22) Ibid., p. 254, table 100.
23) Ibid., p. 311, table 109.
24) Ibid., pp. 269-273.
25) Zenkoku keizai chosa kikan rengokai chosen shibu (Korean Chapter, National Federation of Economic Investigation Agencies), *1941 and 42 Chosen Keizai Nenpo (Korean Economic Yearbook)*, (Tokyo: Kaizosha, 1943), p. 141
26) M. Himeno, ibid., p. 156, table 64.
27) Chun-suk Auh, *Hangug sin gyoyug-sa (New Korean Educational History)*, (Seoul: Hyŏndae gyoyug chongsŏ Pub. Co., 1964), pp. 151-158.
28) Korean Government-General, *1942 Korean Government-General Statistical Yearbook*, (Seoul: Daikaido, 1944), pp. 197-228.
29) M. Himeno, ibid., pp. 35-40.
30) Korean Government-General, *Gaijin no mitaru Saikin no Chosen (Korea Observed by Foreigners Recently)*, Survey Material No. 35, 1932.
31) The data in this section were mainly taken from Minoru Himeno's book mentioned above.
32) Gi-baeg Lee, *Hangug-sa sinron (New Korean History)*, (Seoul: Iljogag, 1967), p. 361.
33) Korean Government-General, ibid., p. 119.
34) M. Himeno, ibid., p. 191, table 78. And also see Masafumi Suzuki, *Present Status of Korean Economy*, (Seoul: Korean Headquarter of Teikoku Chiho Gyosei Gakkai, 1939), p. 456.
35) E. de S. Brunner, ibid., pp. 110-111.
36) Korean Government-General, *1942 Korean Government-General Statistical Yearbook*, 1944, pp, 459-460.

37) Chun-suk Auh, ibid., p. 255.
38) Ibid., p. 347.
39) Korean Government-General, ibid., pp. 222-226.
40) Ibid., pp. 26-35.
41) Man-gap Lee, "Values Expressed in the Independence Press," pp. 593-623.
42) Besides Yong-ha Shin's book mentioned earlier, Gwang-rin Lee's recent work would be useful; see *Hangug gaehwa sasang yŏngu (A Study on Enlightenment Thought)*, (Seoul: Iljogag, 1979).
43) As to the development of Christianity in rural Korea during the Japanese period, see Brunner's report on "Rural Korea."
44) Gag-jong Lee, "Josŏn minjog sasang byŏnchŏn ŭi gaeyo (Outline of Change of the Korean Nationalist Thoughts)" *Josŏn gwa josŏn minjog (Korea and Korean People)*, (Seoul: Josŏn sasang tongsinsa, 1927), pp. 60-61.
45) *Minjog, gug-ga-sa (Nation and National History)*; the first volume of *Hangug munhwa-sa daegye (System of Korean Cultural History)* published by the Institute of the National Cultural Studies, Korea University, 1964, pp. 719-737.
46) Gag-jong Lee, ibid., pp. 64-65.
47) Man-gap Lee, *Hangug nongchon sahoe ui gujo wa byŏnhwa (The Social Structure of Korean Village and Its Change)*, (Seoul: Seoul National University Press, 1973), pp. 96-99.
48) National Agricultural Cooperative Federation, *Hangug nongŏb ŭi bunsŏg (Analysis of Korean Agriculture)*, 1963, pp. 175-181.
49) Man-gap Lee, "Social Organization" in *A City in Transition*, (Seoul: Hollym, 1971), edited by M.G. Lee and H.R. Barringer p. 374.
50) Man-gap Lee, "Sengo ni okeru kankoku kajoku no henka (The Change of Korean Family after World War II)" in *Kajoku Hendo no Shakaigaku (Sociology of Family Change)*, (Tokyo: Baifukan, 1973), edited by K. Aoi and K. Masuda, pp. 166-177.
51) Jae-mo Yang et. al., *Hangug nongchon sahoe ŭi gajog gyehoeg (Family Planning in the Korean Rural Community)*, (Seoul: Yonsei University Press, 1966), p. 182.

Socio-cultural Factors Bearing on Economic Development

Introduction

Among the factors which are involved in the economic development of a community or a nation, the most important are, needless to say, economic. Is there a sufficient amount of capital? How about technology, resources, and market situations? These may be the primary questions people usually raise. However, it is evident that these are not exclusive factors for economic development.

Of those non-economic factors, the administrative competence of a government seems to be very important. It may be particularly so in Korea, where the government is the largest and strongest enterprise. It can mobilize the largest amounts of capital, resources and manpower in the nation.[1] Another important non-economic factor may be the international situation surrounding a given country. If a country has unfavorable conditions such as a serious threat of military invasion or difficulty in diplomatic relationships with other countries, she may hardly avoid economic hardship. But these two kinds of topics are beyond the realm of sociology.

One more area that is regarded as important for economic development is the socio-cultural. Since Max Weber claimed the relationship between the protestant ethic and capitalist spirit, the socio-cultural factors including social structure and values are considered to be essential for discussing economic development. This trend has been particularly intensified by the discussion of

---

* Presented at the Seminar on South Korean Industrialization which was held at the University of Hawaii and sponsored by the Social Science Research Council in 1977.

the problem of economic development in developing countries where the socio-cultural elements are greatly different from those of the developed.

Economic behavior is a kind of human behavior, and human behavior is not conducted by homo economicus as a rational being but by actual human beings who have bodies and behave with feelings in a given situation. If his living conditions are comfortable, everything he needs is provided, and he does not have any threat or challenge;[2] in other words, if he does not have any serious and urgent problem, he will not make an effort to solve such a problem. And also, if he has a strong culture which regards this world as unreal, evanescent, then he will naturally disvalue success and withdraw from the material world.

However, there are so many socio-cultural factors involved in economic behavior. Hoselitz has stated[3] that economic development may be related to a form of social behavior oriented toward achievement, universalism, and functional specificity. These are concepts in the theory of pattern variables[4] put forth by Talcot Parsons. Moore[5] has presented an even more complicated scheme concerning industrialization. He has discussed four factors, which may be considered to bring about industrialization: ideological, institutional, organizational, and motivational factors. If we are going to examine all factors according to Moore's scheme, it would take a tremendous amount of work.

Therefore, the writer is going to discuss some major factors which he regards to have been closely related to economic development in Korea.[6]

Before entering the discussion of the factors, however, he is going to give a brief explanation of the structural features of the Korean society after the liberation from Japanese control and the social situation around the time of the student uprising in 1960 as the social setting in which these factors have been working for economic development.[7]

Structural Features of Korean Society after the Liberation

In 1945 Korea was liberated with the victory of the Allied Forces. Until that time Korea was under the colonial control of Japan, her neighbor. Japan was militaristic and anti-democratic, and most ruthless among the colonial dominators.[8] She strictly prohibited not only political activities by the Koreans, but also their economic and other social activities which might have strengthened their ability to be autonomous. She made every effort to obliterate even the Korean culture and forced Koreans to change their name to conform to Japanese style.

The great majority of those who were on the top of the social ladder during the Japanese colonial period were Japanese. They monopolized almost all important positions in modern social organizations including even the head of police branch offices in small communities, and occupied a great part of the wealth in the society. The Koreans who could be in the top class of the society were those who cooperated with the Japanese colonialists, big land owners, and a few people who were involved in business or professional jobs. One of the most distinct features during this period was that the Korean farmers, whose population was about 80 per cent of the entire Korean population, were continuously caught in downward vertical mobility.[9]

Japanese people built many industrial firms mainly in the northern part of Korea for exploiting Koreans and preparing further intrusion into China. This trend was intensified particularly in the late period of her colonial domination as she prepared for carrying out the big war.[10] The majority of the workers in these firms were Koreans, and there were evidently some engineers and clerks. It is assumed that a considerable number of them came down south after the liberation, though there are no accurate statistical data on it.

After the liberation, the Japanese colonial forces lost power suddenly and had to withdraw from Korea in a short period of time. This is very important for understanding the structural change of the Korean society thereafter. All that they left behind, such as the modern organizations they had operated, high social positions they had kept, and property they had owned including their farming land, belonged either to the Korean government or the Korean people who were mainly the former middle class, though some of the old upper class might also have shared some of them. This is one of the reasons why the Korean people became anti-communists. It is not difficult to guess that the Korean middle class including the intellectuals would become favorable to communism,[11] if they saw that colonial elements would be persistent or the old upper class would still be in power.

The second distinct feature that we could observe was extreme social confusion. Korea was suddenly separated from Japan of which she had been, though unwillingly, one part, and was again divided into two parts under completely different ideologies. She was drastically shifted from the totalitarian system of wartime to an open system without control. Moreover, the U.S. military government did not have any concrete policy for immediate action to improve the social confusion except for basic democratic principles, and they allowed the communists to take all possible actions for revolution and intensify social disturbances. And also the number of those who had strong leadership and ability enough to operate the modern state of organizations was very limited. The social confusion went to the extreme during the Korean War. During this period, many old conservatives who did not have eyes for the future obviously failed in adjusting to the changing situations.

The third important feature was the land reform. The land reform in South Korea was enacted only in 1949. But many farmers seemed to buy much land from their former land owners at relatively cheap prices. At any rate, about two thirds of the farmers became independent farmers due to the land reform.[12]

Many economists seem to be rather critical of the effectiveness of the land reform.[13] From a sociological point of view, however, the land reform seems to have brought some favorable results. Because of the land reform, the tradition-bound landowners who were parasites to the farmers who were without productive work were ruined, and the economic basis of *yangban* kinship organizations became weakened considerably. On the other hand, the lay farmers could become more cooperative among themselves for their communal interests on an equal basis. This may be another reason why communism could not get support from the people in the rural community.

The fourth distinct feature is educational development. The importance of education for modernization was strongly recognized by the pioneers of modern Korea since its very beginning in the late 19th century.[14] And during the Japanese ruling age many Korean people who had strong aspirations for independence made enormous efforts for developing modern education. Consequently, the Korean government adopted a compulsory education system, though it was a great economic burden to the government.

Social Situations around 1960

Syngman Rhee's regime collapsed in the spring of 1960 due to the students' uprising. The students fiercely blamed the President and the Liberal Party under his leadership for their unjust manipulations in the presidential election and for their deeply-rooted corruption. Their actions have been highly evaluated as the brave who fought for democracy. It seems to be very important, however, to observe the socio-economic conditions hidden under the surface.

The people who were active in the society right after the

liberation might be considered as mainly from the former middle class, and the core of them who tried to take initiative and responsibility for the destiny of Korea might be considered as the intellectuals including religious people, journalists, and professionals in various fields. There were some Koreans in the upper section of the society, but many of them could not appear and move actively in the society because they were strongly criticized as collaborators with Japanese imperialism. Those who moved around actively in modern institutions might appear to be similar to each other in terms of socio-economic standing. There were, of course, many poorer people under the middle class, but they might be regarded to be basically the same, as they all were exploited people.

The new Korean society could not be as equalitarian as expected. Some people, mainly from the middle class, were rising up to the upper stratum of the society in the process of allocating resources such as the Japanese properties in the beginning, the foreign aid later, and loans from outside recently. Those who had to stay in the original class might have feelings of relative deprivation to some extent, looking at those who had been in a similar economic situation and suddenly rose to high status. Then, they might be more likely to interpret that those new upper class could go up with unjust conduct, and that they, themselves, could not go up, not because they were incompetent or lazy, but because they were honest. This mentality of the middle class seems to be one of the bases for the uprising by the students who were mostly from the middle class. In addition to this, there was another, more direct cause for their action; that is, the strong discontent of the college or high school graduates. The number of college students greatly increased after the liberation, particularly during and after the Korean War, because the college students had the privilege to postpone military service until their graduation on the one hand, and because the colleges admitted more students than the quota authorized by the Ministry of Education in order to manage or expand the schools.[15]

Most college graduates entered the army which needed manpower tremendously. Therefore it was not a serious problem for them to find a job after graduation for the time being. After the truce talks, however, the army did not need more soldiers then those for regular recruitment, and instead, it had to decrease manpower because some temporary wartime military organizations were gradually disorganized. Consequently strong streams of jobseekers were being poured out into society both from the schools and the army. But it was almost impossible for them to find jobs. Then it is quite natural that they became critical of the society and the government.

Discontentment of the middle class was also strongly represented by the religious people, the journalists and the intellectuals. They themselves belonged to the middle class, but they thought they were elite, and that their role of giving influence to the society had been magnificent for some years after the liberation, but that it had declined to some extent. Moreover, they were concerned with social justice by the very nature of the profession they were engaged in, and they were closely related with the middle class such as students, newspaper subscribers, and believers in the carrying out of their jobs.

Discontent was not limited only to the middle class in cities. The small landowners in rural areas were ruined drastically. Many big absentee landowners in cities might have been ruined also, though some of them could find jobs with which they might be happy in the new society after the Japanese had left, or their children who had had advanced training before or after the liberation could sustain jobs already. But the situations with the small landowners in the villages might have gotten worse, because they had less ability to make successful adjustment to the changing society. Yet they were still influential in rural politics, and they often expressed their critical attitude toward the Liberal Party either overtly or covertly.

The April 19th uprising happened under this social climate. After Syngman Rhee's government collapsed, the students, the strongest pressure group at that time, continuously made active campaign for fair and just elections, democratization, elimination of corruption, and austerities for the time being, but their interest was shifted to the issues of national unification and daily-life economic difficulty of the people.

Meanwhile, some ideological implications were involved in their issues, and finally they raised a question; liberty or bread? This dichotomy obviously suggested the people selected bread rather than liberty. It might have appealed to the people, to some extent, because many of them were sick of various kinds of demonstrations and they observed serious social disintegration without any good economic perspectives. The military coup overthrew John M. Chang's weak government.

The Military revolutionary committee pledged six points, one of which was the establishment of a self-supporting economy. And also a leading newspaper indicated economic difficulty including the prevailing unemployment as one of the causes for the coup.[16] According to the results of a survey which was carried out by the military government, what the respondents most strongly wanted for the government to do was to solve the unemployment problem, and the second item they indicated was to control inflation.[17] So serious was the economic situation. Faced with this challenge, the military government was very anxious to bring about the miracle of rapid economic development.

Some Favorable Factors

1. Challenge and Stability

It is often said that the political stability of a nation is important for a continuously planned economic development, and it seems to be true to some degree. If a society is in serious political confusion for a long period of time, no sound economic policy can be planned and implemented. It is more so in a country like Korea where private sectors are very weak and government dominates almost all important resources.

However, high political stability may not necessarily guarantee high economic growth either. Without challenges government may not make great efforts to bring development. Korean government has had two major challenges; one is the militaristic threat from the communists in north Korea; and another, economic poverty. No government could get support from the people without successfully dealing with these two problems.

The strong pressure to force the government to fulfill these requirements came mainly from the middle class as stated earlier, not only because they recognized the importance and urgency of these problems, but because they were unhappy with their status inconsistency. Therefore, the government had to take efficient action for coping with the problems. It is now almost common sense that the government in a developing country should take strong action for rapid economic development, as it was also often maintained by Korean intellectuals for some time in the early 60s. Around that time pro-government party leaders seemed to try to develop a working ideology of democracy which would justify strong action by the government, and the words of "administrative democracy" and "national democracy" were often talked about.[18]

In fact, however, whenever the government tried to take action, the intellectuals became critical of it. They were inclined to think that strong action by the government would be for their maintenance of power. And also, did not like it by their nature as intellectuals, because strong action by the government usually would limit the freedom of intellectual activities. Therefore, the protests by the intellectuals and students against it were often attempted.

Howevr, the protests by the intellectuals had limitations in the intensity of action. They did not want their action to result in chaos that the north Korean communists could take advantage of to invade or disturb the south. Therefore, they hoped the protests might go as far as stimulating the government to be responsible for economic development and social justice. They did not want it to go so far as to destroy the basic social order.

2. Acceptance of the Free Enterprise System

The free enterprise system was generally taken for granted by the Korean people, since they have been strongly unfavorable to communism and favorable to the Western countries. The Korean intellectuals did not, of course, support it without reservations. They recognized that a superior in power, wealth, or knowledge will destroy an inferior in free competition, and that the application of this evolutionary principle without limitation would be against the democratic ethic that a human being should have equal basic rights. This critical thought of liberalism seems to have existed for sometime after the liberation.

Generally speaking, however, even the Korean intellectuals seem far less critical of the ethical relevance of the free enterprise system than those in other developing countries which were colonized by the Western capitalist countries. Particularly after the Korean War, they have become less critical of it, though they have maintained development of welfare programs in order to eliminate or decrease the undesirable effects of the free enterprise system.

The general acceptance of the free enterprise system might have given great influence to economic activities in Korea. It can be easily imagined that if the unfavorable attitude of Koreans toward the free enterprise system was very strong, the entrepreneurs would not be able to mobilize laborers as they wanted because of the pressure from the labor unions, though it cannot be also denied that it encouraged some entrepreneurs to treat workers in an improper way.

3. Korean Nationalism

It is said that the nationalism of a country is closely related to industrialization.[19] Since Korea has only one ethnic group and one culture and language, it may not be difficult to maintain national integration and mobilization of the people toward one national goal. Furthermore, the Koreans' attitudinal traits formed through their historical experiences for the past one century may have promoted it.

As stated earlier, Koreans are very friendly to the Western countries, particularly to the United States. This trait has been intensified not only because Korea was saved both from Japanese colonial control and the north Korean communist invasion by the United States, but also many people who have taken important roles in the various fields, such as military organizations, educational and cultural institutions, and business circles, were trained in the United States from the early period of Korean independence. Therefore, the Korean people are more likely to accept and introduce new ideas and devices from the United States or other Western countries without much suspicion.

Korean people in general have anti-Japanese feelings; though it has changed slightly, as the formal relationship between the two countries was normalized and the mutual relationship among the United States, Japan, and Korea has been developed. And also the fact that many influential people were trained under the Japanese system might make it easy for them to understand Japan and to introduce new ideas from it. But they do not think that the Japanese people are trustworthy, and seem to be furious with Japanese attitude which tends to be one of looking down on Koreans. Therefore, the Japanese are a competing reference for

Koreans, while the Americans are a friendly one.

Koreans are very anti-communist. Their attitude toward communists seems to have been changing recently as diversification has been taking place in the communist bloc; but as far as their attitude toward the north Korean communists is concerned, it is definitely negative. Thus, the Korean people seem to be ready to make all possible efforts to defend themselves from the communist threat.

4. Education

It is widely accepted that education is one of the most important factors for bringing rapid development. However, education may not necessarily bring good results as used to be considered. In education one needs teachers, facilities, and materials. The expenditure for financing wide compulsory education may be a great burden for a developing country which has many poor people who need immediate assistance. In addition to that, the meaning of education for the individuals who have it is different from that of the government who must provide it. The government expects the students to contribute to the nation after graduation; but the individuals regard it as the means to high status, wealth, prestige, or some other personal thing. If there is no institutional avenue to obtain it, it may function as a factor to intensifying social unrest.[20] This was painfully experienced in Korea for some time, particularly around the April 19th student uprising, and the voice that argued education would cause the ruin of the nation was heard.

However, education in Korea began to function positively as the first economic development plan was carried out after 1962. Unless the policies of developing education, which included a compulsory education system, were not actively implemented, continuous economic development might not be successfully accomplished. Now, as the economic development is going more rapidly than expected, the labor shortage of skilled workers and engineers seems to be sharply recognized.

5. Pragmatic Attitude

Even Koreans are apt to consider that the *yangban* values and their social characters represent Koreans as a whole. Of course, it can hardly be denied that the lay people were influenced by the *yangban* culture to some extent, but it must be critically examined as to what extent the people of low status or those in the provinces remote from Seoul, who were alienated from power during the Yi-dynasty, adhered to *yangban* values. As a matter of fact, the *yangban* wanted to monopolize many of them in order to demonstrate their nobility.

After the liberation, the old *yangban* class fell and the lay people could enjoy equal rights with the former upper class. And it is not the people of *yangban* origin but those of the lower status who could make more successful adjustment to the chaotic, drastically changing society. Even during the Japanese period, many non-*yangban* people seemed to have risen up in the society, and those who were most active for national independence seem to have originated in this status group. But in the postliberation period they could find a far wider stage on which they could be active.

The Korean people have developed the ability to adapt to the changing reality in the process of change. A lot of people came down to the south from the north at all kinds of risks. And almost all Koreans in the south had to move to safer places during the war. Some of them stayed in strange cities away from their original homes for several years. Under this circumstance, they had to throw out all traditional elements which would not function. Thus they became very pragmatic.

Another reason why the Koreans are pragmatic can be found in their culture. There is a saying that the Koreans are not religious. There may be some different opinions on this argument. But it may be well said that the Koreans are not strongly attached to religious beliefs which are likely to disvalue this world. Religions are said to be fundamentally concerned with death. The Koreans' religious practice as to death is ancestor worship, but actually ancestor worship is the worship of himself who attends the ceremony. He may think his soul after death will stay at home with his children, and have the same service by them.[21] Even those who believe Christianity or Buddhism seem to have more or less the same trait. And it is interesting to note that the leaders in the different religions have often unified together in the movements to save their nation.[22] Thus, the Koreans seem likely to change their religion according to reality rather than to stick to it in spite of social change.

6. Elevation of Women's Status

There is one more important thing that should not be overlooked in discussing the economic development in Korea, though it is usually ignored. That is the role of Korean women. Korea has maintained a culture which has discriminated against females for a long period of time. It is not clear whether it was so in the Koryo-dynasty or in the earlier times.

Nobody will deny that females were looked down upon in *yangban* families and strictly prohibited to show up outside the home. But females of lower classes had more freedom to move out of their homes, although they were held in contempt. And even in a *yangban* family it may be questionable to say in general terms that females were looked down, because an elder sister was respected by her younger brother, and mother held power over her children to some extent.

The attitude of Koreans toward women has been changed by the influence of Christianity, modern education, and Western culture through mass communications on the one hand, and the roles of women were expanded and diversified by the increase of job opportunity for them on the other, particularly during World War II. The status of women was greatly enhanced after the liberation mainly because the democratic institutions which emphasized equal rights with both sexes were introduced.

The roles of women also were tremendously increased. Firstly, women had to take care of their family when husbands had to hide themselves or be absent under the communist control or war situation. Secondly, they had to earn money through peddling, *gye* business, or other means because the salary of their husbands was usually not sufficient. Thirdly, many things required women to be involved in social activities. The most important thing among others was to provide their children with better education. They had to get all the information about it and to make good provisions for it.

That women can move around freely in the society is conductive to the economic development in the sense that the labor force is increased. It is even more so if the labor is of good quality and inexpensive. Besides this, there is another important matter. That is that the Korean women might be less oriented to tradition than their husbands in some aspects. Since they were discriminated against under the traditional *yangban* culture, they are eager to eliminate those elements which may be unfavorable to them, although they may not claim it manifestly. They are strongly interested in the happy life with their husbands and children, and want to avoid any disturbance from other kinsmen. Sons are not important for them because they inherit the family lineage, but because they expect sons to take care of them after retirement.[23] They are very anxious to give the best education to their children, and are quite ready to accept all sacrifices for providing better opportunities to their children. Korean women have very strong aspirations for a better life, and are extremely vital. In this respect, their hidden contribution to the economic development should not be under-evaluated.

Some Unfavorable Factors

So far we have indicated 6 items as favorable socio-cultural factors for the economic development of Korea. Now, it is time to discuss the unfavorable factors. If we miss them, we may hardly avoid the criticism of being unfair. Reviewing the socio-cultural characteristics in Korea, however, there do not seem to be many serious factors to impede economic development, though there are some, of course.

A status seeking attitude might be one of them. During the traditional period, status was all important, even if it was in the form of a formal title without actual power or substantial rewards. All titles one had were recorded in one's genealogy, and his offspring were proud of them. This trait is still strong even now. Because of this value orientation, some of the Korean people are more strongly concerned with saving face and having status symbols rather than achievement and performance in their occupational activities.[24]

Another unfavorable factor would be familism. The idea of encouraging one to preserve his family tradition and to promote strong ties among family members may not necessarily be a negative factor which impedes economic development; it can be a positive factor. However, the Koreans are not likely to develop communal ties on the individual basis in community beyond the family solidarity. And also the particularism on the basis of familism may hinder the universal application of norms in modern social organizations, and may aggravate corruption and waste of time and money for unproductive activities.

The Korean familism seems to have one more undesirable aspect. The Korean people still preserve a strong boy preference attitude.[25] Many people want to have at least one son, hopefully two. Some women say that they would allow their husband to have a concubine in order to have a son who can inherit the family lineage, if they could not give birth to boy. Because of this attitude, the population of Korea has been increased.

Apart from the traditional values, there is another negative factor, that is, the gap between the ideal institutions and reality. The new social institutions after the liberation were mainly planned or initiated by the intellectuals who were generally idealistic and inclined to ignore the actual conditions for accomplishing the ideals.[26] For example, the democratic system of giving the voting right to everybody over twenty is, of course, desirable, and can definitely function well, if one is independent mentally as well as economically. But it showed some dysfunction in its early stage, since there were many ignorant and poor people who could not judge their real representatives. This kind of gap can be observed more or less in modern institutions concerning education, labor, and others too.

Since the institutions could not fit the reality as expected, a dual system of institutional arrangements—one, the institutional regulations, and another, the customary norms—was widely practiced. And this practice has obviously caused inefficient activities and misconduct. For example, in compulsory education all expenditure for elementary education was to be provided by the government. But since the financial support for it by the government was insufficient, many schools used the Parents Teachers Association as a tool for collecting money from the parents.

Conclusion

If we ignore the non-economic factors beyond the sociological realm, such as the administrative efficiency in the bureaucratic organizations and the international situations surrounding Korea, one of the most important socio-cultural factors that can be considered to be involved in the economic development in Korea is the downfall of the traditionally oriented upper class, most of whom would be the landowners of *yangban* background, and the emergence of the former middle class as active members in the society after the liberation. This is particularly important because the former middle class were less attracted to Confucianism, hence more favorable to the new ideas to bring about changes.

This structural change in the Korean society took place during the period of extreme social confusion after the liberation. The social confusion, coupled with the Korean War, forced the Koreans to abandon many traditional elements to a great extent, and made them very pragmatic, although the attitudinal change toward materialism might have originated partly in their way of thinking to appreciate this worldliness.

From the motivational aspect, the Korean nationalism, fostered during the despotic Japanese colonization period and also by the invasion of the north Korean Communists, must be reckoned as another important factor. Korean nationalism has encouraged the Koreans to be active in introducing western ideas and modern social institutions as a means to deal with Japan and defend themselves from any possible invasion from the north.

There is no question education plays a very important role in the rapid economic development. Korea has made an enormous effort to upgrade its educational system with introduction of compulsory education since the liberation. However, it was a great economic burden for the government in the beginning, hence further contributed to the intensification of social unrest. But it began to make a substantial contribution to the successful accomplishment of the first five year economic development plan as soon as it was implemented.

In addition to education, the changing role of women should not be neglected. The status of Korean women has been elevated partly through the introduction of democratic institutions and partly through their active role in the chaotic social situations.

Generally speaking, Korea does not seem to have any serious factor that stands in the way of economic development from the sociological point of view. Particularly, the facts that Koreans have a strong aspiration for economic betterment, that there is a plenty of manpower for high productivity at a cheap wage, and that they want to keep the basic social order to avoid the recurrence of communist aggression are most favorable factors for rapid industrialization in Korea. With these they could overcome the challenges such as poverty, population pressure, and both internal and external conflicts. At the same time, it must be admitted that there are minor unfavorable factors. The attitude to seek status eagerly, and the gap between the ideals of social institutions and reality may impede economic development. Among others, however, the most important matter to be taken into account in bringing about continous economic development seems to incorporate social development with economic development so that internal social tension may be successfully controlled before it becomes serious

〔NOTES〕

1) Japanese newspaper writers suggested the bureaucratic organization operated by able technocrats along with the advisory brain of intellectuals as the tools of rapid economic growth in Korea. See "Bei-chu-so no tofuku ajia gaiko wo kaidoku suru" (To interpret diplomacy of the United States, China, and Soviet Russia in north-east Asia), *The Chuo-koron*, May issue, 1977, pp. 174-5.
2) Toynbee pointed out that optimum challenges would develop civilizations. Arnold J. Toynbee, *A study of History*, vols. I-VI, abridged by D.C. Somervell, (New York: Oxford University Press, 1946), pp. 187 -208.
3) Bert F. Hoselitz, *Sociological Aspects of Economic Growth*, (New York: The Free Press, 1960), p. 59.
4) Parsons indicated five pairs of pattern variables; affectivity versus affective neutrality, self-interest versus collective interest, universalism

versus particularism, achievement versus ascription(later changed to performance versus quality), and specificity versus diffuseness. See Talcott Parsons, *The Social System*, (Glencoe, Illinois: The Free Press, 1951), p. 58.

5) Wilbert E. Moore, "The Social Framework of Economic Development," in Ralph Braibanti and Joseph J. Spengler (eds.), *Tradition, Values and Socio-Economic Development*, (Durham: Duke University Press, 1961), pp. 57-82. Later, Moore gave a similar discussion in his book, *Social Change*, (Englewood Cliffs, New Jersy: Prentice-Hall, Inc., 1963), pp. 89-112.

6) The writer presented a paper, "Sociological Implications of Modernization in Korea," at the annual conference of the Association for the Asian Studies in 1967. He also wrote an article, "Socio-cultural Conditions of Economic Development" (in Korean), according to Moore's scheme. This article is included in *Theory and Reality of Korean Economic Development*, Vol. 1 (Part of Theory and Policy), ed. by The Office of Planning Coordinator in the Cabinet, (Seoul, 1969), pp. 52-87.

7) Recently the writer wrote three articles which are concerned with the social change in Korea: (1) "Structural Change of Korean Society" (in Japanese), (2) "Socio-cultural Context of Modernization in Korea," (3) "Characteristics of Social Change in Korea." The first one is included in *Asian Cultural Studies*, No. 9, December 1977. International Christian University in Tokyo. The second is seen in this book with a different title, "Social Change in Korea," and the third is included in *Economic Development and Social Change in Korea* ed. by T.W. Shin, et al., (Frankfurt: Campus Verlag, 1980).

8) *Chosen no genron to seso (Press and Social Climate in Korea)*, a secret compilation published by Document Section, Secretariat, Korean Government-General, Survey Material No. 21 (the publishing date is unknown).

9) According to statistics, the proportion of independent farmers to the farm population decreased from 22.3% to 19.2% during the period between 1918 and 1937, while the proportion of tenants increased from 38.1% to 55.1% during the same period of time. See Minoru Himeno, *Chosen keizai zuhyo (Statistical Tables of Korean Economy)*, Korea

Statistical Association, 1940, p. 168.

10) Andrew J. Grajdenzev described that the industrial potentiality of Korea just before the end of World War Ⅱ was almost as large as that of Italy in the monograph entitled *Korea Looks Ahead* which was published by the American Council, Institute of Pacific Relations, Inc., in 1944.

11) We may find one of the best examples in Vietnam. Once the writer was involved in public opinion research sponsored by a leading Korean newspaper. He found that the highly educated people and professionals showed the most critical attitude toward both the pro-government and opposite conservative parties.

12) No official data are available about the number of tenants after the land reform. According to a study the writer did in 6 Korean villages in 1958, however, out of 336 households investigated including 39 non-farming households (9.8%), 201 (59.8%) were independent farmers, 20 (5.9%) pure tenants, and 49 (14.6%) partly owner-partly tenants. See Man-gap Lee, *Hangug nongchon sahoe ŭi gujo wa byŏnhwa* (*The Social Structure of the Korean Village and Its Change*), (Seoul: Seoul National University Press, 1973), p. 84.

13) National Agricultural Cooperative Federation, *Hangug nong-ŏb ŭi bunsŏg* (*Analysis of Korean Agriculture*), (Seoul, 1963), pp. 178-180.

14) Yong-ha Shin, *Dognib hyŏbhoe yŏngu* (*Studies on Independence Association*), (Seoul: Iljogag, 1975), p. 223.

15) According to *Daehan gyoyug yŏn-gam* (*Yearbook of Korean Education*) of 1953 and 1960, the total number of college students in 1945 (after the liberation) was only 7,110, but it was increased to 33,542 in 1952, and again increased to 75,107 which is a little more than 10 times of the number of 1945.

16) See the editorial, "Underlying Causes," *Korea Times*, May 17, 1961.

17) The percentage of the respondents who indicated "the solution of unemployment" was 42.9%, and 19.5% of the respondents pointed out "the control of inflation." See the *Gyŏnghyang Daily News*, June 14, 1961.

18) See Hyeog-in Lyu, "Bag daetongryŏng ŭl umjigin saramdŭl" (Those Who Help President Park), *Shin-dong-a*, October 1964, pp. 144-165.

19) W.E. Moore, *Social Change*, p. 94.

20) Robert K. Merton, "Social Structure and Anomie," *Social Theory and Social Structure*, (Glencoe, Illinois: The Free Press, 1957). See also Man-gap Lee, "This Problem of the Intelligentsia," *Atlas*, June, 1961. (This is an English summary of his paper contributed to *Sasang-gye* monthly, February issue, 1961).

21) William E. Biernatzki, S.J., Luke Jin-chang Im, and Anselm K.Min, *Korean Catholicism in the 70s*, (Maryknoll, New York: Orbis, 1975), pp. 14-25.

22) The best example may be found in the fact that the majority of 33 persons who signed the Independence Declaration of March 1st, 1919 were the leaders in the various religious groups. Even now, those from different religious groups often meet together for discussion on public problems.

23) Jae-mo Yang, et al., *Hangug nongchon sahoe wa gajog gyehoeg (Korean Rural Community and Family Planning)*, (Seoul: Yonsei University Press, 1966), pp. 66-68.

24) This may look to be somewhat against Kyong-dong Kim's observation. See Kyong-dong Kim, "Industrialization and Industrialism," which was presented at the conference of *Industrialization in Korea* organized by the International Liaison Committee for Research on Korea in 1971. He says that "the Korean works are strongly committed to achievement orientations typical of the Protestant ethic of early Western modernization..." But this is about the attitudes of the workers, not of those from the upper class or the middle who seem to have been more strongly oriented to status than the workers.

25) See Hyo-jae Lee, "Seoul-si gajog ŭi sahoehag-jŏg gochal" (Sociological Consideration on Families in Seoul City), *Idae Nonchong*, 1960, and Bom-mo Chung et al., *Psychological Perspectives: Family Planning in Korea*, (Seoul: Korean Institute for Research in the Behavioral Sciences, 1972), Table C-5, p. 410.

26) Man-gap Lee, "Social Organizations," *A City in Transition*, an ILC-ORK-SID research report, ed. by Man-gap Lee, and Herbert R. Barringer, (Seoul: Hollym, 1971), p. 374.

II

CHANGES IN RURAL AND URBAN COMMUNITIES

Consanguineous Group and Its Function in the Korean Community*

The Traditional Family

In principle, the family system of Korea is generally based on patriarchy, and members of a family descended from their ancestors along paternal lines use the family name with identification of the place of origin of their ancestors in order to differentiate themselves from families of different origins. They are always aware that they are offspring of the same ancestor, and marriage among themselves is strictly prohibited.

Human relations within a family have been governed by the norms of Confucianism. It was strictly observed by those of the *yangban*, or the scholar-officials, who upheld Confucianism as their basic ideology, but it seemed that it was less strict in the lower classes. Most emphasized in family relations at filial obedience, discrimination between husbands and wives, and order in terms of age differentiation. Thus, it compelled the children, wives, and juniors to become absolutely obedient toward their parents, husbands, and seniors, respectively. Particularly, the freedom of women was restricted to the extent that they were kept from the presence of men or from engaging in social activities outside their homes.

Those who occupied the most important positions in the family were parents, husbands, and sons. In the pre-modern age, fathers held an absolute power in the family, and it lasted until their death. Sons were regarded far more important than daughters.

---

* This paper was presnted at The Ninth International Family Research Seminar in Tokyo in 1965. It is included in Families in *East and West: Socialization Process and Kinship Ties*, ed. by Reuben Hill and Rene König, (The Hague: Mouton & Co., 1970), Chap. 18.

Principal reasons were that in the first place those who could inherit the lineage, prestige and fortunes of their families were sons; secondly, sons were charged with the responsibility of conducting services in memory of their ancestors; thirdly, sons would take care of their old parents: and lastly, only sons could become officials, or make a living for their family. Naturally, it was an important duty for women to bear children. Incapability to bear a child, along with insolence toward her parents-in-law, were considered the most serious defects on the part of a woman, possibly causing her removal from the family of her husband. Although those of *yangban* often adopted their sons from thir brothers or near kin, it was seldom that they adopted heirs from those who had no blood relation with them. Among the *sangmin*, or the commoner, often sons of concubines could become heirs, but in the case of *yangban*, they were unable to hold the *yangban* status of their father.[1)]

Nothing is more important in the Korean family than the services to the memory of their ancestors. There are several kinds of these services. In the family of *yangban*, they hold services for all those who died in the previous four generations. The offspring of the ancestors of the previous four generations were considered very near kin. The services in such a family were divided into two; one called *gijesa* to give a memorial service to their ancestors on the day of their death, and one called *charejesa* to pay tribute to their forefathers by seasons. It is known that they did perform the seasonal services more often in the past, but now they pay tribute to their family ancestors on January 1st and August 15th by the lunar calendar besides *gijesa*. Such services are always held by the head family. They do not hold services at home for their ancestors of more than five generations ago. Instead, members of the family assemble before the grave at a certain period to pay tribute to their ancestors. This is what we call *sihyangje*. The service of *sihyangje* is usually given by the members of a consanguineous group.

What I call a 'consanguineous group' in this paper is the aggregation of the offspring under the same ancestors over the four generations, which is larger than the kingroup. Such a consanguineous group is always a group of those related by blood, but not necessarily a group living in a certain place. Some members may be scattered around the various provinces. In the past, however, most of them lived in the villages near the graves of their ancestors. Those who have been living together still in the same village usually compose substantially a consanguineous group.

Organization of a Consanguineous Group and Its Activites

It is known that in Korea there are many villages wherein a predominant consanguineous group exists.[2] Sometimes they are called consanguineous villages. The people who are the members of a consanguineous group in a village fall in the category of *yangban* class or quasi-*yangban*. The *sangmin* were economically and politically incapable of maintaining their consanguineous unity and living together, since they belonged to those holding high social status and were under the strict control of the local governor who had close relations with the *yangban*. Often it can be found that *sangmin* of the same family origin cluster in a village, but they are just living there together without any organized activity.

The villages inhabitated by a consanguineous group of *yangban* class can be broadly divided into two kinds: one has some sort of organized activity, and the other none. Where there are the graves of the common ancestors over the four generations, a certain organization is needed for holding services to the memory of the ancestors. It is common that those of a consanguineous group who do not have the graves as such in their vicinity would not have any organized activity unless they have leaders to work out some activity for other purposes. Even then, they often maintain a close relationship with the consanguineous group in other areas where there are graves of their ancestors.

The *yangban* in the Yi-dynasty thought their foremost obligation as offspring was to uphold the virtues inherited from their forefathers, attach a great importance to the graves of their ancestors, and solemnly hold services for ancestor worship according to the ideology of Confucianism. Among the reasons for having respect for the graveyard is not only the idea of worshipping their ancestors but also the long-cherished belief that their future generations would not be able to achieve their prosperity unless a good site were chosen for the location of the graveyard according to the *pungsu* theory (Taoistic theory that interprets the terrain feature in connection with good luck and bad luck).

It was common for the descendants to have more respect toward their ancestors who had either earned a high position in the bureaucratic hierarchy, high virtue, or fame for their achievements eliciting a high respect from the people. It was stemmed from the fact that by respecting their ancestors, they could identify themselves as the descendants of such-and-such distinguished figures and, accordingly, they could enjoy a social prestige corresponding to their status. They kept a record of their family tree to show clearly who were the descendants of such-and-such persons who had held such-and-such social status. The genealogieal record shows the collateral descendants and their status, achievements, and location of their graves. It also records the family background of their wives but usually not that of their daughters.

The formal organization of a consanguineous group is generally called *jonghoe*. The consanguineous association may be composed of the descendants of the first ancestor of the whole consanguineous group or of an intermediate originator of its minor branch. Some consanguineous groups might trace back to their ancestors of a thousand years ago, but mostly they went back around thirty generations. The reasons were, I believe, that when a new ruling class was formed at the time of the founding of the Yi-dynasty, a certain family saw the need of combining the members of their family to attain prosperity for them by forming their own separate group on the basis of their affinity by blood, putting themselves in the center of the family members, and by uncovering their common ancestors of over four to five generations before whom they could identify.

The offspring of the same ancestor are automatically admitted into *munjung* or *jongjung*, that is, consanguineous group. However, they do not necessarily participate in the activities of the *jonghoe*. Most of those living in the urban areas, and even rural areas which are far from their consanguineous center, do not have any tie with the association. The consanguineous group composed of the offspring of the first ancestor is the largest one, but such a large group is usually divided into several branches.

Some of them want to establish a small *munjung* to brighten their own section of the larger consanguineous group by respecting one of their intermediate ancestors who gained some prominence in the society, and try to make themselves distinct from other remote families. Again this small branch would be divided into other smaller branches. Each branch, however, does not always become a *munjung*. Sometimes even the smallest *munjung* has several sects in it. One could be a member of both small or smaller *munjung* and major *munjung* as he could be a member of both small and large communities. Every *munjung*, small or large, has its own consanguineous association. It is generally located at the village near the graves of their ancestors who originated the consanguineous group. However, it is often located at a metropolitan area which has no direct concern with the grave, when there are many wide-spread members or socially powerful members of the consanguineous group or if the location is considered favorable for their communications and activities. In the case of the general consanguineous group centering around the first ancestor, the association is usually established in a large city such as Seoul. Needless to say, there are communications among the associations of the various levels.

Each *munjung* has a representative called *munjang* (chief of *munjung*). As a rule, the chief of the *munjung* is to be the highest—first, in terms of the generational orders; second, in terms of ages; and then in virtue. However, some family groups consider age as the primary criterion in determining the order of precedence within the consanguineous group. The chief of a consanguineous group is not only a symbolic representative of the group, but also that of the consanguineous association which deals with the business of the group. But he seldom exercises power. He has under his control a man called *yusa* who takes the role of the general manager. He operates the association and is responsible for the implementation of its business plans.

In most cases, the association has one *yusa*, but sometimes it has several men in such capacity; not because the work load is heavy, but because it is desirable to eliminate the possible complaints that might come from various branches in the group. The manager carries out his routine business at his own discretion, but he consults with the elders and powerful men in the group before making decisions on relatively important matters. In some instances, the association has several councillors and honor advisors. Usually the advisor is a man of power or wealth in the consanguineous group. In the annually-held general meeting, the staff are elected, but actually most of them are rather informally nominated on the advice of the powerful elders in the group. The staff including *yusa* are not paid any salary.

The general meeting of the consanguineous association is normally held in *jesil* around the time of *sihyangje* in which many members participate. The *jesil* is the assembly place for members of the consanguineous group. It is sometimes used as the house to prepare the memorial services, and as a place to accommodate those who come from other areas to attend the services.

In most cases, it is a firm, tile-roofed house with an extraordinary shape, built at the location of the graves of their respectable ancestors. The items discussed at the general meeting of the association are: (1) memorial services, (2) management of the farm land, *wito*, prepared for the deceased ancestors, (3) financial problems, (4) maintenance of *jesil*, (5) election of staff of the association, and (6) miscellaneous problems. The most important things above all are the matters concerning the memorial services and graves. Although there recently has been a move in some consanguineous groups to promote the education of their children, it is not thus far shown that they have made any noteworthy progress in this activity. The consanguineous group rarely has had any plan for pursuing productive work or any other mutually cooperative endeavor. In the past, before World War II, many consanguineous groups organized a mutual assistance system among the members, but this kind of system gradually vanished by itself after the War as the value of the fund dropped.

What constituted the fund for the consanguineous association were the donated land and forest for the memorial services. The land reform ruled that the size of such land, namely *wito*, should be no more than 400 *pyŏngs* (one *pyŏng* is about 3.3 square meters) per grave, but they can still own the same size of the land handed down from generation to generation, as they have many graves of ancestors to whom no land was attached originally. Those who cultivate the land are called *myojig* (guardian of the grave). They are different from ordinary tenants and are under the control of the *yusa*. The employer and employee relation in such case takes more or less a pre-modern characteristic. They do not pay the form rent like tenants, but with the income from the land they defray the expenses for and look after the memorial services. Nowadays, there are many cases where poor members of the consanguineous group take this kind of job, while in the past only those with low social status did it. Though the donated land is the only financial base of supporting the activities of the consanguineous group, sometimes extra funds are raised from the members for emergency use; for instance, when the group feels it necessary to expand their *wito* or repair the *jesil*, they rely on the contributions from the members of the group who are wealthy or powerful, or famous, mainly in the urban areas.

In the past, *sihyangje* was observed twice a year in summer and autumn, but now it is observed in October by the lunar calendar with no exception, as it is the season of leisure after harvest when those living in the distant provinces may have free time to attend the services. Usually attendants are those in the vicinity of the grave, but many also come from far places. Some services are attended by several hundreds of the group. The services normally start with the grave of the earliest ancestor, and go down to the later ones in accordance with the order of precedence. Even when the graves are scattered around the various parts of the country, services are usually held by the order of precedence, and so are the dates arranged for the services. If there are many ancestors' graves around the village, the service takes many days, at the cost of other business.

For the service to the memory of the prominent ancestors, for whom *wito* was prepared, the service itself tends to be held more pompously. On the contrary, people show a tendency of simplifying the services for their mediocre forefathers by using a tiny portion of income earned from *wito*, or just by reducing the complexity to bowing to the graves. In some other cases, a consanguineous group is living in a place where their forefather is apotheosized in *sŏwŏn*, or the learning institute. Since the institute is a Confucian school, it is operated by the Confucian scholars. Thus, it has no formal connection with the particular consanguineous group. But in case such an institute is incapable of operating itself, it often obtains some support from the consanguineous group. They must help support the institute, willingly or unwillingly, because their ancestors are worshipped by others, and it would damage their prestige if the institute were to be ruined.

Human Relations Bearing on the Consanguineous Group

The head family is a family that is inherited by the eldest male descendant of a particular *munjung*. The head family may be one that is representing only a small *munjung* or a large one of higher level. The head family was respected by other members within the same *munjung* because it formed the main lineage, observed the memorial services and was responsible for preserving the family tradition.

However, the tendency of respecting the head family has been decreasing because of the following reasons: the former leaders who had supported the consanguineous group became poorer after the proclamation of the land reform; moreover, sometimes, the head family which is generally conservative, stayed poor because of failure to adjust itself to the rapid social changes; the head family has lost sympathy from the fellow members by misappropriation, such as selling the property of the consanguineous group; and, also, even the idea of keeping a strong unity of the consanguineous group is withering away among the younger people.

There is not any particular functional relation in everyday life of the members of the consanguineous group and the consanguineous association, although they can use vessels and other equipment for the rituals owned by the association. The association does not control or interfere with the conduct of its members. It occasionally happens that when a member does something which would bring disgrace to the consanguineous group, such as marriage with a person of lower status, the elders or the powerful members of the consanguineous group, not the association istelf, would informally discuss the problem and give him a warning. If he does not follow the warning, he will be isolated in the village. In the past, the isolated person could not continue to live in the village. Even now, people try to avoid such misconduct, lest they should be subject to the criticism of their family, because it would bring them trouble. But the elders are less influential than before.

It may be easier for members of the same consanguineous group to become friendly with each other than with those who are not members. Actually, they seldom live closely with each other unless they are near-kin, and also there does not seem to be any special activity of assistance or mutual cooperation. It is common that often a conflict unknowingly exists among those of a consanguineous group, if there are competing branches in it. Such conflict does not appear on the surface. However, it would appear on the surface, if the conflict were to make them lose face, or if the interests of both branches were in conflict. Also, when the difference of their present social status is considerably wide, they may be less friendly with each other than with the unrelated persons, even though they are of the same ancestor of generations ago.

It is also widely observed that there would be an internal conflict among the people when two or more different consanguineous groups exist in a village. In the past such conflict often appeared on the surface. It seems that such conflict was generally caused by extreme competition for social prestige and jealousy of those who were prosperous, but more specifically, they fervently quarreled with each other in a struggle to secure good sites for graves. Naturally, their struggle was extremely severe because of their belief that the prosperity of their future generations depended on the property of the graves. While in peace, they were on friendly terms, and married each other, as they held the same high social status. Nevertheless, their dispute could emerge on the surface whenever the interests of both sides were in conflict.

As noted in the beginning of this paper, in the age of the Yi-dynasty the *sangmin* depended on the *yangban* class in terms of economy, power, and prestige, and consequently, were subject to the consanguineous group which held the high status. Even under the rule of Japan, they were still under the pressure of the *yangban*. Most of the *sangmin* worked as tenants for the landlords who were mainly of *yangban* origin.

However, a great change was brought to the farms after the day of liberation. First of all, because of a democratic atmosphere which was newly created, the *yangban* could no longer despise the *sangmin*. Moreover, there were many progressive youths among those of *yangban* who thought that such discrimination was not necessary. Secondly, most of *sangmin* rose from tenants to land owners, while many of *yangban* landlords declined. Consequently, the economic inequality almost disappeared, and both *yangban* and *sangmin* farmers became equal. Thirdly, the family groups of *yangban* could no longer have their strong leaders in the villages because most of them moved to the urban areas. Fourthly, the activity for the entire village was urged as the administrative control became stronger. Accordingly, the villagers had more chances of discussing and solving their problems together regardless of their past status.

Under the government of Japan, a positive effort was made to achieve the unity of the village, according to the needs of the Japanese colonialism. During World War II, this effort became more active owing to the war policy of impressment and mobilization of labor power. After the War, such efforts for achieving unity were expanded according to the needs of maintaining public security and in order to increase farm productivity.

Today, it has become very difficult to find the practice of discriminating *yangban* and *sangmin* in the every day life of the villagers, since such tendency has remarkably diminished. But still in many villages the tendency remains in the matter of arranging marriages, by being strict about the background and social status. A recent survey in the village of a famous consanguineous group shows that many of the *yangban* populace were not unfavorable to marriage between *yangban* and *sangmin*. This attitude is presumed to be very unusual among those of *yangban* in other villages. They only opposed strongly the marriage with *chŏnmin*, or the lowest class, of whom there are only a few in the rural villages.[3] However, the rural people of *yangban* background are much less concerned over the marriage between *yangban* and *sangmin*, particularly when the partner happens to be the bride of *sangmin*. It is because of the fact that the woman adopts the status of her husband after marriage.

Sometimes the discrimination between *yangban* and *sangmin* is also observable in the mode of their conversation. In strongly traditional villages of the consanguineous group, it is often noticed that the *yangban* speak impolitely to the *sangmin*. After the liberation there was an argument between *yangban* and *sangmin* over carrying the hearse in some villages. The argument was started because the *yangban* expected the *sangmin* to carry the hearse of the *yangban* as they had done in the past, and *sangmin* said that they could not do so any more unless *yangban* would do likewise. This did occur at the village where the *yangban* did not have a common consanguineous basis.

Changing Social Functions of the Consanguineous Group

Along with Confucian academic circles, the consanguineous groups, dispersed over the farm villages, were the core for protecting the traditional Confucian norm of the *yangban* class and maintaining social orderliness. The local bureaucrats were only able to exercise power with their support. Besides, the consanguineous group, being a pressure group and family oriented, deferred the promotion of the welfare of the entire nation, brought disorder in the discipline of the bureaucracy, and made enforcement of the law difficult. The *yangban* enjoyed their leisure time, pursued the prestige and prosperity of their own family, and failed to inspire production and labor.

The consanguineous group consequently prevented the nation from bringing about changes and progress. It further deprived the individual family of its independence from kinship control and the independent activity of an individual member of the family. Especially, it suppressed the freedom of activity of youth with new ideas, prevented the women from improving their position and acting in freedom. The consanguineous groups also deferred the unity of the villagers by discriminating against the lower classes, such as *sangmin* and *chŏnmin*. Whenever a problem of the community arose, it was usually solved in the name of the consanguineous group and in its interest.

As they were protected by the authority and were in a favorable position economically, the *sangmin* could not resist them. As pointed out in several parts of this paper, today the consanguineous group has been considerably weakened and deprived of its functions. However, the consanguineous group still has considerable influence because of political reasons. Candidates who run for election to the National Assembly or the local assembly attempt to win a bundle of votes from the components of the consanguineous groups, who are under the influence of the powerful members of the group in the village, by associating with the latter. On the other hand, the consanguineous leaders in the village may hold the power in the village, place themselves in a favorable position, and secure the funds for the consanguineous activities through association with the former. It may be very difficult for the politicians and other powerful men of consanguineous group to reject the recommendations or requests made by their kinsmen. Frequently, they are willing to help fellow members. Therefore, the consanguineous group in Korea still plays a powerful political role in maintaining the *status quo* of pre-modern characteristics in Korean society. However, there is a growing tendency in Korea today for the rural people to be less influenced by the leaders in the consanguineous groups and to exercise their voting right by their own judgement, as they receive more and more education and possess more new ideas.

[NOTES]

1) Social classes during the Yi-dynasty may be classified as follow:
    a. *Yangban* who are chiefly the family members of the royal officials or their offspring down to the four generations, former *yangban*, and *yangban's* relatives.
    b. *Jung-in*, technical specialists in the central government.
    c. *Sangmin*, composed of assistants to the royal officials who were supposed to contribute mainly to the local government without payment, tenant farmers, merchants etc.,
    d. *Chŏnmin*, composed of domestic servants, entertainers, butchers, fortune tellers, necromancers etc.

    Besides these four major status categories, there were some other status groups such as *hyangban* and *toban*, and *sŏ-ŏl*, but these may not be so important for the present discussion.
2) E. Zensho, *Chosen no shuraku* (*Village in Korea*), Vol. III, (Keijo: Chosen Government General, 1935), p. 217.

3) Taik-kyoo Kim, *Dongjog burag ŭi saenghwal gujo yŏngu* (*The Cultural Structure of a Consanguineous Village*), (Daegu: Chŏng-gu College Press, 1964), pp. 132-3.

Politics in a Korean Village[1]

The 1966 census of the Republic of Korea showed that about 67 per cent of the population lived in rural areas.[2] Although the flow of population to metropolitan areas precipitated by industrial growth and other conditions is gradually changing the demographic map of Korea, the distribution is likely to continue in present proportions for some years to come.

As in most non-Western countries, the contrasts between rural and urban areas are very marked in Korea. Although the rural areas are undergoing change, the process is little affected by the currents of Western civilization. The residues of the past remain strong. Standards of living and education are lower than in the urban areas, and communications and transportation are less convenient. The sociopolitical structures and behavior patterns are also considerably different, and understanding of these is essential for a proper general understanding of the workings of politics in Korea.

Geographical and Administrative Characteristics of Korean Rural Areas

The Republic of Korea is divided into two special cities (*Seoul* and *Busan*) and nine provinces. Each province is, in turn, divided into cities and counties(*gun*). There are 139 counties as of 1965. In number of administrative units, the island province of *Jeju* is the smallest, with only one city and two counties. The next

---

* This article was prepared in 1969 in order to contribute to a book about "Korean Society," but the plan to publish the book was canceled by some reason.

smallest is North *Chungchŏng*, with two cities and ten counties. The largest province, North *Gyŏngsang*, has five cities and 24 counties. The average county population is about 140,000.

Each county office is responsible for the general administration in its area and is under the direction of a chief county officer appointed by the central government. The county has never been a self-governing body and consequently there is no representative assembly. The police function in each county is conducted by a police station which is independent of the county office, though both organizations are controlled by the central Ministry of Home Affairs through the provincial government. In each county there are also various governmental agencies, such as the health station, agriculture extension station, tax office, and forestry and soil conservation agency, which carry out specific functions.

Usually a county is composed of one *ŭb* and about ten *myŏn*. The *ŭb* is a small town having a population between twenty and fifty thousand. It serves as the county seat, and usually is a town with some modern organizations such as banks, factories, and shops, and governmental agencies.

The lowest administrative unit in rural area is the *myŏn*. The *myŏn* office provides general administration; a police branch office is charged with the security of the district and is separate from the *myŏn* office. Often, but not necessarily, the *myŏn* office is in the economic center of the district. The police branch is more likely to be stationed in the economic center or at an important traffic point for convenience in maintaining security.

Sometimes the *myŏn* and police branch offices will be in isolated places without a village nearby, but even in such cases they are usually in the central part of the district and convenient to transportation. If there is a socio-economic center in the district, it might be obviously more desirable for these agencies to be there; conflict between different areas in the district, however, may prevent their moving to the more convenient site.

Some *myŏn* have only a small socio-economic center composed of shops and eating places. A somewhat larger center will have a market which is open every fifth day, together with other facilities such as a bus stop, barber shop, newspaper distribution agency, drug store, and hospital. Economically more important centers may have also branch agencies of banks. Some centers, while similar to the *ŭb* in appearance, fall short because the population is not large enough.

The *myŏn*, or township, is divided, further, into about ten *ri* or *dong*. The terms refer to the same thing, the only difference being that in general "*ri*" is used in the central part of the republic and "*dong*" in the southern part. The *ri* (or *dong*) is a supplementary administrative district, under a *ri* chief who, while doing his own work for a living, works also for the government and, since he does not maintain an office, keeps official records at home.

There is no fixed population size for the *ri*. Some *ri* have more than a hundred households, but this large a number is rather unusual. The *ri* shown on government maps are not necessarily the actual *ri* administrative districts at the present time. Although some *ri* on the map still remain as administrative districts, many others have been divided further into two or three minor districts with a *ri* chief in each. For example, *Waeryang-dong*, in *Gunwi* County, North *Gyŏngsang* Province, appears as an administrative district on the map, but it is actually divided in first, second, and third *Waeryang-dongs*. The subdividing of the former *ri* districts was carried out recently, partly because villages in the district were scattered in remote places and partly because the population of the villages had increased to a point where one *ri* chief was not able to discharge his duty efficiently.

The *ri* itself is divided into units known as *ban*. Under the Liberal Party (1959) the government reorganized the *ban* into *bang*, which was a slightly larger unit. The old *ban* system was restored after the Party lost power in 1960. Unlike the *ri* or the *myŏn*, the *ban* is not a territorial unit; it applies to a grouping of households. All the households in a *ri* are divided into *ban*. Over each *ban* is a chief, representing his group, who assists the *ri* chief.

Many *ri* have several "natural villages"; some have only one, but typically there are more.[3] A natural village may be defined as a cluster of rural houses situated at some distance from other collectivities. The common term in the countryside for the natural village is *burag*. Although sometimes this word is used alternatively for *maŭl*, a distinction can be made. The natural village may have minor groups of houses which are separated by a relatively short distance, say fifty or one hundred yards, or several hundred yards at most, and the word for these minor groups of houses is *maŭl*. In the past, when there were fewer houses in one place, a natural village and a *maŭl* could be the one and the same. Even now, in many cases, the village can be a *maŭl*, but close inspection may show that the village comprises more than one *maŭl*. Rarely, a collection of houses which to the outsider appears to be one *maŭl* is actually divided into two different *maŭl* and the people there distinguish between them; two or more *maŭl* may have been originally separate and now appear to be combined because of the increase in the number of houses. The *maŭl* often gets its proper name from a geographical characteristic, but it may be named after the family of the predominant consanguineous group in it.

In most cases, the people of a *maŭl* have a high sense of social identity which has been developed in a long process of village life. They may have slight or latent feelings of conflict or competition with those of another *maŭl* while keeping up friendly relations on the surface.

When foreigners apply the English word "village" to a Korean rural community, they may fail to indicate a particular area, and confusion in terminology can result. Usually "village" means the natural village, but the word may be applied to the *ri*, or even to the *myŏn*. In the present study it will be used to refer to the *ri*, and the focus will be primarily on it rather than on either the natural village or the *myŏn*, because the *ri* is not only the most clearly defined lowest administrative district, but also is the area in which the rural people have relatively more integrated organizational activities.

As to the physical appearance of the Korean rural community, there is no open country, as seen in the United States, in which individual farm houses are dispersed here and there. Some few farm houses may be found apart in isolated places, but most of them cluster together to form a *maŭl*. The clay-walled houses have roofs of thatch, except where well-to-do farmers have chosen to roof their homes with tile. Some villages have a mill powered by electric generators. There is usualy a small store and a *jumag*, where meals and drinks are available. There are also villages, although not many, which have a public hall, school, or church.

Modern social organizations with specific functions, except the agriculture cooperative, will rarely be found in a village, unless it is a community center convenient for transportation. In some villages will be seen a relatively large tile-roofed house which does not appear to be an ordinary dwelling. It may be a *jesil* which is owned by a consanguineous group of *yangban* (the aristocrats or the upper class families) and is used for ancestor worship ceremonies or as a meeting place for the group members. In other cases it may be *sŏwŏn*, which is an academy for the local Confucianists.

Village Social Structure

In Korean rural society most of the people are deeply involved in the family. There may be some who do not have their own family, in which case they are usually attached to a family to whom they are not related by blood. The social status of the individual thus is defined by the socio-economic condition of the family head or other responsible member and also by the family background for many generations. Even today it is very easy for rural people to know the past social status of their ancestors, because many families have stayed in the same area, although not necessarily in the same village, for long periods of time.

There are three basic factors to be taken into consideration for understanding the general social structure of the Korean rural village. These are consanguineous kin relationship, traditional social status, and economic status.[4]

The consanguineous kin relationship embraces families who are descended from an identifiable common ancestor along the paternal line and who share the same family name and place of origin. People with the same family name are not necessarily related by consanguineity unless they share also the place of origin of their first known ancestor. Far more extensive than the usual kin group of relatives, the consanguineous kin group includes persons who are related to each other as offspring of a common ancestor of four generations back.

The consanguineous kin group has been formed mainly among those of *yangban* or quasi-*yangban* status. In traditional Korean society those of lower status could not maintain extended and well-integrated kinship relations, since they had neither sufficient economic and political means nor the actual need to do so. The lower classes did not have any distinguished ancestors to revere in their worship ceremonies and were not required by the Confucian code to hold worship rites for their ancestors except for the parents.[5]

In times past, the ancestor worship ceremonies were the main function of the consanguineous group. Consequently, the first factor, consanguineous kin relationship, was closely connected with the second, the traditional social-status system, in determining a person's situation in society.

The third factor, economic status, was not as significant, at least not overtly. The most crucial requirement for power, prestige, and high economic standing as well, was an official position in the government. Not all *yangban* families were wealthy, and indeed they were supposed not to be concerned with monetary matters, though many of them were wealthy landowners. Some took the role of core members in supporting the consanguineous kin group.

More recently, during the Japanese period (1910~1945), while ownership of land remained the primary source of rural wealth, positions in the governmental agencies and public associations became very important for attaining high economic status. This was owing to the modernization of the bureaucracy, together with the development of modern business enterprises. The same trend continues today. The more desirable and better-paid positions are obtained mainly through educational training and relations with politically influential persons. In obtaining positions, persons of the *yangban* and quasi-*yangban* classes have more advantages, that is to say more educational opportunity and contact with officialdom, than those without strong kinship background.

In rural Korea there are many villages where families with a common ancestral origin and surname live together to form a consanguineous group. Sometimes there are other consanguineous groups of different origin in the same village. In other cases, the groups do not necessarily have a formal kinship organization. But if the village is the place of origin of the first ancestor or of any distinguished intermediary ancestor of a particular consanguineous group, then that group uaually has its own formal kinship organization, or *jonghoe*.

The offspring of the identified first ancestor automatically belong to the largest group of *jongjung* or *munjung*. In turn, the *jong-*

jung is split into branch groups of minor *jongjung* if there is a respectable intermediary ancestor after the first and his direct male offspring want to serve him in a special worship ceremony to distinguish themselves from other member families of the larger consanguineous group. This branch group may again be split, further, if another distinguished ancestor has appeared in later generations and his descendants want to carry on observances in memory of him. It is possible, therefore, for a person to belong to several *jongjung* of different levels. In the same village there may be several minor branches which belong to the major consanguineous group. Although conflict between branches is not a matter of course, the offspring of a concubine of a particular ancestor, for example, will usually be discriminated against to some extent by those born of a legitimate wife. In traditional society the children of a concubine would not enjoy the same *yangban* status as those of a legitimate wife.

The consanguineous association, or *jonghoe*, is based on a particular consanguineous group. Not all consanguineous groups form an association, since there are two major conditions that must be present. First, there must be a strong sense of solidarity impelling the members to worship an ancestor. Second, some kind of economic foundation must exist or be established to provide for the ceremony. The seat of a consanguineous association is usually the village containing the grave of the worshiped ancestor.

A consanguineous association has officers such as the *munjang*, or chief of the consanguineous group, and the *yusa*, or secretary. The *munjang* serves as the symbolic representative of the group. He is selected by ascriptive traits such as seniority in genealogical order and age. Accordingly, he is very old. The actual administration of the association is performed by the *yusa*, who is nominated by the elders of the consanguineous group. In general, each association has one *yusa*, but, though rare, there are some associations which have two or three *yusa* who represent their respective branches within the consanguineous group.

The main functions of a consanguineous association are to maintain the graves of the ancestors, to hold seasonal ancestor worship ceremonies, and to manage the properties of the association such as the *wito* and the *jesil*. The *wito* is the farm land which has been secured by the contributions of the kinship members (mainly the wealthy members) in order to carry out the functions of the association. Besides the *wito*, many kinship associations own the unused land where the graves of the ancestors are situated. The *wito* and grave sites are managed by a *myojig* (grave custodians) or *sanjig* (mountain custodians) hired by the association.

In addition to the functions just mentioned, the association may have some programs to promote cooperation among its members, to support the *jong-ga*, or chief family, of the consanguineous group. The *jong-ga* is the family successively descended from the eldest son in each generation. In the past, many consanguineous groups had a kind of cooperative organization for mutual security among the member families. Most of these disappeared after the Second World War, when their funds became valueless owing to economic inflation.

The consanguineous association does not overtly interfere in the private affairs of the individual member families, but the opinions of the leaders may effectively exert covert pressures on any family which has brought disgrace to the group. The authority of the aged leaders is declining, but it still seems to be strong.

In some villages there is a *sŏwŏn*, or reading academy, established to memorialize and revere prominent Confucian scholars. The *sŏwŏn* is supported by the local circle of Confucianists and does not have a formal relationship with any consanguineous association. It is inevitable, however, that an association will provide some economic support if the academy is in the same village and if one of its ancestors is revered there. Most local Confucianists are not wealthy enough to maintain a *sŏwŏn* alone; on the other hand, the con sanguineous association may not be happy to see it fall ruin, since it is a glorious symbol of their kinship status in the community.

Traditional Social Status

In the Yi-dynasty the status system had seven components: (1) the royal families, (2) the *yangban*, (3) the *hyangban* and *toban*, (4) the *jung-in*, (5) the *sŏ-ŏl*, (6) the *sangmin*, and (7) the *chŏnmin*.[6] In a strict sense, the *yangban* may be defined as the direct ancestors and offsprings of a person who kept a qualified position in the government, ranging to four generations above and four generations below him along the paternal line. The *hyangban* and *toban* were people who had been *yangban* but were downgraded because no qualified official appeared among their family members in four generations, although the *toban* had less prestige than the *hyangban*. Both the *hyangban* and the *toban* groups enjoyed some power and prestige in their community. People who comprised the *jung-in* were the technocrats in the central government, such as medical doctors, translators, and historiographers. The *sŏ-ŏl* were offspring of the *yangban* through ther concubines. The *sangmin* were commoners, who were mostly engaged in farming, commerce, or handcrafts (the *ajŏn*, who worked in the local government without payment, were also included in this class). The lowest class, the *chŏnmin*, were slave-like servants in the governmental agencies and private families, but also included butchers, dancers, fortune tellers, and the like.

In contemporary Korean rural society, status backgrounds are largely in three major categories: *yangban*, *sangmin*, and *chŏnmin*. Probably the *yangban* with whom some rural people identify themselves are not genuine *yangban* but rather *hyangban* or *toban*. Sometimes even those of the *ajŏn* class identify themselves with the *yangban*. In general, people are to be taken as *yangban* if they are recognized as such in the community, regardless of the reliability of their alleged origin.

In some rural areas the *sangmin* are known as *jung-in*, but this is an improper usage of the term. Persons of *chŏnmin* origin are now few in rural society because most of this class have migrated to the cities. There are many villages which do not have even one *chŏnmin* family. This class, therefore, is not of much significance in the rural social structure.

It seems that during the Yi-dynasty, many of the high-prestige *yangban* usually lived in Seoul or in places fairly close by. *Gyŏng-gi* and *Chungchŏng* provinces, mainly south of the *Han* River, were perhaps the areas where most of them had their original home bases. Some appear to have lived in *Gyŏngsang* and *Jŏnla*, and, rarely, in other provinces.

Those of *yangban* descent who are found in the rural areas today tend to live in rather secluded places together with their relatives and other fellow members of the same consanguineous group. In contrast, those of *sangmin* descent reside along the roads, or in other places relatively exposed to outsiders, and as individual families without consanguineous kin relationship. Formerly, *yangban* would not live in predominantly *sangmin* villages but now *yangban* families are frequently found there.

There are no physical features by which *yangban* and *sangmin* can be distinguished. In the past, *yangban* had hats and clothes different from those of the lower classes, but these are no longer worn. Some of *yangban* origin, however, continue to keep a genealogical book and to discriminate against those of *sangmin* origin, especially by avoiding intermarriage. Another mode of such discrimination when talking to *sangmin* is the use of status terminology. This has greatly declined since the Second World War, but it may be occasionally observed in a village where a powerful consanguineous group has been dominant over the *sangmin* for many generations. This pattern of interclass relationship seems to be strongest in the northern part of North *Gyŏngsang*.

In recent years, in at least one village a conflict arose over the carrying of the coffin of a *yangban* during a funeral ceremony. It had been customary that *sangmin* youths would carry the coffin, but they refused to do so, because the *yangban* group did not accept the proposal that *yangban* should reciprocate by carrying the coffin of a *sangmin*. In another village, some leading members of the consanguineous group tried to persuade their fellow members to practice egalitarian treatment of the *sangmin*, but were unsuccessful.[7]

Both cases might be extremes. Today, those of *yangban* and *sangmin* origin do not appear to have any conspicuous conflicts in daily life, even though a covert sense of superiority among the *yangban* may cause overt conflict on some occasions. During the Korean War, when refugees came and settled in some villages, their family background remained unknown and the native villagers did not show any strong interest in it. Such cases suggest that distinctions between *yangban* and *sangmin* are largely fading and are persistent mainly among villagers whose relationships have followed for many generations the practices of the dynastic period.

Discrimination may be practiced, however, even among persons of the same family names and origins if their status backgrounds are different.

For example, several *Bag* (surname) families of *Miryang* (original place) lived in the same village but in different *maŭl*. Those in one *maŭl* were of *yangban* descent and, despite a common consanguineous background, did not have much contact with those in the other *maŭl*, who were *sangmin*. Instead, the *yangban Bag* families had close relations with other *yangban* families of different family names.[8]

Where two different consanguineous groups reside in one village, they are usually in latent conflict or at least in competition. On the surface, they get along well with each other and maintain friendly cooperation. Moreover they are often related by marriage. Even so, the two groups will not be in accord. There is likely to be long-standing friction over property, or political and economic conflicts may have existed between their ancestors.

Typically, the struggle to secure choice grave sites has been one of the causes of serious strife among different consanguineous groups. The geomantic belief that a favorable site for an ancestor's grave will bring prosperity to his offspring is still strong in Korea.

Economic Status

The economic status of the rural people may be evaluated primarily according to the family income. There are two major sources of income: (1) land and (2) occupations other than farming.

(1) The economic status of a person whose income comes from agriculture depends mainly upon the amount of land he owns and cultivates. So far, government statistics have been concerned with the amount of land a farmer cultivates rather than what he owns. For a better understanding of the economic status of the farmers and their social and political roles, however, land owned seems to be more important. Governmental statistics show the average amount of land cultivated per farm household to be 2.721 *pyŏng* (about 2.2 acres) as of 1965.[9] No official figure is available as to the average amount of land owned per farm household.

Research in a limited area in 1958 found the average amount of land owned per farm household to be 2.239 *pyŏng*.[10] A Study in 1959 covering a wider area found that 82.7 per cent of the respondents owned some farm land: 39.1 per cent possessed 2,000 *pyŏng* (about 1.6 acres) or more and 43.6 per cent had less than 2,000 *pyŏng*.[11] This suggests the small scale of landholdings among Korean famrers.

The 1958 research found the economic strata of the farm households in terms of the ownership of land as indicated in ⟨Table 1⟩.[12]

Table 1. Economic Strata

	Number	Per Cent
Landlord	6	1.0
Part landlord, part owner-farmer	31	4.9
Owner-farmer	395	62.3
Part owner, part tenant farmer	85	13.4
Tenant farmer	62	9.8
Farm laborer	25	3.9
Non-farming	25	3.9
No response	5	0.8
Total	634	100.0

A distinct characteristic to be noted in this sample is that the great majority of the farmers, roughly two third, were owner-farmers. This implies that most were almost equal in economic standing and might have a sense of independence to some extent, although not that they were economically independent enough to support their families fully and to make progress. Many of them had moved up from the status of tenant farmer after the land reform of 1949 and thus, at any rate, were in a better situation than formerly.

About 20 per cent of the sample farming population was composed of tenants or farm laborers. Since the land reform, no absentee landownership or tenancy is allowed, but in spite of the restriction by law those who do not have enough of land must rent from others who have an excess of land. Although in the sample the number of landowners not engaged in farming is very small compared to the number of tenants, there can be no doubt that the actual number of landowners was larger, and was disguised because of restriction.

The big landowners in the Japanese period were not necessarily of *yangban* descent. As was noted earlier, the *yangban* had high status because of their official positions and as a rule were not allowed to own land; yet they were allowed to control land while in office. Also, under the Confucian ethic they were not supposed to have an interest in money matters; and indeed there were many poor *yangban* but generally speaking, the *yangban* were much wealthier than the lower classes. Particularly in the latter period of the Yi-dynasty, when the administration became disorderly and corruption widely prevailed, powerful *yangban* could usurp land from weak people and hold it without registering it with the government. In the Japanese period many *yangban* became legal landowners. Although persons of lower status could also become landowners, the wealthy *yangban* landowners through their consanguineous group integration continued to have a powerful influence in community affairs.

In 1949 the land reform deprived absentee landowners who lived in the city of their major economic holdings in the rural areas. Of course, they could continue to maintain social relations with their relatives and friends there. At the same time the landowners who were living in the villages were downgraded to ordinary owner-farmers and many became equivalent to tenants in economic standing.

In spite of these sweeping changes, the former landowners have remained influential to some degree, particularly in the villages where they have support of their dominant consanguineous group. One reason for this is that the consanguineous group has not been completely dissolved as an organization. It still has an economic foundation in the *wito* (see above), and may have the support of members of the group who have moved out of the village and become rich or powerful. Another reason is that many officials and clerks who are working in the governmental agencies or in other modern social organizations are from the high-prestige *yangban* consanguineous groups. Accordingly, the former landowners who are related to them have better opportunities to impose influence on the community than do the former peasants.

(2) There are various sources of non-agricultural income, but they may be classified into three major categories. In the first category are the regularly salaried from governmental, public, educational, or industrial organizations. The village dwellers who work in these organizations usually have access to income from land cultivated by some of their family members or rented to other farmers.

Persons who get salaries in addition to income from land have the highest economic standing among the villagers. Some are former *sangmin* peasants but most are of the *yangban* class, since few peasants can afford to give their children the education required for these jobs. These persons do not appear to be directly involved in village politics, partly because they work outside their villages and partly because they are forbidden by the nature of their jobs to be involved in politics. Yet they undoubtedly have some significant indirect influence on village politics, since they have important information, useful experience and knowledge, and contacts with local authorities. Those persons who are active in village politics today seem to be those who were once in these occupational fields.

In the second category of non-agricultural income are occupations in private business. Formerly managers of mills predominated. However, in many villages, private ownership of mills has disappeared, as mills were absorbed in agricultural cooperative projects. Since few large business enterprises other than mills have ever existed in most of the villages, the most common job in this category is commercial business on a small scale. Most of the merchants are peddlers rather than shop owners. For some this is a full-time occupation; but for others it is an occasional supplement to farm income. In general, the merchants or peddlers do not seem to be involved in politics, except some whose economic situation is relatively stable.

The third source of non-farm income comprises jobs that occasionally become available, such as road consruction. Those who work at these jobs have neither land to cultivate nor money to invest and are also likely to be unskilled. They are similar to the peddlers in economic standing and in education and social background. Primarily they depend on work as farm laborers for their livelihood. Along with the peddlers and tenants, they are the poorest people in the village and seem to be without interest in politics.

Village Politics

The *ri* chief is responsible for village administration. His duties are to receive, disseminate, and execute instructions from the *myŏn* office or police branch, and to report on the situation in the *ri* to these organizations, in cooperation with the *ban* chiefs. He also serves as the representative of the *ri* to the outside world. In order to carry out his duties, he holds village meetings in which each household head takes part in settling any serious village problems.

When the Liberal Party was in power (1953~1960), the *ri* chief was selected by the villagers, but formal elections were rather rare; when they were held, the procedure was not strict, except where some serious conflict existed in the village. In general, the informal leaders of villages—often called *yuji*, and comprising retired *myŏn* chiefs or *ri* chiefs, *myŏn* council members, or other experienced and trustworthy elders—would reach an agreement to select an adequate person as the new *ri* chief, after which the chosen candidate would be nominated and accepted in the village meeting. In the process of selecting a new *ri* chief, the recommendations and suggestions of the former *ri* chief and the administrative agencies would also be significant.

Near the end of the Liberal Party period, the government attempted to employ an appointment instead of an election system. But this policy was cancelled by the government of the Democrat Party which was in power for less than one year after the April (1960) uprising of students. Succeeding military and the Democratic Republican Party regimes applied the appointment system not only to the selection of the *ri* chief, but also to the selection of some higher level administrative chiefs. Consequently, the central government is able to impose a stronger pressure on village politics. In practice, however, the process of selecting the *ri* chief may not be greatly different.

The role of the *ri* chief was originally established for the convenience of administrators rather than villagers. Particularly during World War Two, under the Japanese, the *ri* chief was compelled to follow Japanese policy which was very much against the economic interests of the farmers. Duties such as collecting rice and other agricultural products, and mobilizing labor power placed him in a conflict between the governmental agencies and the villagers.

This conflict declined greatly under Syngman Rhee's regime. But even in this period, the government was more concerned with political manipulation than with helping the villagers. Under these circumstances, the major concern of the *ri* chief was to prevent suffering among the villagers while dealing successfully with the administrators.

The authority of the *ri* chief to control the villagers is not clearly defined. If he is competent, he may be able to impose his ideas on the villagers. But this may be rather unusual, since he has no legal authority to solve a problem, to approve or disapprove any request, or to regulate village affairs. He has no office, no budget, and no personnel at his disposal. He is similar to a class representative in school. In the past when government agencies gave him only a few routine tasks his work was relatively easy. In the past decade, however, his work has become not only more time-consuming, but also more demanding as villagers are becoming more perceptive about community development actions.

The *ri* chief became busier as the ambitious military government strongly pushed the local government to carry out more development projects. Even this lowest governmental agency frequently had to present accurate "briefing" reports to higher echelon officials and other authorized visitors. Then, too, the *ri* chief had to keep up-to-date records about the village situation and to report them to the governmental agencies without delay. Moreover, the *ri* chief usually must assume chairmanship of the *ri* unit of the Agricultural Cooperative Association which has been active since the military government was established.

The *ri* chief's job has become more demanding as the number of educated persons has increased. In 1958 more than eighty per cent of household heads over the age of forty in a specific place had no formal education but almost all of their children were educated.[13] Another study done six years later in a different village, indicated that about half of the household heads had some formal education.[14] Furthermore, most of the adult males below the age of forty have had military experience. This might lead to greater rational thinking and effective problem-solving as well as more frequent protests against what they think is unreasonable, or undemocratic.

All these trends require a more competent *ri* chief. Since the *ri* chief is recruited from among the younger people, he is likely to be more active and efficient in his administrative practices today than previously. Where once he was inclined to follow passively only the directions from the government, now he seems to be more active in seeking means of development.

The government provided no remuneration to the *ri* chief until several years ago. The only reward was provided by the villagers. It is a general custom that the villagers, except some poor families, donate some of their summer and autumn crops, mostly barley and rice, for his effort. Recently, however, the government began to provide allowances to the *ri* chief and accordingly, he is becoming more of a bureaucratic agent than a volunteer. While competition for the position of the *ri* chief previously existed in some villages, this trend has intensified greatly since the remuneration began.

The important problems of a village are discussed in the general village meeting which is often called *daedong-hoe*. Important information and instructions coming from the government are also announced in this meeting. The general village meeting is held neither frequently nor regularly. The only regular meeting is that held some time after the harvest in order to settle accounts and to discuss the past year and the prospects for the coming year. The reward to the *ri* chief is given at this occasion. Usually a party follows the meeting.

A general meeting is convened whenever some urgent problems arise such as meeting the needs of the villagers. More often, it aids in complying with governmental directives such as collecting grains, mobilizing labor, or accomplishing special projects as the "seven years plan for food production increase."[15] During elections, educational programs about the procedure might be carried out. It seems that some suggestions to support the government party were given on these occasions during the period of the Liberal Party.

The participants at the meeting are the representatives of the households, usually the heads. Women may attend but this is very rare. In some villages, the distinguished *yuji* such as a former *myŏn* chief may occupy the seat of honor. Occasionally an official attends the meeting, if the governmental agency has a strong interest in the agenda.

In most of these meetings, the conclusions that are reached seem to be in compliance with both the intention of the government and the opinions of the *yuji*. However, since the discussion also reflects the opinions of the villagers, it might not proceed smoothly if there is any conflict in the village. The opinions of women and young people are rarely expressed in the meeting but as many male adult villagers are coming to have more formal education, their suggested solutions are likely to be increasingly rational and progressive. In the past rapid progress in social development was hindered by the rural people's lack of education and reluctance to accept modern technology. Today, this is no longer a serious barrier.

Social Organizations and Politics in the Village

Besides the family and the consanguineous kin group, there are other social organizations in the village. These may be categorized by the degree of spontaneous participation by the members. The first type is initiated by the desire of the members. The second is an intermediary type between the first and third, which is formed by pressures or strong recommendations of officials outside of the village.

In the first category, the most prevalent organization is the *gye*. This traditional mutual assistance organization can be further subdivided into two types. One raises money to assist members in special occasions such as funerals, weddings or sixtieth birthdays. Another makes each member save money for his own personal use or to purchase for shared usage some necessary but expensive item such as a sewing machine. The first type is traditional and widely practiced, while the second is a more recent trend, influenced by the *gye* activity in the city. Other examples of voluntary organizations are the 4-H Clubs and the Youth Clubs. These are formed by ambitious young men in many villages, but most are not very active, mainly because of the lack of economic foundation and persistent incentive. The *gye* organizations are rather informal and usually do not have written regulations. They are never involved in political matters. The 4-H Clubs and Youth Clubs are relatively formal and the latter have potential for raising a voice in village politics, even though they are not supposed to take an overt political role.

The intermediary category includes the agricultural cooperative, irrigation association, irrigation *gye*, forestry *gye*, community development *gye* and the like. They are organized by enthusiastic, influential leaders and pushed by the local government. These *gye* organizations are a little different from those in the first category. Actually, they are modern small scale cooperative groups using the traditional name of *gye* mainly to stimulate spontaneous participation of the members. These organizations may be based either on the village unit or the *myŏn* unit. They are relatively active, since the government provides some financial aid, and they usually bring some benefits to the members. Occasionally, they may be accompanied by governmental supervision, sometimes with dishonest political intent. Pro-government village leaders staff these organizations and usually receive many favors.

The third category of social organizations consists mainly of political or ideological groups on a nationwide scale. Their lowest branches are usually formed in the *gun* or *myŏn*. They are established by pro-government political leaders and are likely to be supported by the government or leading parties. There may be a few organizations in this category which are neutral or opposed to the government. Many of the political organizations claim as members villagers who have no interest in them are and not even aware of their membership. Consequently, these organizations are usually not active in the village. During election campaigns, however, some of these groups become political instruments of the government party. This trend was particularly distinct during the

Liberal Party period. In general though most villagers regard social organizations inspired by the government as paper groups which do not provide service but collect membership fees and only bother them with an occasional political speech.

There are other important social organizations, mostly religious, which deserve special attention. Christian churches exist in some villages, but rarely have a regular minister. Usually a minister comes to the village from the city on Sundays or whenever a service is necessary; otherwise, presbyters operate the church without ministers. Rural churches in general seem to be concerned only with religious activities and are never involved in politics.

Buddhist temples or other religious institutes may be observed near villages, althongh less frequently than the Christian churches, and these too have no social activity other than religion. The Confucian Association is organized on a nationwide basis with local branches. The Confucianists may have both religious and non-religious activities centering around the *hyang-gyo*, the community Confusican school(which actually has no students), and the *sŏwŏn*. Even today, a few Confucianists may be influential in politics because they have the organizational support of the Confucian Association and are respected in the community. But their political role has been declining greatly.

The elementary and middle (presently, high) schools were very important tools for the Japanese government, particularly during World War II. After the independence of Korea, the schools influenced politics only by advocating Korean nationalism and basic principles of national policy. Data is not abundant on the political attitude of teachers but they do not seem to have a strong interest either in village affairs or in local politics. They are likely to keep some social distance from the ordinary villagers. While they appear to be strongly concerned with their personal advancement, they are apt to be frustrated, regarding themselves as deserted educators.

Leadership Structure within the Village[16]

The leadership structure of the village during the Yi-dynasty is not clear. However, we may be able to draw a rough picture based on some empirical findings on the contemporary Korean rural society. In the pre-modern society, it is assumed that the *yangban* or quasi-*yangban* families had strong political power because of their economic dominance over the people of lower status in the same village and neighboring villages. The other people who were not bound to particular families of high status might be controlled directly by the local government.

The power of eminent *yangban* families derive firstly from their economic and political privileges; secondly from the support of their respective well-integrated consanguineous groups, and thirdly from their strong tie with other *yangban* families in the community which formed the local circle of Confucianistic scholars. The local governors did not have enough power to control these *yangban*. Therefore, the solidarity in consanguineous groups was far stronger than in the village as a whole. Even in a village where no consanguineous group existed, the villagers had no organizational activities with political implications. The only likely group activities were for agricultural productions, shamanistic village festivals, and recreational activities.

The leadership structure in the present rural village takes a variety of forms, determined largely by both kinship and traditional status background of the villagers. At least five types can be distinguished.

Type A is a leadership structure in which all villagers are equally independent and the leaders support each other without serious conflicts. The formal leaders such as the *ri* chief are also supported by the informal leaders. This type is often found in a village where no dominant consanguineous or status group exists and is conducive to democratic development.

Type B is frequently observed in villages with only one dominant consanguineous group. The formal leaders appear to come mainly from the members of this group and are supported by the informal leaders also from the group. Individuals who do not belong to this consanguineous group may stay away from village politics or may support the formal and informal leaders but without much enthusiasm. During elections, the group members will support the same candidate if the group is well integrated. This pattern of leadership structure is fairly stable, but suffers from the inability to promote village-wide cooperative activity.

Type C is often found in villages where two or three different competitive *yangban* consanguineous groups exist. Here the *ri* chief will be selected from among members of the stronger group, and the other group(s) may or may not support him, depending upon the degree of potential conflict between the groups. At election time each group often votes its own candidate. Obviously, this type of village has difficulty in achieving integration, although serious conflicts do not occur very frequently. This leadership pattern can also be found in villages in which there are two conflicting branches of the same consanguineous group.

Leadership type D occurs in the very rare case where a *yangban* consanguineous group and a group of *sangmin* have the same family name and a common place of origin. The latter group might also be called consanguineous but it does not have a formal association. It is just a cluster of people who are supposedly descended from a common ancestor but who do not practice ancestor worship ceremonies on the basis of consanguinity. In the only observed village of this type there was no close contact between the two groups, but the *ri* chief who came from the *sangmin* did not, in fact, have any particular difficulty in his administration, since the leader of the *yangban* consanguineous group, who was the deputy *myŏn* chief, supported him strongly.

Changes in Rural and Urban Communities 159

Pattern of Leadership Structure in Village

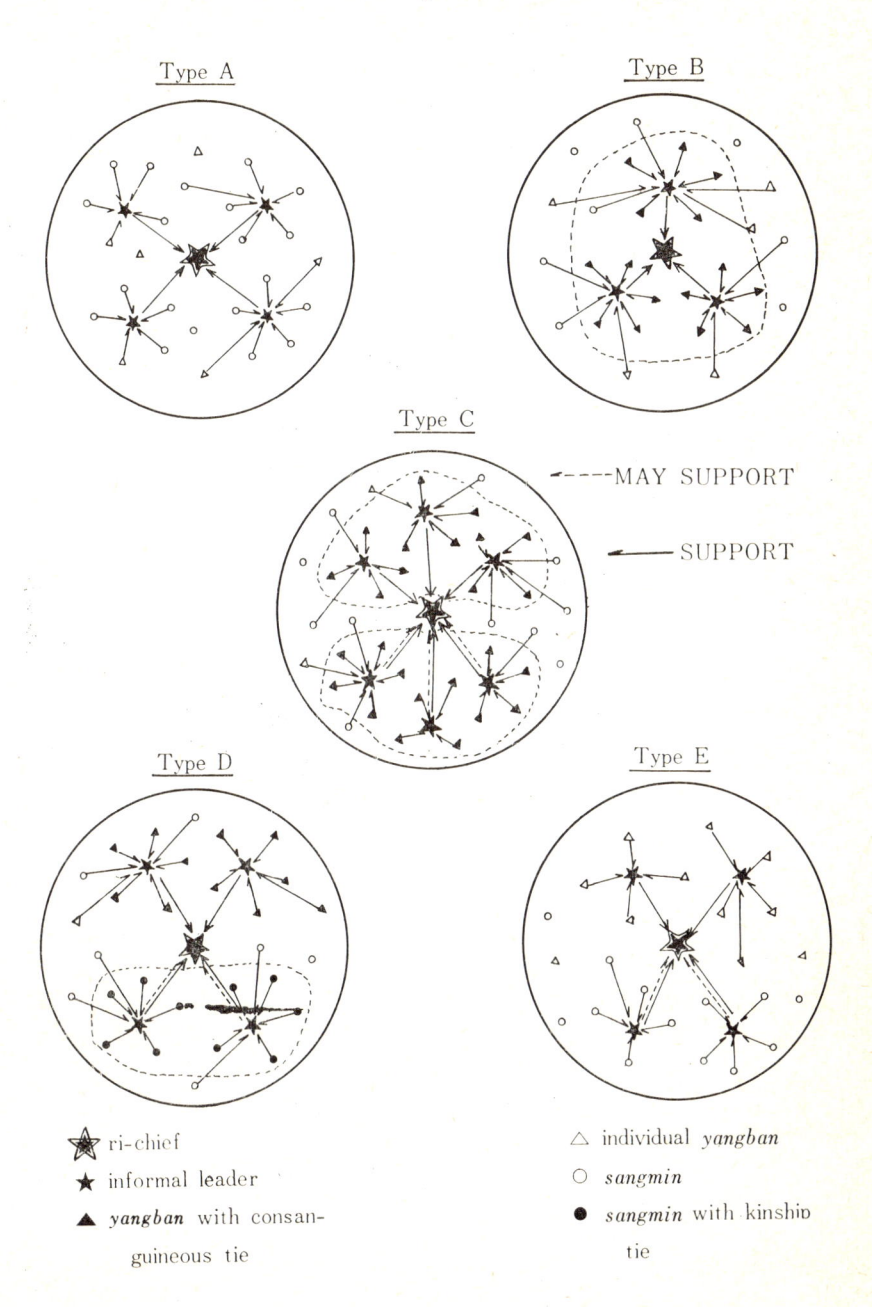

Type A

Type B

Type C

----- MAY SUPPORT

⟵ SUPPORT

Type D

Type E

☆ ri-chief
★ informal leader
▲ yangban with consan-
   guineous tie

△ individual *yangban*
○ *sangmin*
● *sangmin* with kinship
   tie

It is fair to say, however, that these two groups can easily come into open conflict as a result of a seemingly casual event such as an insult of one group by the other.

The final type E is another rare case. It occurs in a village where there is no dominant consanguineous group but where two groups of people with different status background, namely, the *yangban* and *sangmin*, exist. Those of *yangban* status have no common consanguineous basis and no particular dominance submission relationships with those of *sangmin* status in previous generations. Therefore, those of *sangmin* origin are unlikely to recognize the *yangban* as superior. However, the *yangban* might want to enjoy special privilege in which case there might be conflict. Such a conflict was described earlier in the episode about carrying a coffin in a funeral ceremony. This village appeared to be the least integrated and in far worse condition than other villages.

Both the consanguineous kin relationship and traditional status background are still basic factors in the leadership structure of the Korean village. However, two recent conditions have tended to alter these patterns. On the one hand, the government has been exercising strong administrative control over the rural villages regardless of these traditional factors, and on the other, the existing consanguineous *yangban* families have been losing their economic basis. At the same time, other factors such as economic standing, occupation, and educational level are becoming more significant. As a result, villagers are becoming more egalitarian and the basis for integration is changing from consanguinity-orientation to community-orientation.

Traits of Village Leaders and Relationship with Governmental Agencies

According to one study,[17] sincerity is the most wanted trait in a desirable leader. Other traits indicated by respondents are generosity, ability to command, brightness, knowledge, and fair mindedness, in that order. Deductively, rural people appreciate a leader who is faithful to his role, is generous but of a strong character, and has ability based on education and experience. The research also found that the most nominated age bracket for leaders was 40~45, followed by 35~40 and 45~50. As noted previously, since the military coup, village leaders are likely to be replaced by younger people, but the villagers still appear to be reluctant to select anyone less than thirty-five years of age. Conversely an old man is respected and may have authority in dealing with his family affairs, but great age is becoming less significant in both formal and informal leadership.

The distinct traits among popular village leaders are their formal education and experience in modern social affairs. In short, they have an ability to deal with village problems effectively. People without education and experience could not maintain high economic standing during the drastically changing period after World War II. The statement that education is an important requirement for village leadership does not mean, however, that the higher the education the better the chance for leadership. While education is essential too much sometimes impedes communication between the educated and the uneducated lay villagers.

Experience in modern social affairs seems to be more important than education. Someone with such experience knows not only what is going on outside the village and how to adjust to it, but also has contact with many influential people in the community. Although a leader is required to have an understanding of modern society he cannot deviate too much from traditional behavior or he will surely encounter strong resistance from the villagers. The villagers do not consciously support the Confucian value system *per se*, but they do feel their moral patterns are proper and they do not want to replace them with unfamiliar ones. Therefore, leaders are mostly conformists as far as their morality is concerned.

As suggested above, leaders are strongly concerned with keeping good relationships with governmental agencies. One without government support can hardly exerise leadership in the rural area. For a long time, people have submissively followed governmental policies and have had a stereotyped notion of government as an absolute authority operated by superior persons. Indeed, the government is still almighty, because it monopolizes most of the resources and means for administrative control. But the local officials are usually from the same community and are very friendly to the people with whom they must deal. The democratic atmosphere after World War II has promoted these friendly relations.

However, the situation is greatly different in the case of the police. Many policemen are not persons of local origin, and do not have frequent contacts with the people. Moreover, the police agencies have special functions to prevent not only illegal acts but also legally permitted antigovernment actions. Sometimes, they may interfere with the ordinary administrations of the *myŏn* office for political reasons.

During the Liberal Party period, the *gun* police office was deeply involved in local politics. In particular, the intelligence section developed very close relationships with pro-government National Assemblymen by giving them secret information and providing other favors. Reciprocally, government party assemblymen influenced the Ministry of Home Affairs to appoint persons congenial to them to fill important positions such as the police chief of *gun* and the chief of intelligence sections.[18] Consequently, rural people are very cautious lest they should be suspected by the government authorities. If a stranger asks a question with political implications they will simply evade him.

In spite of the power of government agencies, appointed leaders are not able to carry out their duties successfully,[19] unless they meet the needs of the villagers.

Opinion Formation and Politics

It may be worthwhile to note the political significance of the *sarang* and other places where villagers meet and talk. The *sarang* is an exterior room of a relatively rich person's house and is mainly used by the male household head and his guests, usually male adults. In the summer, they usually gather in a specially prepared open place under the shadow of a big tree or on a river side and relax, exchange information, and informally discuss various problems. Young people may attend, but they stay in the background without participating in the conversation. There are some opinion leaders at these gatherings, mostly the *yuji* of the village, but the very aged or the most distinguished persons rarely attend. Generally, opinion leaders do not talk much. However, if the topic is important, or if an erroneous opinion is being promoted, or if an argument ensues, they become actively involved in settling the controversy.

Major discussion topics are largely derived from the mass media or from information obtained from outside the village. Since the *yuji* has the most frequent contacts with the outside world he provides many of the interesting items. News is usually selective and distorted, being mixed with the private opinion of the transmitter.

During the early Liberal Party period a few villagers had access to mass media, but most relied on word of mouth for information about the outside. In later Liberal Party stages a new communication system was introduced and it became increasingly widespread after the military coup. The system consists of a single stationary amplifier broadcasting the voices of individual speakers. In 1964, about half of the villagers in *Pyŏngtaeg* county used this system, indicating that today far more rural people receive organnized information more rapidly than previously.[20] However, this applies only to information transmitted by radio; the number of subscribers to newspapers has not increased significantly. Moreover, commercial radio broadcasting does not reach the more distant parts of the countryside. There are two powerful nationwide broadcasting networks. One is operated by the government; the other is commercial but seems to have a special relationship with the government. Therefore, the contents of radio programs are generally controlled by the government directly or indirectly.

As radio became more popular, women and children are learning more about life outside their village. Apparently, however, they are not too interested in radio programs dealing with political and economic affairs and find personal communication about local social affairs more significant.

Politics outside the Village

It is assumed that the territorial boundaries of each *myŏn* district were originally determined for administrative convenience. In other words, rulers probably decided the boundaries on the basis of controlling the people rather than of providing for their social development. The rural people did not care much about these matters, for most of them were confined to the village and were farming for survival.

Today, with villagers having more frequent contacts with the outside, particularly with local governmental agencies and market centers, present *myŏn* districts are presenting some serious problems. The pattern of the *myŏn* district is ideal only when it sufficiently meets the needs of communal life and when the administrative agencies are located in the social and economic center. In fact, however, many existing *myŏn* districts do not coincide with the actual community and often contain parts of different communities.[21] The people in one area often do not share common social and economic interests with those in the other, and each may have its own market.

The conflict between the areas seems to have become more distinct since World War II mainly because of the change in local politics. Beginning in the Liberal Party period, the *myŏn* chief was elected by the people and his role in making decisions became more significant. He was given the authority to allocate fertilizer, rice, and other supplies for social welfare, and to decide the priority and sites of various projects.

A secondary cause of conflict is the increase in functional activities. For example, a school may be located in one community and persons living in another may be inconvenienced by the distance. Therefore each community competes intensely in the election of the *myŏn* chief and the location of govermental agencies. If an area loses in the *myŏn* chief election, it makes every effort to put a representative in the position of the deputy *myŏn* chief. There have been attempts in some *myŏns* to move the *myŏn* office or police branch from one community to another, and these usually caused strong conflict between two areas. Given these circumstances, it is often difficult for the *myŏn* chief to exercise fair policies effectively. On the one hand, he is pressed to give favors to the area he represents, and on the other, he easily becomes a target for complaints by the other area. Wanting to be fair he might simply allocate funds or supplies equally to both areas, disregarding the actual benefits for the entire *myŏn*.

There is another factor which causes inefficiency and unfairness of *myŏn* administration. This is the political influence of the National Assemblyman. The *myŏn* chief has special relationship with the assemblyman who represents that district. The assemblyman is more deeply concerned with the persistent maintenance of his power than with the beneficial development of the entire area. Consequently, he is more likely to push the *myŏn* chief to implement policies which will result in immediate political benefits for himself, regardless of long range effect to the district.

Generally, the candidates for *myŏn* chief came from consanguineous groups because such members had higher prestige, better education, greater experience and more influential supporters than non-members. The competition for the position of *myŏn* chief was often between two consanguineous groups in two different villages. The leftist movement, active in the rural area for some years after World War II, was said to be related to this consanguineous factor. When one consanguineous group came into power, the other competing group became very critical and was readily influenced by the leftist organization, although often not convinced ideologically.

Although the consanguineous group is becoming disorganized, it is not yet weak enough to allow its members independent political behavior. For a time in traditional society, upper class Korean people were attached to their family, group of relatives, and consanguineous group on the one hand, and to their own status group on the other, in addition to their government. Those of the lower class identified with the government and/or families of higher status. There was no other distinctive social organizations. Moreover, the community-orientation was far weaker than either the status or family-orientation. The people did not develop a strong sense of devotion to their community.

In contemporary rural society, some modern social organizations have appeared but they usually exist in the town and most villagers do not have a significant relationship with these groups. Therefore, they have no particular economic interest which may stimulate them to form a specific political opinion. The question of who will be elected is actually not of great concern to them. Under these circumstances, they may easily follow the suggestions of the influential leader of their family or consanguineous group. They have no reason to refuse it and, if they do, it may still cause serious trouble for them (《Table 2》).

Table 2. Factors Influencing Voting Behavior in *Ŭb* and *Myŏn* Chief Election[22]

	ŭb	village
Relatives	12.0	34.3
Money	30.7	11.2
Local *yuji*	16.0	15.4
Governmental pressure	7.3	4.7
Territorial conflict	4.7	6.5
Others	12.7	9.5
Do not know	16.6	18.4
	100.0%	100.0%

A candidate for the National Assembly tries to maintain a close relationship with influential leaders of the consanguineous groups in the appropriate election districts, for he knows that he will be able to get mass support through these leaders. Therefore, he willingly contributes to these consanguineous groups for such purposes as maintaining the *jesil* or *sŏwŏn* which are related to the groups and also does various favors for them.[23] For example, he provides concessions, recommends them for appointments—very often as trustee members of irrigation associations—and arranges employment for them or their children. At the same time, the local consanguineous group leaders are themselves anxious to maintain close contacts with these politicians in order to pursue their economic and political interests. Often, therefore, the supposedly democratic political system is operated on the basis of undemocratic, traditional social structure.

Local Autonomy in the Rural Area

Local autonomy was practiced in Korea for more than ten years but has been suspended since the military coup. According to the amended Constitution of 1962, the system of self-governing administration is to be revived and its lowest unit defined as the *gun* district, instead of the *myŏn*, but the implementation of this has been postponed indefinitely. Local autonomy has been urged only half-heartedly by the opposition parties, and there is no distinctive sign that the populace wants the establishment of local assemblies.

A study conducted in 1964 showed that in the subject area about one-half of village respondents expressed negative opinions concerning the establishment of the *myŏn* assembly, while those in the *ŭb* were slightly more favorable to that of the *ŭb* assembly.[24]

This finding indicates the lack of benefits achieved by local assemblies in the past. Considering the survey responses as well as other social conditions, the basic reasons for the dysfunctions may be classified as follows:

First, the local assembly does not have a substantial budget. The greater part of its budget is determined by the central government and most of the items for expenditure are fixed at the higher level in advance. Consequently, the local assembly actually does not have much to decide.

Second, most of the rural people are engaged in self-supplying agriculture and they do not have frequent outside economic and social contacts. Even their relationship to the market is not significant, so that they have no particular need to protect their economic interests through the local assembly. The farmers have strong interests in the price and distribution of fertilizer, the price of rice, and perhaps the irrigation project. However, these problems are too big to be solved by the local assembly. Therefore, the agenda for discussion in the local assembly would not be directly concerned with their immediate economic interests.

Third, there is no effective communication between the local governmental agencies or political organizations and the local inhabitants. There are local radio stations and newspapers, but these are not much concerned with what happens in the smaller areas. Therefore, the local people are not informed about news concerning the governmental agencies, problems in the community, possible solutions for them, and criticisms of local politics. Once the assemblymen are elected they no longer maintain functional ties with the people. Under these circumstances, the people do not understand why the assemblymen should be elected and what they actually do. They are thought to be busy seeking personal concessions and advantages, indulging in power struggles, engaging in dirty factional conflicts, and wasting time and money for unnecessary banquets and entertainment.

Finally, the people have neither a strong recognition of democracy nor much experience in developing their community through the democratic process. (An attempt to measure rural attitude toward democracy by the Guttman scaling technique failed due to unsatisfactory reproducibility. This may have been caused by a wrong application of the technique, but more likely because the assumption of a consistent undimensional continuum in their attitude toward democracy is not warranted.)[25] The Korean people, particularly in the countryside, have been accustomed to seek personal favors from the government rather than to develop the community as a whole through the universalistic, democratic approach. They are likely to be more concerned with themselves and their own families rather than about their community. They conform to the existing norms of the family elders and of governmental officials, rather than to raising problems, discussing alternatives, and reaching solution through the democratic process.

While the above observations about the local assembly may to some degree be applied to the National Assembly, the latter case is somewhat different. For example, the National Assembly deals with matters closely concerned with the economic problems of the rural people. Secondly, the newspaper and radio provide information on the National Assembly. Thirdly, since the National Assemblymen are widely known, the people of an area represented by a particular assemblyman have some personal interest in his activity. For these reasons, most of the rural people say that the National Assembly is useful, though they are slightly less favorable to it than those in the urban areas.[26]

The fact that most rural people voiced negative opinions concerning the local assembly does not mean that they do not have aspirations to participate in politics or that they leave politics to the local governments. On the contrary, many of them seem to have strong interests in some specific aspects of politics and they usually talk about political matters in their informal discussions. It is true that they lack democratic experience but they do have democratic aspirations. Evidence to support this view is well shown by the opinion of the great majority of the villagers that the chief of the local government must be elected. This seems to indicate that they do recognize the significant role of local administrators and do want to participate in the democratic process.[27]

[NOTES]

1) It is especially important to note that this article was prepared in 1967, because the Korean rural situation has been rather drastically changed in many ways since that time.
2) Economic Planning Board, *Korea Statistical Yearbook*, (Seoul: EPB, 1970), p. 31.
3) Man-gap Lee, *Hangug nongchon sahoe ŭi gujo wa byŏnhwa* (*The Social Structure of the Korean Village and Its Change*), (Seoul: Seoul National University Press, 1973), pp. 21-25.
4) Ibid. pp. 3-13.
5) The rule is indicated in *Gyŏng-gug daejŏn* (one of the legal codes established during the Yi-dynasty). See Bongsa-jo of the Ye-jŏn part in the book.
6) Tokutaro Tanaka, "Chosen no shakai kaikyu (Social Class in Korea)," *Chosen*, a monthly magazine published by the Korean Government-General, March, 1921, p. 58.
7) Man-gap Lee, ibid., p. 44.
8) This was observed in one village during the field research on "the

Social Structure of the Korean Village and Its Change" which was undertaken by the author, but it is only covertly implied in the report. See pp. 32-35 and pp. 149-150 of the book.
9) Economic Planning Board, *Korea Statistical Yearbook*, (Seoul: EPB, 1966), p. 55.
10) Man-gap Lee, ibid., p. 52.
11) Whang-Kyung Koh, et al., *Hangug nongchon gajog ŭi yŏngu (A Study on the Korean Rural Family)*, (Seoul: Seoul National University Press, 1963), p. 208.
12) Ibid., p. 206.
13) Man-gap Lee, ibid., p. 50.
14) Man-gap Lee, "Jiyŏg sahoe danche siltae (Situation of the Local Community)," in *Jibang jachi danche pyobon josa jonghab bogosŏ (Sample Survey Report of the Local Self-governing Body)*, (Seoul: Local Government Research Committee, Ministry of Home Affairs, 1965), Section II, p. 90.
15) This plan was implemented from 1965.
16) This part is largely based on the writer's observation on "The Social Structure of the Korean Village and Its Change." See Chapter 10, Part I of the book (pp. 137-153). This chapter was translated into English by Dr. Glenn D. Paige in 1961 under the title "Korean Village Politics and Leadership" (mimeographed).
17) Ibid., p. 145.
18) It may be rather difficult to find any academic document to prove this, but the author observed it by himself.
19) The author found that after Syngman Rhee lost power local government chief rarely tried to appoint *ri*-chiefs against public opinion in village, although his regime enacted the law to abolish the system of electing *ri* chiefs toward the end of his rule.
20) Man-gap Lee, "Situation of the Local Community" in *Sample Survey Report of the Local Self-governing Body (Pyŏngtaeg* survey), pp. 98-102.
21) Man-gap Lee, *The Social Structure of the Korean Village and Its Change*, pp. 25-27. This was also observed in the *Pyŏngtaeg* survey. See pp. 95-96 of the *Sample Survey Report*.
22) *Pyŏngtaeg* survey, pp. 107-108.

23) Man-gap Lee, *The Social Structure of the Korean Village and Its Change, op. cit.*, pp. 59-60.
24) *Pyŏngtaeg* survey, p. 105.
25) Ibid., p. 104.
26) When this article was written, the writer probably referred to a certain finding by one of the participants in the *Pŏngtaeg* survey. However, there is no way to confirm it now, since nobody, neither the author nor the publisher has the copy of the article.
27) Man-gap Lee, ibid., p. 312. Actually this part was included in the original manuscript of the writer's report on the *Pŏngtaeg* survey, although it did not appear in the published report.

Rural People and Their Modernization

The Rural Community before the Liberation

1. The Stagnant Society

The modernization of Korea was not originally generated by the creative ideas and aspirations of Korean people as a necessary process of its social development, but rather was stimulated by the influence from outside, as generally seen in other underdeveloped countries. The society of the Yi-dynasty can hardly be called feudalistic, in a strict sense, compared to those of the Western countries or even Japan.[1]

It was an agricultural and centralized bureaucratic state devoid of variety, ruled by the *yangban*, or scholar-officials, under the king's charismatic authority. The king had nothing in particular to do but check the emergence of any political force which would overthrow the existing ruling order, while the *yangban* were simply absorbed in seeking status in the government which assured both wealth and prestige. The local governors were not feudalistic lords as those in the pre-modern Western countries, but merely officials appointed by the king and transferred from one post to another. There was no necessity for them to maintain strong solidarity with the provincial populace to form an integrated political unity and promote production in order to defend their territory from the possible aggression of competing forces.

The social organizations passionately sustained by the *yangban* class were the family, kinship, and larger consanguineous groups with which families under the same ancestor were associated.

---

* Presented at the International Conference on the "Problems of Modernization in Asia," held at the Korea University in 1965.

A stern family order was also kept up by maintaining absolute obedience to the family-head, distinction between both sexes, and respect for the aged, all in accordance with Confucian norms. Family consolidation was achieved by admiring the achievements of the ancestry, and by boasting of the family's glorious status through rituals of ancestor worship. Among the functions of ancestor worship, other than the promotion of family and kinship consolidation, there was a religious one. It is a general belief that after death one's soul would be consoled by his descendants. So everybody has been eager to have sons who are supposed to be successors of the family, take care of their old parents, and have responsibility for ancestor worship.[2] Thus, Confucianism, though it is not intrinsically a religion, has functioned to meet the religious needs of the people to some extent.

Another organization set up by the *yangban* was the class system of sholar-officials. Upholding Confucianism as a supreme ideology of life, the *yangban* constituted a ruling circle through daily get-togethers at the *hyang-gyo*, or Community Academy, and the *sŏwŏn*, or Reading School. Though agriculture was highly esteemed by the *yangban* class, other productive activities were looked down upon. Wealth was considered not valuable at least overtly, but it is quite readily assumed that everybody earnestly wanted wealth deep in their hearts. However, wealth naturally followed one's success in officialdom. As a matter of fact, a good many *yangban* took advantage of their power for the exploitation of common people, usurped national property, and indulged in bribery and graft.

The general populace had neither any ideology of its own, nor did it have a self-governing body in which such an ideology was rooted. Subordinated to government control and to the command of the *yangban*, the spiritual life of commoners was confined to the traditional customs and primitive beliefs in conformity to Confucian norms.

2. Japanese Domination

That stagnant, traditional society was shaken at last by the infiltration of foreign capitalistic forces. Faced directly with the political and military pressures of these forces as well as the impact rendered by modern civilizations, the *yangban* were divided into two political groups: one of radicals who insisted upon the nation's enlightenment, and another of conservatists who remained attached to the old traditions. These groups subdivided into pro-Chinese, pro-Russian, or pro-Japanese forces and so forth, each conspiring with the pertinent foreign power. It was at this tumultuous period when a commoners' insurrection took place, led by some politically-minded leaders who belonged to an indigenous religious force called *Donghag*, or Eastern Learning. But, such a situation was not resolved by the Korean people themselves; Korea in the long run fell prey to Japanese colonialism.

As a capitalistic country endeavoring to infiltrate deep into Korea, Japan imposed some reforms on Korea, including the abolition of the old status system. After 1910 Japanese authorities in Korea stepped up a reshuffle of the administrative structure, and modern private land ownership was initiated at the same time under a large scale research project.[3] As a result, the classes of landowners, independent farmers, and tenant-farmers became distinguishable. An urbanization along with industrialization was also accentuated, and a new type of human relationship was promoted in compliance with a new legal-rational structure on the basis of social contract.

With the administrative control reaching deep down to the lowest units of administration, unity of the village as a whole was strengthened. In particular, this unity was intensified as Japan carried out a war policy at the end of her rule. Another important change in this period was the founding of a modern school system in rural areas; thus the number of farmers receiving school education gradually increased.

Korea's modernization by Japan, however, had considerable limitation in that (1) Japan herself retained certain backward social characteristics of her own, and (2) Japan only exploited Korea as a tool for her own development. Japan, being late in transforming herself into a capitalistic state, constituted an absolute militaristic Emperor system, and employed policies aiming at preserving a considerable portion of her feudalistic characteristics. With such policies, her colonial domination of Korea was not fundamentally divergent from her basic line. Japan might be said to have set up a modern social system in Korea, mainly in urban areas, but all such performances served only to benefit the Japanese.[4] Very few Koreans could be relatively favored by the Japanese policies, but they were mostly those whom Japan needed for maintaining her goals. They were chiefly the descendants of old *yangban* or land-owners who adhered to the traditional Confucian norms which seemed to inspire the people to conform to the existing order. It is a widely known fact that a majority of farmers continued to be ruined and some of them were forced to emigrate to urban areas or foreign lands due to the economic pressure during Japanese domination. Tenancy disputes became a serious problem in this period.[5]

Meanwhile, the Korean people reacted in various ways to the internal and external situation in this transitory period from the end of the Yi-dynasty through the Japanese domination. When foreign powers began struggling to infiltrate Korea, a minute portion of the *yangban* participated in the modernization movement; but it was substantially pushed by the young men of the classes between the *yangban* and the commoner, including the *jung-in*, or technical officials of the central government, who were much discontented with the existing conditions and had some education. One of the earliest organization representing these people's progressive opinions was the *Dognib Hyŏbhoe*, or the Independence

Association. The ideas of the group about the nation's modernization were rather naive. It seems that during the Japanese domination those who were sincerely concerned with the destiny of Korea were mostly dedicated to the work of education, journalism, culture, and religion. It is also presumed that they made great efforts toward national independence, consciously resisting the Japanese colonialism. The lay farmers, however, were never conscious of their own role in the work of national modernization, though their awakening and development were persistently emphasized by the above intellectuals.

As to the rural populace of Korea at the time of liberation from Japan, it was composed of a majority of tenant farmers and a slender proportion of independent farmers, agricultural laborers, indigenous landowners, and some *saŭm*, or field managers hired by absentee landlords.[6] There were also a few people who fell in the categories of merchant, government official, clerk, teacher, and others engaged in non-agricultural enterprises. Most of them, the former part of the populace mentioned above, seem to have had little contact even with *ŭb*-level towns.

The rural people were under the authoritarian patriarchal control of the traditional family institution. While the men of higher pre-modern status, particularly the *yangban*, were hardly free from the bond of consanguineous organization, it could not exist among the farmers of lower status. It might be said that the social integration based on the village community as a whole was greatly promoted through administrative control. While in the villages where the population was largely composed of lay farmers, the social relations were rather based on individual equality, the solidarities in the villages where those of higher status were predominant were often obstructed by the discrimination between the different statuses.[7] Aside from those unities, however, the lay people could never develop any modern interest group except for a few land-owners and influential persons.

Social Changes since the Liberation

1. Land Reform

Right after the liberation, it was generally recognized that tenants should be freed from the old tenancy system. Land reform was strongly expected by many intellectuals and social leaders. Even landlords could not oppose land reform in principle, because (1) some powerful owners of land had been pro-Japanese and were in no position to discuss social matters after the nation recovered her independence, and (2) others began to expect a promising future in other economic activities in a new, emancipated, and independent nation even though their farm lands would have been lost. Comparatively less powerful indigenous landowners, the most vulnerable to such a reform, could choose no alternative at all because there was no organization with which they could construct a social force to oppose the reform. With all these inspiring factors present at that time, however, farmers themselves were completely devoid of abilities to take initiatives over the land readjustment project.

A land reform was officially initiated in 1949, but the rents of the farm fields previously owned by Japanese already had become much cheaper. At the same time, it is supposed, absentee landlords hurriedly sold their fields at low prices for fear of some prospective results unfavorable to them which might occur in the wake of land reform.[8] In this way, tenant-farmers were satisfied in coming to possess their own farm-fields quite unexpectedly even before the land reform. The effects of the land reform including the preceding change of landownership may be discussed in the following way. First of all, the land reform was carried out in such a mild and smooth atmosphere that there was no detectable tension at all, and this might have made farmers unable to evolve autonomous activities through organizations aimed at the promotion of their self-interests.

Secondly, the reform resulted in the formation of a thick populace of independent farmers. Therefore farmers became more homogeneous in terms of economic standards and self-reliant. Nevertheless, the conditions following the reform being unfavorable for farmers in some sense, the pauperization of farmers has been accelerated ever since.[9] It would still be hard to expect the emergence of progressive farmers willing to dedicate themselves to the cultivation of an enlarged production process and a renovated form of agricultural administration.

Thirdly, in the wake of the land readjustment, the consanguineous bond of the *yangban*, the core of the pre-modern force, was gradually undermined because it lost its economic basis. In particular, many rich persons who had formed the backbone of kinship consolidations lost their own lands as a result of the reform. However, as they were permitted to keep with them some part of their lands for use in ancestor worship, the consanguineous unions whose main function was to hold ancestor worship rituals have continued as a stronghold for pre-modern elements, imposing hindrances to the modernization of the rural society to some extent.

Fourthly, even after the reform, many former laborers and tenants, who had not possessed land at all or had owned a little, still remain as the same tenant-farmers or laborers as before. This was because the reform was carried out to allocate farm-fields only to those who registered as tenant-farmers at the end of the Japanese domination

2. Participation in Politics

Another important change since the liberation was that people for the first time became entitled to participate in elections. It must be a fact of great significance that the rural people who, as the least educated and the least conscious of public matters, never had political means to demonstrate their own rights and represent themselves in their own interests, became fully entitled to exercise their right to vote. Through participation in elections they have come to maintain their own concept about democracy and have come to be interested in politics gradually. But it is believed that they have not been able to utilize this valuable right for their betterment.[10]

As to the reasons and causes for the improper practices in farmers' voting, we can take into account the following: first, some rural people, who are uneducated and economically poor, might easily have cast their votes for the candidates who actually were not the right men to represent their interests. Secondly, consanguineous ties have influenced voting behavior. Though such solidarity has been much weakened as pointed out above, powerful men of kin groups still take on important roles in rural communities. These persons are in position as to keep close contact with influential relatives stationed in urban areas. Such relationships are readily utilized by politicians for collecting the votes of family members in local districts. Thirdly, administrative agencies can exert implicit pressures over rural people by suggesting that they cast votes for the candidates of the ruling party, through various organizations, or through the elders or the village chief, who are influential and are closely tied with local administrative agencies such as the *myŏn* office.

Though Korean people generally seem politically inactive, the rural people might be less active yet. They are not much interested in the election of representatives nor in the functions of the National Assembly. It might be said, however, that a substantial number of farmers show relatively strong interest as far as the National Assembly is concerned, while they seem to be fairly negative in their attitude toward local congresses.[11] Apart from the low standard of education and political consciousness of farmers, there are other fundamental reasons for the fact that they do not join actively in politics. First, local self-government bodies are mostly dependent on the central government in terms of budget; they are devoid of the financial resources necessary for the autonomous management of community projects. Secondly, in many cases the local administrative district, *myŏn*, does not correspond with the actual community set up by the people's socioeconomic necessities. Thus it frequently does not function as an organic community. Thirdly, all the socioeconomic activities are confined within the boundary of community so that villagers usually are not in close connection with markets at higher-level communities. Thus such villages do not have any spontaneous "interest group." In this way only a few people show willingness to join in politics for the augmentation of their own interests. Fourth, local assemblies are severed from villagers because there exist no public, independent media that would possibly render proper communication between local assemblies and villagers.

3. Other Social Causes Accentuating Change

The third type of social change since the nation's liberation was that the government and other social organizations have given stimuli to the rural people through various projects. Until 1960 the Liberal Party government had done nothing in particular for farmers except for making hard efforts to manipulate them for political objectives. The government set out a community development project and a cooperative union movement in rural areas toward the end of the Liberal Party regime. The community development projects involved quite limited activities not only in number but also in district. In many cases the projects were not really effective in serving the national economic development. The cooperative union movement resulted in a failure, too, because the union was nothing but a uniform, government-initiated organization lacking credit activities; and so the farmers hesitated to join in.

On the other hand, the Democratic Party government extemporaneously started the National Construction Projects. These projects underwent some modifications by the military administration. A few years immediately after the military revolution was the era in which the government conducted very ambitious projects, and thus rural areas seem to have been greatly stimulated in this period. First, the Agricultural Bank system was transformed into a new cooperative union which has credit functions. For this reason, the cooperatives became more attractive to the rural people than before. Second, the military administration took measures to wipe out usurious loans in rural areas; and, in spite of some serious side effects, these measures caused a new tendency for rural people to rely on more reasonable, mercenary transactions rather than on the traditional, irresolute relationship. Third, through the government-run National Reconstruction Movement, activities fostering the rationalization of life were accentuated. Fourth, radio-amplification facilities were widely established so that the size of the radio target-audience increased rapidly. Fifth, the family planning program was initiated as a national policy. With the wide recognition of increasing economic difficulty and population pressure, the program has been strongly pushed throughout the nation. Nevertheless, further objective evaluation is necessary in order to calculate correctly the results of such government projects which mobilized so much money and effort on the part of the administration.

The above are items of momentous change the rural populace has gone through since the nation was emancipated from Japan. However, no change was achieved by the voluntary, conscious efforts on the part of Korean farmers themselves; all were merely attained by the government or public organizations, with farmers just obeying. Other than such important changes brought about by the government, we must here take into account the Korean War. It might be said that the War itself didn't have such an immediate influence over rural communities since it lasted only a short span of time, occurring chiefly along the main roads and in cities; but the War made almost all Korean young men undertake military training. While they went through army life, they had new experiences in a totally unimagined, unexpected form at; such as organizational activity, scientific techniques, army discipline, sense and sensibility, and the like. Another result the War brought was a mass movement of population from area to area; and in this way many refugees from different parts of the nation settled down in rural communities.

Some Factors Related to Modernization

1. Traditional Value and Belief

So far we have discussed the social changes since the national liberation in 1945. Now let us pass over to the elements that encourage or discourage the modernization of rural communities at the present time. A widely accepted notion is that one of the most essential elements discouraging modernization is the traditional ideas about the way of life. It is attributed to Confucianism which is rooted in the family system, that the modernization of Korea is being delayed because this philosophical ideal despises productive activities other than agriculture. No doubt, Confucianism was responsible in the past for preventing the people from becoming independent and progressive. It may be said, however, that it does not restrain the people's adaptability to ever-fluctuating society as much as is usually believed. It is a system of ideas oriented toward the secular world rather than a religion oriented to the future world after death. Moreover, while Confucianism was not deeply internalized into the personality of laymen, the great majority of Koreans, many of them influential *yangban* who were a stronghold of this religious faith, have removed to urban areas, and their offspring have received modern education earlier than any other social group.

Confucianism is still partially responsible for setting impediments on the road to the nation's modernization, in view of the fact that it has emphasized the devotion to family rather than to community and forbidden autonomous activities of women and young people; and that, obeying the teachings of Confucianism, the people preferred formalism, spending too much money on such ceremonial occasions as marriage, ancestor worship ritual, funerals and so forth. But they have been changing much of their Confucian attitude, with some feeling of resistance, while adjusting to reality. One of the Confucian aspects still remaining the most intact is the discipline of filial piety. Even this aspect, along with a series of social changes, has been greatly modified.

The status and role of the female in society, in particular, have been in transformation. Korean people often have abandoned without much hesitation anything whatever of a Confucian essence whenever they regarded it advantageous to do so.

Traditional aspects that are most hard to eliminate today are the practice of ancestor worship which functions somewhat religiously, and the *pungsu* theory, or a Taoistic belief in the effects of geographical characteristics, particularly around a tomb site. It has been emphasized that the most unfavorable demerit of ancestor worship was over-expenditure, but not to be less stressed here is that ancestor worship has (1) only given accent to the father-son relationship while disregarding the status of the female in family relationships, (2) encouraged the whole family union so strongly as to discourage individual freedom, and (3) sometime accelerated conflicts among different family groups in a community.

Though Confucianism has been antagonistic to the modernization of Korea, it has, on the other hand, performed the important function of perserving family integration and preventing young family members from deviant behavior. At present, the Confucian originated ancestor worship and the tradition of blood solidarity would necessarily be weakened in the rural area. Thus the autonomy of the individual family, equal relationship between the male and female, and freer activities of younger generations would be accentuated, too. We may see, on the other hand, both family and social disintegrations take place today while the Confucian ethics rapidly disappear in the urban area which is subject to the unregulated influences of Western culture from various sources.

One of the facts foreigners might find strange in the Korean rural community is that no predominant religious organization exists. In many foreign countries religious bodies generally take a role at the center of life in the community as a whole, but nothing as such is found in rural areas of this country. Though there are Confucian-oriented institutions like *hyang-gyo*, or Community Academy, and *sŏwŏn*, or Reading Place, these are only established for the *yangban* and the Confucianist. Besides, these organizations today exert little influence on the routine life of the general populace. Other religious bodies are found, such as the Christian church or the Buddhist monastery, and only a few people seem to belong to them.

The fact that the Korean people lack a predominant religion is of great significance in view of the modernization of the country. The Korean people can easily take any means useful for their betterment, as they do not have strong religious beliefs which often forbid the utilization of new means. However, for this reason it has been very hard to inspire the people to devote themselves to modernization work in a universal spiritual bond supported by the majority of the people.[12]

Instead of a religion, Koreans seem to have had a tendency to rely on such superstitious faiths as prophesy, the *pungsu* theory, necromancy and what not. These superstitions are widely spread especially among the rural people who are generally old and uneducated. They are inclined to be fatalistic, always accepting one's lot without trying to overcome it. To such people, the power of a Heaven which reigns over all natural phenomena, and that of officials who reign over the society, are too mighty and absolute to challenge in an attempt for better living standards.

2. Education

Commoners as well as women had not been able to enjoy opportunities of education at all before Korea began the work of modernization. Leaders of the country for the first time stressed modern education around the end of the Yi-dynasty, being confident that education was the only means to achieve independence.[13] The general populace also began to recognize that only the educated successfully adapted to the ever-changing social situations and secured high status, and that the uneducated were looked down upon and were faced with a lot of inconveniences in public life. Today Koreans are regarded as people with exceptionally strong aspirations for educating children in spite of their economic conditions.

There are still a great number of illiterates in rural areas though the compulsory education system has been in effect since the liberation. Important problems are chiefly discussed and decided at the village meeting in which all household heads are supposed to participate. According to research conducted by this writer at a certain rural area about six years ago, 60 per cent of the household heads were men over 40, and 80 per cent of them never received formal school education. Conversely, only 20 per cent of those under 40 were without formal education.[14] So it is quite expectable that in the near future such village meetings will be composed of men with formal education who will be more rational in their thinking and more self-assertive.

Along with this fact, it must be noted again that a great majority of young men in agricultural areas have experienced military life. It is also noteworthy that since the military coup of 1961 the younger generations have exerted a more powerful influence on daily living in rural areas. This is because the government since the coup has appointed younger people to the offices of local administrative bodies on the one hand, and because the official activities, especially those of cooperative unions, were so increased that active, younger people naturally had to take charge of the office in place of old men, on the other hand. It is an inspiring fact that nowadays the number of young men of willingness who are well aware of their own problems and of how to solve them reasonably, is ever increasing, and that they have come to take part in the process of resolving such problems common to the community, acting as the nucleus. At the same time, however, it might be presumed that, if they cannot have satisfactory prospects for achieving their rising goals, they will either be frustrated or try to seek some radical means, as it has happened among the young intellectuals.

The fast swelling of the target-audience of radio broadcasting in rural communities must be taken into account as another momentous change in addition to the development of education. Research conducted recently at a rural community shows that about 50 per cent of the households use radios.[15] Radio broadcasting has allowed the rural people to get more information more rapidly, and at the same time enjoy recreation as well as a rationalization of routine living. In the meantime, the desire for greater consumption has become stronger, too.

3. Functional Relationship with the Outside

Getting rid of consanguineous unions, the rural populace today is becoming more united on a community basis, and further shows a tendency toward strengthening solidarities in terms of economic interests, though it is still weak. Unified action on the basis of the village community helps resolve common problems in a democratic way. In fact, however, this has been promoted by necessity on the part of the government agencies in an attempt to control the people, and not by the desire of the people themselves. During the Japanese domination, particularly during World War II, the government authorities officially controlled the people through the *myŏn* office, police dispatches and the head of the village so as to mobilize labor and deliver war goods. Informally, the leaders of the community who were comparatively rich and respected by the laymen in line with traditional concepts were asked to help maintain such control. Right after the nation's emancipation from Japanese occupation, similar political controls were exerted over the populace by the government in an attempt to establish social security, and to acquire the people's support for the ruling party. The fact that autonomous activities of the people were considerably increased after the national liberation was the only aspect quite characteristically different from the situation in the period of Japanese control.

Community solidarity in the last several years has been promoted by the agricultural cooperatives. Until recent years, the traditional forms of social cooperation were those such as *gye*, or a sort of cooperation system for raising funds or labor for the occasions of death or the like, and *pumasi*, individual labor exchange. Modern types of village solidarities looking forward to economic development of the whole community were not encouraged at all. Hence, it might be said that the agricultural cooperative is a project which promises to result in favorable change for rural communities. But such projects have been initiated not only by official authorities but also developed in a wholesale manner. Farmers are taking part in these cooperatives because they are urged to do so by officials on the one hand, and because, on the other hand they can get loans only in this manner. Although the agricultural cooperative unions hold such activities as common procurement and sales, and are managed by the cooperation of all members, the activities cannot yet be considered brisk and effective.

For the agricultural cooperative unions to perform full-fledged functions, it is a prerequisite that agricultural management should be diversified so that the production of marketable merchandise is increased. Thus agricultural communities shall be closely related to market and modern productive systems, and be able to secure economic development.

Im this manner, morever, farmers will escape the confined social life at the village level and enjoy better, organic socio-economic activities together with adjacent villages on a wider community level. So far the government has made certain efforts merely to improve technology and customs in a stereotyped way. The government has not endeavored to inspire entrepreneurs to inter-link the agricultural economy with industries in urban areas. The authorities themselves make the most powerful enterprise in the nation, yet they have not tried up very hard to invest in such projects. In reality, both the administration and the politicians, though they had always stressed policies to benefit the farming populace, had done nothing but maintain measures to manipulate farmers; and these brought only great losses to them.

Other reasons for the fact that the economic activities of farmers are not closely tied with higher-level communities follow: (1) local district differentiation is not in accord with rural economic life; it is set up only for the purpose of carrying out official business; (2) official control within the boundaries of such local administrative districts is so strict that spontaneous economic development on the part of farming people has been very much obstructed. We can see quite often that within a *myŏn* district there exist two different actual communities conflicting with each other, thereby checking integrated political and economic activities.[16]

For the reasons mentioned above, farmers' activities through social associations are very feeble. The social associations, even though they have worked, have seldom reached to the villages in their functioning. Additionally, almost all the staff members of such organizations have not been farmers but those who have been interested in other matters such as politics, or business. It may sound very paradoxical, that more men participated in social associations in rural villages than in *ŭb*-level towns. However, a lot of them have been generally supported by the government overtly or covertly, and have been established with an economic, and political aim of manipulating the farmers. It is easier to establish such organizations, without any strong reaction by farmers, in small villages than in *ŭb*-level communities. The administrative agencies, anyway, can easily gain more fruitful results in the exercise of control propaganda in the small villages.

However, this is because that nowadays even farmers are becoming more and more reluctant to accept the administrative controls even while they superficially pretend to obey the government.

Conclusion

The illiteracy, traditional custom, and lack of techniques on the part of farmers are not to be taken as the only reasons for the delaying of the nation's economic progress. It is not true that for modernization every man should be a master of proper modernized information and techniques. Nor must all traditional customs which are regarded as obstacles to modernization necessarily be eradicated at once. Neither is it that agricultural people must necessarily be trained for information and techniques toward their own self-modernization.

In rural communities today there is a growing number of men who know how to employ modern information and techniques. These people are emerging as a new force exercising powerful influence over the whole community. Though Korean farmers, just as their counterparts in foreign countries, are conservative as well as too cautious, they seem to be comparatively ready to accept such techniques once they are sure that such techniques will surely bring them increased income. That they lack sufficient capital and experience is attributed to the fact that they are quite indecisive in engaging in a new form of productive activity. At the same time, it would be very hard for the individual farmer to engage in both market transactions and farming. Therefore, if the government, agricultural cooperatives, and entrepreneurs help them by providing the needed capital, information, and techniques, by guaranteeing reasonable prices for their future products, and by affording incentives to make them reorganize an organic community by themselves, farmers will gladly work hard.[17] It is also desirable that the authorities establish as many industrial bodies as possible in the centers of agricultural areas to use idle labor forces and resources. Consequently, rural people will voluntarily be united in functional groups and will actively participate in social and political activities which are desperately necessary for the progress of democracy. Furthermore, they will gladly devote themselves to the work of the elimination of discrepancies in the economic and cultural standards between the urban and rural areas, and achieve the elevation of their living standards.

[NOTES]

1) E.O. Reischauer, "Special Features in the History of Japan," *Japan-America Forum*, Nov. 1964, pp. 10-12.
    T. Hatata did not characterize the Yi-dynasty as feudalistic in his work, *Chosen-si (Korean History)*, (Tokyo: Iwanami Shoten, 1953).
2) Too-hun Kim, *Hangug gajog jedo yŏngu (Study on the Family System in Korea)*, (Seoul: The Eulyoo Pub. Co., 1949), p. 279.
3) Hong-jin Chong, "Nongchon sahoe ŭi baljŏn (Development of Rural Society)," *Nongchon sahoe-hag (Rural Sociology)*, ed. by Korean Rural Sociological Society, 1965, p. 54.
4) E. de S. Brunner, "Rural Korea," *The Christian Mission in Relation to Rural Problems*, (New York: International Missionary Council, 1928), pp. 116-117.
5) Man-gap Lee, "Nongchon sahoe gyechŭng (Social Stratification in Rural

Society)," *Nongchon sahoe-hag (Rural Sociology)*, ed. by Korean Rural Sociological Society, 1965, pp. 182-183.
6) Man-gap Lee, *Hangug nongchon ŭi sahoe gujo (The Social Structure of the Korean Village)*, (Seoul: The Korean Research Center, 1960), pp. 105-110.
7) Whang-kyung Koh, et al., *Hangug nongchon gajog ŭi yŏngu (A Study on Korean Rural Family)*, (Seoul: Seoul National University Press, 1963), pp. 198-203.
8) Taik-kyoo Kim, *Dongjog burag ŭi saenghwal gujo yŏngu (The Cultural Structure of a Consanguineous Village)*, (Daegu: Chŏng-gu Colle-ge Press, 1964), p. 223.
9) The National Agricultural Cooperative Federation, *Agricultural Year Book*, 1964, p. 140, Part 1.
10) Chŏn-joo Yoon, *Hangug jŏngchi chegye sŏsŏl (Introduction to Korean Political System)*, (Seoul: Munun dang, 1962), p. 419.
11) Man-gap Lee, *Social Associations in Rural Community*, which is not published yet.
12) Bert F. Hoselitz, "Tradition and Economic Growth," *Tradition, Values, and Socio-economic Development*, ed. by R. Braibanti and J.J. Spengler, (Durham: Duke University Press, 1961), pp. 84-85.
13) The first modern newspaper in Korea, *Dognib Sinmun (The Independence Press)*, stressed the necessity of education with a great enthusiasm.
14) *The Social Structure of the Korean Village, op. cit.*, pp. 62-64.
15) Jai-chun Yoo, "Communication Source in Rural Community," *The Sinmun pyŏngron (Journalism Review)*, No. 9, Jan. 1965, p. 54.
16) *The Social Structure of the Korean Village, op. cit.*, pp. 29-32.
17) Wilbert E. Moore, *Social Change*, (Englewood Cliff, N.J.: Prentice-Hall, Inc., 1963), p. 61.

Some Problems Democracy Faces in Rural Areas

Some Factors Related to the Development of Democracy

1. Family System and Kinship Group Union[1]

Yangban(scholar-officials) who were the ruling class in the traditional society have maintained unity of family and kinship group through strong patriarchal controls. In their (*yangban*) family, offspring, juniors and women folk could hardly enjoy independent personalities; and the family itself, in most cases, lost its independence due to the solid unity of the kinship group. They have oppressed the low inhabitants of the village or ones near it with political power, economic superiority and social prestige. Owing to this, efforts designed to bring about common development, on equal basis, of the people in a community could only be weak.

The old-fashioned status system disappeared perfunctorily at the turn of 19th century, but the *yangban* class continued to wield power over the commoner because it was economically superior. However, kinship group unity of the *yangban* class was weakened seriously because, on the one hand, the *yangban* and the commoner became almost equal economically since the land reform of 1949; and, on the other hand, unity on a village basis was encouraged through modern administrative organizations. Yet, they are still in a superior position to the commoner because they have their relatives in the same area or in nearby cities who have influence.

During election campaigns, candidates, considering advantages of kinship group, try to muster the support of those who have influ-

---

* Presented at the seminar on "Democracy and Development in South-East Asia," in Kuala Lumpur in 1966.

ence in the kinship group. Also, it is necessary, in the interest of both individuals and the groups, for leaders of the groups to have connections with politicians related to their groups or other statesmen whom they befriend through the related politicians. If a leader of a rural kinship group supports a certain politician, the members of the group normally support him too. For there are not many groups that are stronger than the kinship group. And since a leader of a kinship group ordinarily represents the opinion of a village, inhabitants of the village who are not members of a kinship group naturally are apt to be influenced by the leader. The survey I conducted indicates that dwellers of a village where there is kinship group are influenced, more than anything else, by their relatives in voting for candidates.[2]

2. Confrontation of Sectional Interests

Traditionally, farmers have lived in villages and their relations outside the village are maintained in two ways. One way is through administrative offices and the other is through markets. Although one or several independent villages form auxilliary admininistrative area under the name of *ri* (or *dong*), there is no administrative office looking after the village or villages. There is only the head of the *ri*, representing the district, who coordinates with administrative offices concerned. An administrative area is called *myŏn* which normally consists of 10 to 15 *ri*, and a *myŏn* office and a police branch are major administrative offices in a *myŏn*.

It is not clear on what basis *myŏn* boundaries were drawn, but it seems that the demarcations were made not so much for the convenience of the farmers as for the convenience of the administrative officers. Until now, the relations farmers voluntarily maintained, whether stimulated by economic needs or other social requirement, were with markets rather than adminstrative offices. The markets are really the center of a community. While there are areas in which administrative offices are located within the markets, they are usually situated outside the markets; and what is more, the administrative area of the *myŏn* in many cases is drawn in contradiction to the area of the community formed around the market, thereby resulting in a divided sphere of livelihood activities.[3] Therefore, elections of *myŏn* chiefs or members of the *myŏn* council in the past were fought, in many cases, not for the immediate economic interest but for the simple emotional conflicts which resulted from the desire to prevent candidates from other areas from carrying the election. And such emotional confrontation frequently prevailed in the decisions of the administration. Thus it is difficult for the *myŏn* to have sectional unity, and the *myŏn* chief usually finds himself in a disadvantageous position when he tries to concentrate on certain projects with a limited budget. Therefore, the *myŏn* chief often divides his budget into two areas with a view to avoiding such trouble, and this process only incurs budgetary waste.

3. Controls by the Authorities

In the past the occupants of the villages have been under the strong control of the authorities concerned. And such controls brought about more sacrifice on the part of the farmers than benefits. Although farmers sometimes revolted against the cruel oppression of the authorities, they usually acquired a habit of absolute obedience to authority. During the reign of the Yi-dynasty which adopted confucianism as guidance for rulers, authorities were considered as noble and omnipotent beings. And the public learned from long experience that to rebel against the authorities brought destruction to self and to family. Such attitudes have not changed conspicuously even now with a democratic system established.

The authorities, especially during the regime of the late Dr. Syngman Rhee, created various organizations and forced farmers to be affiliated with them. Superficially, such organizations existed for the benefit of the farmers, but often they were used as an indirect means of controlling villagers. During the Japanese occupation and the period preceding it, the farmers did not have freedom to form organizations for their common interest. Since the emancipation in 1945, they have enjoyed, to a certain extent, liberty to establish such groups. However, the farmers do not feel the need for having such organizations because their economic activities are based simply on self-sufficiency and because of their extremely family based thinking; nor could they afford economically to maintain the organizations. As for their voluntary organizations, there are unofficial cooperative bodies for aiding marriage or funeral ceremonies, youth organizations, and 4H Clubs designed to help farmers improve their lives or improve morale. But such groups are not developed to the extent that they have great influence.

The leaders of villages are forced into a position, whether they want it or not, where, in most cases they cannot help but cooperate with the authorities. The leaders can be divided into two categories. One category is the *ri* chiefs who have formal administrative responsibility, and the other is the influential seniors in the villages. The latter are usually those who have served as *ri* chief or equivalent positions in the past, and the former is normally a person whom the influential seniors recommended. A *ri* chief cannot perform his job smoothly without the support of such unofficial leaders of a village. He is are under direct control of the authorities, and influential seniors normally assume advisory roles to the authorities or key positions in semi-official organizations.

Furthermore, the authorities have at their disposal mass media which provide information to the farmers. Most of the newspapers in the country are politically independent and run by civilian hands, but a large majority of the farmers are not in a position economically to subscribe to them; and there are still many in rural areas who are not literate enough to read newspapers. Conversely, it is much easier for semi-official newspapers to reach the farmers because such newspapers do not have to worry much about running in the red. After the collapse of Syngman Rhee's regime, serveral private broadcasting stations were established but due to their weak power capacity, they cannot reach most of the rural areas. About 50 per cent of the farmers listen to radio broadcasting, but they listen mainly to the government-operated broadcasting station.[4]

The administrative authorities are expected in principle to be politically neutral and officials seem to want to stay that way. However, as an election approaches, those in power establish, with a view to staying in power, policies wooing popular support, and there is trend to use the budget for that purpose. Moreover, it has become more frequent for the authorities to use administrative offices, especially police, for political purposes. The latest survey[5] indicates disappearance, at least superficially, of pressures from the authorities during elections; but previously there was frequent overt pressure from the authorities.

4. Economic Nonspecialization and Poverty

As long as the farmers are engaged in farming on a scale that would provide only for their own consumption, they would not feel the necessity to discard traditional modes of life and to make joint efforts for pursuit of political and economic interests. Their major concerns in farming are a reasonable level of crop prices, a supply of timely and adequate amounts of chemical fertilizer, and adequate measures for fighting drought and flood. The first two problems are related with basic policies of the government which are too big to be solved by the farmers of a village through submitting their consensus of opinion; and it is also impossible for the farmers to have a nationwide network designed to bring about unity in recommending what ought to be done. The last problem derives purely from nature and the only thing farmers can do in case of natural calamity is to cooperate with each other.

If the farmers produced crops for sale and had frequent transaction with markets, they would unite in pursuit of common economic interests and gradually they would get interested in the political field as well. However, the farmers cannot expect to have close relations with markets through crop sale alone, and this is more so when most of the crop is used for their own food. Although agricultural cooperatives were established several years ago, they are not performing their original roles satisfactorily because they are greatly influenced by the government. The farmers living in villages near urban areas nowadays have relatively closer relations with markets, but such villages are very limited in number.

Another reason explaining why farmers lack political goals and why it is difficult for them to be united for their own interest is that most of the farmers do not have the means to expand their farmlands, and some of them are a having hard time providing food for their family. Therefore, most of the farmers expect to receive assistance from others rather than unite themselves for their own development. Such farmers are easily "bought" with meager material assistance or temptation during elctions, and they are not capable of deciding whom they should elect to represent them.

5. Education and Value System

Important factors to be considered when discussing democracy in the rural area are farmers' education and their value system. According to my observation,[6] Korean farmers still live in old-fashioned ways, but they are not too deep-rooted in traditional custom, and because of this they are not likely to be a serious barrier to economic development. Traditional ideas in Korea have derived mainly from Confucianism but they have ben adhered to principally by the *yangban*. To the commoner, the bond has not been a strong one. Since the land reform social status of commoners improved to the point where they enjoy equal rights with the *yangban*. The commoners can flexibly adjust their behavior to reality in order to pursue economic benefits. They keep living in a traditional mode only because they have no favorable chance of which they can be sure, nor do they have the means to create such an opportunity by themselves.

Education will enable the farmers to successfully accommodate themselves to reality and to maintain their independence. Pioneers of modern Korea emphasized and implemented the view that development of the country can be brought about only through education.[7] And the farmers witnessed that educated men made a success of their lives. Therefore, farmers have willingly gone through all hardships to educate their offspring. Yet there remains a considerable amount of illiteracy among females and elders. Problems of a village are discussed at the meeting of family heads; but according to a survey of an area seven years ago, 65 per cent of the family heads were over 40 years of age, and 80 per cent of that 65 per cent did not even attend primary school. Since ignorant heads are superior in number, and because seniority sways more power in decision making, it is clear that solutions of the meeting tend to be more conservative and inefficient. However, the number of those who received education increases dramatically below the age of 40. In short this phenomenon indicates that the number of those who are rational in thinking, and who want to be independent and more democratic is increasing in rural areas.[8]

Representative Government in Rural Areas

Local inhabitants were not strongly opposed when it was decided at the end of Syngman Rhee's regime that the chiefs of *ri*, *myŏn* and county would be appointed. Nevertheless, an absolute majority of rural dwellers now want to replace the current appointment system with an election system. Yet they seem to be divided equally over installation of *myŏn* or county councils.

It appears that opposition to installation of the councils is based on the belief that the councils are only the ornaments of democracy, that they cause useless troubles between council members and their lackeys, and that council members are dawdling while wasting government money. Like the central council, major functions of local councils are examination of budget and recommendation or approval of policies on behalf of the inhabitants. But because of the following the councils do not seem to be efficient. First, about half of the budget for a local autonomous body is met by government subsidy, and because of this there is not much chance for local councils to reflect their opinions in formulating the budget. They merely approve the scale of the budget and of projects which have already been set by the central government. Second, there are no communications media through which people can be informed about happenings between local councils and administrative offices nor can people's opinions be transmitted to local councils or administrative organizations, and there is seldom any interest group mediating politics. There are newspapers at the provinicial level reporting major articles, but below that level there is no medium to assume that role. Therefore, once local councils are established after election, it will be difficult for them adequately to reflect the opinions of the people; and, what is more, there is possibility that they might do things counter to the general interest.

In *ŭb* which is a town a district equivalent to *myŏn*, more people seem to favor the establishment of councils. There are more people in *ŭb* than in *myŏn* who are educated, and who know how to utilize mass media, and who cannot, because actual needs demand, be indifferent to politics. Still, most of the *ŭb* occupants are engaged in small business or farming or daily labors. They don't yet feel the needs to unite in their common interest, nor do they have the competence to do that. Power structure is formed through a vote of the people; but once the power structure is established, it acts regardless of the interests of the voters; and this phenomenon, although there is difference in degree, applies as well to higher levels—provincial or even national—administrative echelons.

Partial Skepticism over Democracy

Although it is hard to find anyone completely skeptical about democracy, there are some Koreans who have, after experiencing democratic social and political behavior during the past 20 years, vague skepticism over efficiency of democratic operation. That doubt is becoming intensified as Koreans painfully feel economic poverty. The conditions of economic poverty may have improved in an absolute sense; however, as the result of population increase and a higher level of knowledge through education and mass communication, there are increasing numbers of people who, not being satisfied with reality, want to pursue the goals of higher positions and more abundant material value. And as their desire for a fast economic growth intensifies, the sense of economic poverty becomes stronger.

The doubt about democracy is spreading, principally in regard to the representative government system. It is pointed out that by giving voting rights to those who have not yet discarded traditional thought as indicated earlier and who are not economically and intellectually independent, a representative government system fails to elect representatives who are truly democratic and progressive and who have the knowledge and will to construct a new society. Secondly, the skeptics consider political parties as groups of those who are blinded by desires for their personal interest and power, and therefore partisans in an effort to maintain the parties and their power, who will not hesitate to raise political funds by any means possible. And by doing so, the doubters believe, they demoralize the people, loosen social discipline, and help weaken the people's sense of sovereignty. Thirdly, they argue that the representative government system often prevents swift and adequate administrative action, and makes it hard for the government or the authorities concerned to push forth projects to which concentrated efforts are given. Thus, the critics of democracy discredit the National Assembly and politicians as a whole, and tacitly expect the appearance of "goodwilled autocracy" or "strong leaders."

Another aspect of democracy at which they are pelting criticisms is the dysfunctional effect established by the democratic idea. Often democracy is recognized as a synonym of freedom. And they believe that in a democratic society some people think freedom means they can do anything they please, thereby bringing disorder to society through encouraging wayward and irresponsible behavior. Secondly, some people believe that free competition makes those with power, wealth, and other means more superior while it drives the poor and powerless to a more difficult situation. Moreover, they insist that because high class people in a backward country, where material resources are short, try to enjoy a living standard as high as that of an advanced country, there is a widening gap between the haves and have-nots and wide-spread luxury among high class people. Thirdly, the critics say that since democratic society is open, there is a strong tendency to import foreign ideas recklessly. Accordingly, good traditional custom and culture are undermined and cultural confusion results because the foreign ideas themselves are too diverse.

Conclusion: Survival of Democracy

It is clear that a democratic system in underdeveloped countries exposes to a certain degree such undesirable points. And it seems that the more there are disappointed people in a society and the more disappointment is aggravated, the more people become impatient and exaggerate the defects. Furthermore, skepticism about democracy seems to become strong when rulers or social leaders fail to have a symbol that can be identified with the people and when the ruler or social leaders are considered to be pursuing wealth or power by any means possible.

Koreans toppled Syngman Rhee's regime when enraged to learn of flagrant violations in the democratic election. The short period following the fall of Rhee's regime saw Korean society enjoying excessive freedom to a dangerous point. Skepticism about democracy was felt strongest during this period. However, people appear to prize democracy after the military rule. There are some conditions in Korean society which are favorable to development of democracy. First of all, there is no one in Korea who has authority through ascription. Although those from the *yangban* class lord it over others in rural areas, they would be a laughingstock if they tried the same thing in the cities. Most of those in the upper class today do not have a glorious background; they have an ordinary background like most of the middle class people. Secondly, there are strong and influential newspapers in Korea which play an important role in inspiring democratic spirit. Thirdly, Korea has a thick layer of educated people who can do things independently. Sometimes educated men can be a danger to democracy when society cannot give them satisfactory positions. Nevertheless, learned men would value democracy more than others. Fourthly, Koreans have experienced and strongly rejected both Japanese totalitarianism and Communist rule.

Democracy in Korea is still vulnerable and there may be many more trials in the future. Development of democracy in advanced democratic nations has never been smooth either.

[NOTES]

1) Man-gap Lee, "Consanguineous Group and Its Function in the Korean Community," which was presented at the 9th International Seminar on Family Research in 1965.
2) This survey was done in 1964 with the tentative title, "Sociological

Study on Local Autonomy," but the report is not published yet.
3) Man-gap Lee, *Hangug nongchon ŭi sahoe gujo (The Social Structure of the Korean Village)*, (Seoul: The Korean Research Center, 1960), pp. 29-32.
4) Jai-chun Yoo, "Communication Source in Rural Community," *The Sinmun pyŏngron (Journalism Review)*, No. 9, Jan. 1965, p. 54.
5) "Sociological Study on Local Autonomy," *op. cit.*
6) Man-gap Lee, "Rural People and Their Modernization," presented at International Conference of the Problems of Modernization in Asia which was held in Seoul in 1965.
7) *Dognib Sinmun (Independence Press)*, the first civilian newspaper published in 1896, stressed education as the most important means of reaching the goal of national independence and development.
8) *The Social Structure of the Korean Village, op. cit.*, pp. 62-64.

Pushing or Pulling?

Background of the Problem

The mass migration of rural people into the urban areas has been looming as one of the serious social problems in the developing countries, especially since World War II, although this steady trend of migration had already begun before the War.

The urban population of Seoul amounted to approximately 200,000 at the end of the 19th century, the time when Korea was about to cast off the traditional form of her society; the population increased to 350,000 by 1930 and to 900,000 by the time of liberation, 1945. Thus during this period, the population of Seoul increased four and one-half times. But it increased to 5,000,000 during the quarter of a century since the liberation.

What causes this mass migration to urban areas? This important question has been asked frequently enough. The answers given by different scholars, however, are not always consistent with each other. The extreme poverty in the rural sectors is usually pointed out as the major factor pushing out the farmers and their families and hence causing the mass migration to the urban areas. According to T.O. Wilkinson,[1] the urban growth in Korea is not a result of the pulling factors existing in the cities, but mostly a result of the pushing factors operating in the rural areas. After studying the change of population in terms of the periods of migration, Chong-Ju Yoon concludes in his paper[2] that the growth of population in Seoul is not caused by pulling factors but by the pushing factors. Hyok Chung argues,[3] on the contrary, that the

---

* Presented at the "International Seminar on Urban Affairs" organized by the Population and Development Studies Center, Seoul National University in 1970.

surplus population in the rural areas is pulled to the cities, mainly for three sets of reasons, categorized as (1) economic, (2) socio-cultural, and (3) geographical factors.

The following are generally considered to be the most significant factors causing the people to move from one place to another. (See the Diagram of Analytical Framework of Migration)

A. Characteristics of the potential migrator
 (1) His value system
 (2) Demographic characteristics of his family
 (3) Socio-economic background of his family
B. Characteristics of the place of origin
 (1) Cultural characteristics
 (2) Socio-economic characteristics
C. Characteristics of the place of destination
 (1) Cultural characteristics
 (2) Socio-economic characteristics
D. Ability of the potential migrant for adjustment
 (1) Ability for cultural adjustment
 (2) Ability for socio-economic adjustment
E. Intermediate Variables
 (1) Natural disasters
 (2) Change in the governmental policy or political events
 (3) Personal or familiar interrelationships
 (4) Historical background

With the above paradigm in mind, we selected 23 factors which were supposed to be causally related to the urban growth in Korea. Which factors among those 23 are most responsible for the migration to Seoul? Are the pushing factors really more contributive than the pulling factors are? Or is the opposite case true?

To identify the causal factors for migrants to Seoul, which is the main aim of this paper, was one of the several objects for a broader and more comprehensive research project. Other important objects of the project were to collect information concerning (1)

Changes in Rural and Urban Communities 207

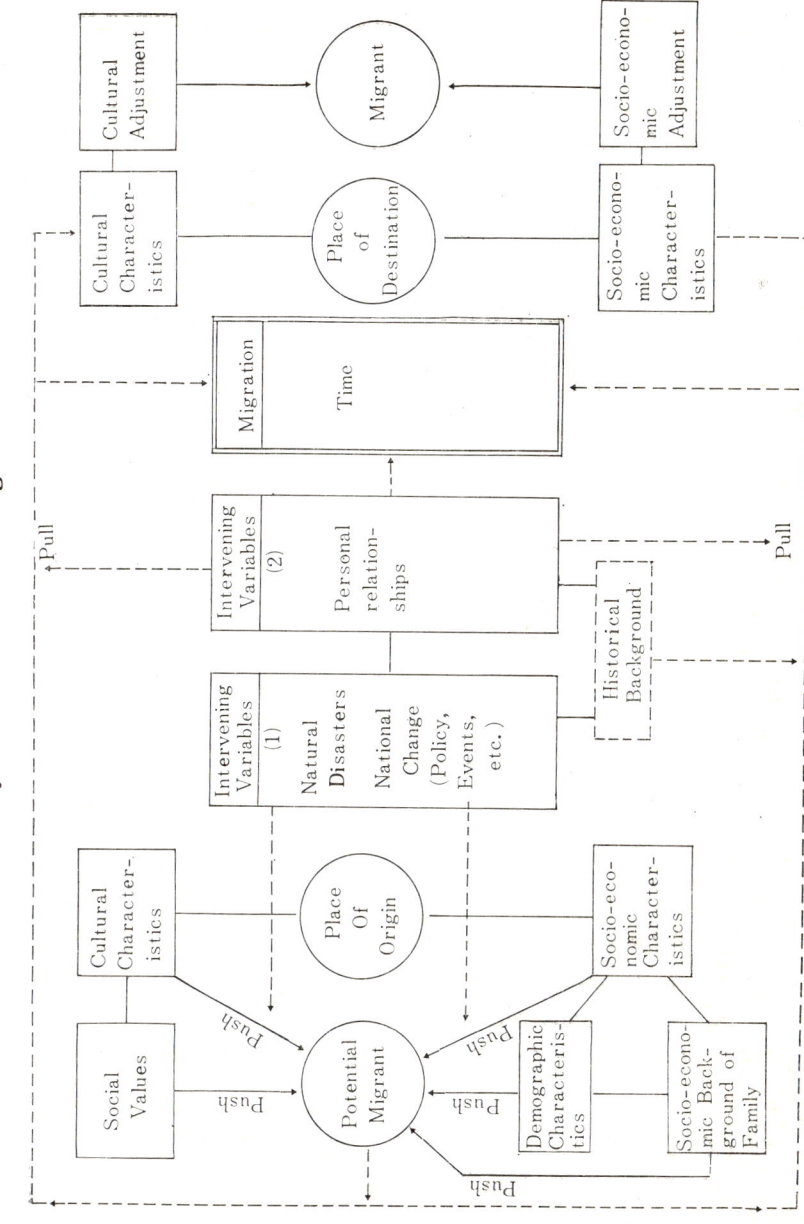

the places where the people lived at the end of Yi-dynasty(around 1890) and other places they moved through before settling down in Seoul, (2) the kinds of occupation they held during the period of transition, and (3) the kinds of problems they had to face in adjusting themselves to the new environment in Seoul.

The 23 factors listed below are considered to be causing the migration to cities.

A. Pushing factors
   (1) Poverty
   (2) War, social turmoil
   (3) Escape from traditional life
   (4) Family bankruptcy
   (5) Social class distinction
   (6) Difficulty with employer
   (7) Natural disasters
   (8) Spread of epidemic
   (9) Land reform

B. Pulling factors
   (1) To find a job
   (2) To establish a private business
   (3) Employment opportunities
   (4) Education
   (5) Cultural resources
   (6) Desire for urban life
   (7) Personal relationships
   (8) Marriage
   (9) Anonymous refuge

C. Other factors (neither pulling nor pushing factors)
   (1) Disease
   (2) To show skill or talent
   (3) Change of office or occupation
   (4) Skills learned in military service
   (5) Superstitious prophecy.

Research Method

The field work for the research was carried out in the fall of 1968. Five hundred households were sampled for the survey. The unit of sampling was households registered in the administrative office of *dong* in Seoul. Sampling procedure was firstly to select at random 43 *dongs* out of 302 administrative *dongs*, secondly to select 3 *bans* out of each *dong* and thirdly to select 4 households randomly from all the households registered in each *ban*. Consquently, 516 households were finally selected as samples. Due to the absence of responses from some households, 505 households were covered in the actual investigation, with 2.1% of sample loss. Although the sampling unit was a household, the actual respondent was to be the head of each household, who was interviewed according to the schedule. In case the head was absent or the interview with him (or her) was impossible for some reason, a person who was acting in the household in place of the head was interviewed.

The research project has several built-in defects. Firstly, since the sampling was done on the basis of the registered households, some non-registered households and some single persons not attached to any household were inevitably excluded from the sampling. But the fact that the project was carried out at the time when the system of residence registration was already enacted must have considerably lowered the number of those exceptional cases. The low-income people usually change their dwelling places more frequently and also the recent migrators to Seoul are likely to live in factory dorms, in the boarding houses or simply with their relatives. Thus, those transient people were not included in the sampling, which is not a negligible defect of this research.

The second defect consists in the fact that the responses to the questions concerning the life situation of the grandfather or the father of the interviewees may not be too reliable, since most of the interviewees did not have exact knowledge about the elder generation of their family. The third weakness of the survey is that, in many cases, the interviewee was not the head of the household but another member of the family. It was difficult in Seoul to interview the head of the household, because he is likely to be out most of the time. But this fact may not have biased the result of the study too much, because presumably most members of the family can provide reliable information about such an important family event as the migration to Seoul.

1. Findings

Out of 505 respondents interviewed, 101 (20.0%) say that their families have been in Seoul for more than three generations. Those who migrated to Seoul during the period between the end of the Yi-dynasty and 1944 are 18.6 per cent of the total number of the migrants. The number of respondents who moved to Seoul after 1945 is 325. This group is 81.4 per cent of the total number of the migrants and 65.1 per cent of the total number of respondents. The period in which the migration movement was most active in our time brackets is between 1954, the year after

Table 1. Number of Migrants by Time Period

Period	No. of respondents	Per cent
∼1944	75	18.6
1945∼1949	74	18.3
1950∼1953	60	14.8
1954∼1959	99	24.5
1960∼1962	39	9.7
1963∼1965	40	9.9
1966∼	17	4.2
Total	404	100.0%

Note: The periods are classified in terms of the historical events.

the ceasefire of the Korean War, and 1959, the year before the April student uprising (⟨Table 1⟩).

In one question we asked the length of time which had passed between the time they decided to move to Seoul and the time of their actual migration. The most frequent response is that they moved immediately after they decided, and the proportion is 26.0 per cent (105) of the total migrants. Those who moved within a half year after the decision are 19.8 per cent (80), and those who moved between a half year and one year after the decision, 16.6 per cent (67). Thus, the total number of the migrants who moved within a year after the decision is far more than half of the migrants. Those who migrated one year after their decision is only 21.6 per cent (87). Among the remainder, 62 (15.3%) people say that they do not know when it was decided, since they did not decide by themselves. Three persons did not indicate the time of decision. Generally speaking, the stability of the society seems to have determined the time span between the decision and actual migration. Namely, the more the society is unstable, the longer the time taken for the practice of migration after the decision to migrate.

In an open ended question, the migrants were asked the causes of their decision. The major causes indicated were classified into arbitrary categories through content analysis. The analysis shows that the most frequent items are occupational matters, such as looking for a job or taking a new job assignment. The total number of persons who referred to job related reasons is 69 (17.1%). The second most frequent category is education for the migrants themselves or their children (62 persons : 15.3%). The third is oppression under the communist regime (35 persons: 8.7%); the fourth, poverty (30: 7.4%); the fifth, the Korean war (20: 5.0 %); the sixth, private business affairs(19: 4.7%); the seventh, desire for an urban life (18: 4.5%). The others(33 persons: 8.2 %) indicated miscellaneous reasons. The remaining 118 persons

(29.2%) did not indicate the possible causes because they did not decide by themselves or they just do not know exactly.

The number of the respondents who say that they decided to move to Seoul for job related reasons increases in relative importance after the ceasefire of the Korean war, when many refugees started to come back to the capital city from the southern parts. The same trend is also observed among the respondents who say that they migrated to Seoul for establishing private business. The number of respondents who say that the major reason for their migration to Seoul was to have educational opportunities there increased slightly after the ceasefire, but the increase does not seem to be statistically very significant. They are rather evenly observed in each period of time. The number of people whose main reason for migration is said to be economic poverty decreased much in the unstable period after the liberation of Korea and in the chaotic time during the Korean War when compared with the period of Japanese control. But it gradually increased again after the ceasefire. The people who say that they came to Seoul becasue of the desire for urban life were represented evenly in every period, although their number is relatively small. Needless to say, most of the respondents who say that the communist oppresion caused their migration came to Seoul between 1945 and 1949.

As mentioned previously, there are twenty-three motivational factors which may possibly induce the people to migrate. These factors were selected after examining the various works which have dealt with the reasons for migration. The respondents were asked whether each of these factors had influenced them when they had decided to migrate to Seoul, and if yes, to what extent they think it had influenced them.

According to the results of the analysis, the factor which was most frequently referred to is to find a job or to take a job; the second most frequent, education; the third, to establish a private business; the fourth, that there were better opportunities for employment in Seoul. It is interesting to note that all of these are pulling factors.

The most important item among the pushing factors seems to be the social turmoil, such as political pressure or war. It comes, after better opportunities for employment, as fifth in the ranking order. As discussed earlier, many people believe that economic poverty is one of the most important factors pushing the rural people to move to the urban areas. But it is only ranked as the eighth, after cultural resources (the sixth) and the desire for urban life (the seventh). Only 86 persons out of 404 respondents (21.3%) indicated that poverty influenced their migration. The ninth most frequently mentioned category is to show skill or talent, and the tenth is change of office or occupation. The last two items are regarded neither as pushing nor pulling factors in our classification (〈Table 2〉).

This ranking order would be changed if a different scale were to be employed. For example, 〈Table 2〉 shows that the score of the category "Change of office or occupation" is larger than that of the category, "to show skill or talent." However, the number of those who indicated that the desire "to show skill or talent" had "greatly" influenced their decision of migration is less than the number of those who pointed "to some extent," while in the category of "change of office or occupation" the number of the respondents who indicated "greatly" is far bigger than the number who marked "to some extent." Therefore, if more weight is given to "greatly" than originally was, the category "change of office or occupation" may become a more influential factor than the category, "to show skill or talent." Generally speaking, however, the present ranking order seems to be relevant enough to show the extent to which the pushing or pulling factors are involved in the decision making for migration.

Reviewing 〈Table 2〉, the factors which influence the decision

Table 2. Extent to which Pushing or Pulling Factors Are Involved in Migration

	Not at all	Slightly	To some extent	Greatly	Do not know	Score	Ranking
Pushing factors							
1. Social turmoil	306	7	9	66	16	223	5
2. Poverty	304	27	25	34	14	179	8
3. Escape from traditional life	315	25	29	17	18	134	11
4. Family bankruptcy	369	2	4	13	16	49	13
5. Social class distinction	376	4	4	5	15	27	16
6. Natural disasters	378	1	4	5	16	24	17
7. Difficulty with employer	380	4	3	1	16	13	19
8. Superstitious prophecy	384	—	2	1	17	7	20
9. Epidemic	387	—	—	1	16	3	22
Pulling factors							
1. To find a job	212	17	24	134	17	467	1
2. Education	237	18	30	101	18	381	2
3. To establish a private business	256	16	21	98	13	352	3
4. Employment opportunity	279	17	28	63	17	262	4
5. Cultural resources	271	39	56	18	20	205	6
6. Desire for urban life	284	34	45	23	18	193	7
7. Personal relationships in city	321	18	28	19	18	131	12
8. Marriage	370	4	5	7	18	35	15
9. Anonymous refuge	375	2	5	3	19	21	18
Other factors							
1. To show skill or talent	322	4	31	29	18	153	9
2. Change of office or occupation	337	2	4	42	19	136	10
3. Military experience	370	2	6	8	18	38	14
4. Land reform	381	3	—	1	19	6	21

Note: Score = figure under "slightly" + figure under "to some extent" × 2 + figure under "greatly" × 3

making about migration "greatly" rather than "to some extent," are factors such as "social turmoil," "family bankruptcy," "looking for a job," "education," "establishing a private business," "employment opportunity," and "change of office or occupation." On the other hand, some other factors such as "escape from the traditional life," "personal relationships in city" and "to show skill or talent," are most often referred to as those influencing the decision to migrate "to some extent" rather than "greatly." Even the factor of poverty may be regarded as belonging to the latter group. It seems to the writer that the latter factors were not sufficient to cause immediate migration, although they might have been slowly persuading the potential migrants for a relatively long period of time of the need for a change. The former stimulated them to fully make their move.

The postulate that the pulling factors are more influential to the decision making of the migrants to Seoul than the pushing factors may not be applicable to the migrants to other cities in Korea. Let us take the migration to *Daegu* as one example.[4]

According to the migration data obtained from a sampling survey in *Daegu* city in 1969, 20.8 per cent (60) out of 289 respondents are people who have lived in *Daegu* for more than three generations, the remainder (73.3%: 212), except a few (5.9%: 17) who did not give relevant responses, are those who migrated to *Daegu*. 49.1 per cent of the total number of respondents came from other parts of the North-*Gyŏngsang* Province of which *Daegu* is the capital city, and 12.1 per cent came from South-*Gyŏngsang* Provinces. 139 (65.6%) out of the total group of migrants (212) say that they came directly from the rural areas.

The reason which was most frequently mentioned for migration is change of office or occupation (21.2%: 45). The second major reason is poverty (17%: 36); the third, looking for a job (10.8 %: 23); the fourth, education (9.9%: 21); the fifth, establishing a private business (9.4%: 20); the sixth, social turmoil(5.7 %: 12); the seventh, desire for urban life (4.7%: 10); the eighth, personal relationships with people living in *Daegu* (3.8 %: 8). Thus, economic poverty is indicated as the most important reason for migration to *Daegu* other than change of office or occupation, which is regarded as neither a pushing nor a pulling factor. This distribution in terms of reasons for migration is greatly different from that of Seoul.

One of the main reasons why the pulling factors, such as finding a job, are more influential in the decision to migrate to Seoul than the pushing factors may come from the fact that the migrants to Seoul are largely from other cities. As shown in the ⟨Table 3⟩, 56.2 per cent of the Seoul migrants originated in rural areas, and 31.2 per cent (126) were from the urban sectors. In other words, a considerable number of the migrants are originally urban people of long standing. If their living places just before the migration to Seoul are identified, we see that 48.0 per cent (194) of the migrants lived in other cities before the migration, while 40.6 per cent (164) came directly from rural settlements.

Table 3. Former Living Places of the Migrants

	Original Place		Place just before migration	
Rural area	227	56.2%	164	40.6%
Ŭb (town)	46	11.4	37	9.2
Urban area	126	31.2	194	48.0
Foreign country	3	0.7	9	2.2
No response	2	0.5	—	—
Total	404	100.0%	404	100.0%

Economic poverty seems to be related to the size of the communities from which the migrants came. It would seem that poverty is likely to influence migration from the rural sectors more than it does migration from urban areas, although the significance level

Table 4. Influence of Poverty on Migrants by Size of Communities from Which They Came

	No.	Yes	Don't know	Total
Rural area	110(67.1%)	46(28.0)	8(4.9)	164(100.0%)
Ŭb(town)	32(86.5%)	5(13.5)	— —	37(100.0%)
Urban area	154(79.4%)	35(18.0)	5(2.6)	194(100.0%)

of the correlation is not high (⟨Table 4⟩).

Seoul is not only the local center but also the national center, while other cities like *Daegu* function only as local centers. Seoul has the extraordinary proportion of wealth, means for business, cultural facilities, and power under the highly centralized government. No one can reasonably expect a comparatively better life style and occupational opportunity who decides to remain in other areas. Therefore, everybody may want to go up to Seoul, and once he lives in Seoul, he may not want to leave it. It is so attractive to many Koreans, not because it is ideal or comfortable, but probably because it may provide a better quality of life. However, it is not the place for everybody. Particularly the farmers, who lack education, money, skill and experience with modern social life, may not easily be able to approach the huge metropolis, except for those who live in the area surounding Seoul and have relatives or friends in the urbanized area. The migration to Seoul may be somewhat similar to the migration of some Koreans to the developed countries. They may attempt to go there, not because the Korean society has pushed them, but because the developed countries attract them.

[NOTES]

1) "The Pattern of Korean Urban Growth," *Rural Sociology*, Vol. 19, No. 1, 1954.
2) "A Study on the In-coming Population of Seoul," *Ingu-munje nonjib*, Vol. 3.

3) "The Analysis of the Concentration of Population on Cities and Its Problems," *Ingu-munje nonjib*, Vol. 1.
4) This is the baseline survey for understanding the sociological characteristics of *Daegu* City including migration. The basic methodology of the survey, particularly the sampling procedure, is very much similar to that of the preceding study of migration to Seoul. The migration problem in *Daegu* is to be reported on by Dr. Barringer, professor of Sociology at the University of Hawaii.

Socio-cultural Aspects of the Community Development Movement in Korea

Introduction

The Korean term *"jiyŏg-sahoe gaebal"* is the translation of the English phrase "community development." It seems rather difficult to define in a simple, distinct term what is meant by community. A common-sense interpretation is that a community means the district in which a group of people live together in a common environment. But a community means more than a social group of people having common ties with the land in which they live. Quite often it means a social group which has common interests not in the land on which it lives but in the mode of their collective life.

Some scholars interpret a community as a group of people living together in an area large enough to make their lives self-sufficient, whereas others hold the view that a community is a small group of families living in a locality—a village, for example.

The word community is used more in reference to a rural society than to an urban one. It is understandable because the collective nature of human lives is more evident in a rural society, and hence the human relationship is personal, comprehensive and lasting, much like a *Gemeinschaft*, while the human relationship in an urban society tends to be self-centered, unilateral and temporary. In this discourse, a community refers to a collective life in a single locality, and the discussion is confined to the rural community.

The fast-paced industrialization and urbanization of our society have given rise to a variety of complex urban problems. Moreover,

---

* Contributed to *Korea Journal*, January 1973.

further acceleration of modernization requires the development of rural communities which have long been steeped in tradition. Our concern for rural development grows greater in view of the widening gap between urban and rural areas, various aspects of which have impeded an integrated, balanced development of our country as a whole.

In a broad perspective, the community development movement in our country can be traced back to the distant past. But as far as this writer knows specifically, "*hyangyag*," rural community activities undertaken chiefly by *yangban*, a social class of nobility and gentry, during the Yi-dynasty were the beginnings of a distinctly organized community movement.

Next came a self-help, revitalizing movement organized and initiated during the Japanese colonial rule of this country. Though the movement had a dubious motivation since it was inspired and carried out forcibly by the Japanese colonialists, it can still be regarded as a kind of a community development. But more noteworthy is the fact that some of our patriotic people voluntarily initiated a rural movement to aid and enlighten our rural populace.

The liberation of our country from the colonial yoke has brought various rural movements. One of them is the 4-H Club movement. Although it was introduced from abroad, it has grown into a nationwide movement with the voluntary participation of rural youth. It may be hard to tell exactly what role the 4-H Club movement played in our rural development. However, if the movement has not produced significant results, it has at least given a highly valuable opportunity to our rural youth to discuss village development problems and seek answers for themselves over the past 20 years.

It was in 1958 that the rural movement began to be called community development in Korea. The first such project was undertaken by the then Ministry of Reconstruction assisted by the then Office of Economic Coordinator (OEC), a U.S. agency for economic assistance. In its initial stage, the government set up a central committee for community development which in turn trained cadres who were to engage in field projects. In the first year, the committee set up model sites in *Ulsan* County of South *Gyŏngsang* Province, *Yŏn-gi* County of South *Chung-chŏng* Province, *Gwang-ju* County of *Gyŏng-gi* Province, and *Jeju-do*, where the cadres, villagers and village leaders embarked on development work. The movement began losing much of its initial drive with the downfall of the government of the Liberal Party and declined further in scale as the succeeding government of the Democratic Party launched a national construction scheme.

Finally, this version of the community development project petered out with the dissolution of the central committee for community development following the May 16, Military Revolution in 1961. Instead, the government carried on the national construction work with emphasis on physical construction. At the same time, the government introduced a nationwide popular campaign for spiritual, ethical and socio-cultural enlightenment through the National Movement Headquarters. These movements, of course, covered the rural regions, but they did not necessarily emphasiz the rural aspects.

Among the rural movements which the government did conduct, one can cite the development projects undertaken through the agricultural cooperatives and the campaign to establish sisterhoods between urban communities and rural villages.

In this year the government began to push the *Saemaŭl* (New Village) Movement on a national scale. It is the first time in our history that the chief executive of our country, with such zeal and deep concern, assumed direct leadership in a rural movement. This dynamic movement, as in any other similar movements which involve human judgments, cannot be entirely free from trials and errors and unexpected side effects. Nevertheless, all agree on the acute need for a resolute rural campaign since the country is beset with grave ethical, economic and social problems bred by the urban-rural gap. This makes the basic significance of such a rural scheme as the *Saemaŭl* Movement indisputable.

My discussion here is not about the *Saemaŭl* Movement *per se*. Yet this doesn't mean that my treatment of the subject is simply a theoretical discussion about the social and cultural aspects of community development without regard to the present reality and circumstances. My interest lies in what I consider as important and urgent needs in social and cultural aspects for rural development, be it the *Saemaŭl* Movement or any other form of community development movement.

Causes of Poverty

To understand why Korea's rural regions are poverty-ridden, it is appropriate to study the structural characteristics of its rural society in light of the process of their changes in historical perspective, for the rural poverty originated in the social structure of the Yi-dynasty.

No doubt, the society during the Yi-dynasty was a highly centralized one dominated by the *yangban* bureaucrats. Their attitude toward human relationships was authoritarian. Largely oriented by a Confucian value system that paid attention to propriety and order in society, not to production and progress, the ruling *yangban* class placed prime emphasis on office holding and personal status. A high official position was the source of fortune and authority.

The limited number of such high posts, naturally caused a heated, often bloody, competition in which many attempted to gain the posts with payoffs and graft. They used all their energies in political infighting and, the welfare of the people living in their communities was out of their concern.

Unlike Europe or Japan, where hostile political groups lived in close confrontation with one another, Korea during the Yi-dynasty was subordinate to China and managed to overcome crises with Chinese support. Consequently, the *yangban* officialdom of the Yi-dynasty did not feel the need as seriously as it should to explore ways to enhance legal protection and advance technical skills in order to increase production. Instead, they were absorbed in attaining high official positions and exploiting and extorting the rural people in order to amass fortunes to back up their status.

Under the circumstances, the agricultural populace, the main force for production, was forced to undergo severe economic and social repression imposed by the officialdom on the one hand and the rural *yangban* class on the other. The economic plight of farmers worsened after the middle period of the Yi-dynasty as the nonproductive *yangban* populace increased, while the number of *sangmin*, the common persons, diminished remarkably. One historical record shows that a considerable number of farmers were saddled with enormous amounts of debt to their land owners at the latter part of the Yi-dynasty.

Not only were they poor, but they were also illiterate. The official language used during the Yi-dynasty was *hanmun*, literary Chinese, which was too recondite for farmers to learn. Moreover, they had no need to learn it because they had no opportunity to use it, living a simple life in the shade of society. Since the ruling *yangban* class virtually monopolized Confucianism and other ideological or technological knowledge for which *hanmun* was the sole means of linguistic expression, there was no need for the common people to learn the language.

Most of our farmers could not learn *hanmun* nor were they able to learn even *hangŭl*, the Korean writing system. Therefore, they lacked a major means of communication with which they could obtain information about what was going on in their society. They had no means with which they could train themselves in making adequate judgments on things or in preparing for changes that were forthcoming.

The social organizations with which our farmers were affiliated were chiefly their families and villages. They had no access to social activities that were larger in scale than such limited organizations. The families of the common people, being economically subordinated to the officialdom and the *yangban* land owners, seldom had a base for independence.

Families in the Yi-dynasty society were understood to have been thoroughly soaked in Confucian ethics. This applies only to the families of the ruling *yangban* class. It is doubtful that the families of the common people were regulated by Confucian ethics as strictly as in the case of the *yangban* families.

Not a few people hold the view that the organizational form of the rural villages during the Yi-dynasty resembled that of a community. One can hardly deny that farmers who were *sangmin* had community organizations within their villages for irrigation, transplanting, cooperation in agricultural production, rituals, recreation and operation of *gye*, a kind of mutual fund, for weddings, funerals and traditional celebration of the 60th birthday anniversary.

In my view, however, such communal activities were insignificant and small in scale as they were conducted under the oppressive yoke of the ruling class which held both power and fortune. The situation did not improve much under the Japanese colonial rule. The abolition of social discrimination and the ensuing social and geographical mobility of the land-based *sangmin* brought about a favorable turn for farmers in general. Doubtless, farmers were freed from the arbitrary exploitation and repression of the *yangban* land-owners who acted as if there were no law. That farmers were assured of security, minimal though it may have been, though it was mainly intended for colonial exploitation, must have provided some relief for them.

Also a boon to the farming populace was the fact that educational opportunities began to appear, while improved farming techniques were introduced, and health and sanitation facilities were more or less renovated.

But economically, the nation as a whole suffered hardship because of the Japanese colonial policy; and the fate of our farmers, a majority of whom were tenants or destitute small-scale owner-operators, became even worse. With the passage of time, an increasing number of farmers became small-scale owner-operators, and small-scale farmers became tenants. As this tendency of social degradation increased, the worsening hardship forced many rural people to break up their families and seek new means of survival.

The Japanese colonial government regarded the farming populace as the main source of their exploitation, and naturally they did not grant farmers freedom of political and social activity, much less any chance to make a collective movement to protect their rights and promote their interests. If they allowed any such movement, they limited it to a minimum and kept it under government guidance or surveillance.

The Japanese colonialists were somewhat more generous to the Korean land owners, but never to the tenant farmers or owner-operators. There was a time when tenant farmers frequently raised disputes, relying on a liberal social climate. But such disputes were constantly suppressed and were totally ruled out toward the end of the Japanese colonial rule.

For a time, the Japanese colonial government had encouraged a self-help revitalizing campaign in farming villages, stressing diligence and savings. But the real intention was to increase output of food grains which the Japanese acutely needed, broaden the base for effective exploitation and make better use of Korea as the logistical depot for the Japanese inroad into the Chinese continent.

It was ridiculous to enforce such a campaign on our farmers who were already deeply debt-ridden and continuously exploited.

Material and economic pressure aside, it was too much to call for self-help and revitalization of the farmers whose traditionally Confucian sense of value demanded absolute obedience of the strong by the weak.

Changes in Rural Society after the Liberation

Korea's rural society underwent many changes after the liberation of the country. The most important one, needless to say, was the land reform. However, it seems that many economists discount the value of the land reform. Some voice the extreme view that the reform was a failure. More people assert that the reform had many defects in it.

One can hardly deny that there were many shortcomings in the land reform from the economic point of view. But from the sociological standpoint, one sees definitely positive aspects.

For one thing, the reform freed many farmers from the exploitation of the land owners. There still are a number of tenant farmers in our rural villages. But so many tenant farmers have been elevated to owner-operators that this represents a truly significant change. Our farmers became far more self-reliant economically than ever before and now enjoy fairly equal economic status. A considerable number of them can look to a better future.

Secondly, the educational level of our farmers has remarkably improved. Many thoughtful Koreans, from the period of the late Yi-dynasty through the days after the Japanese colonial government, observed that the illiteracy of our farmers was the chief cause of their poverty and noted the importance of education as a means to help them overcome their economic difficulty.

As a result, there were consistent and strenuous campaigns led by such considerate persons to enlighten and educate the rural populace. Such efforts intensified with the adoption of a compulsory educational system after the liberation. The rate of illiteracy declined sharply. In 1958, this writer made a survey of several rural villages which showed that more than 80 per cent of those aged 40 or older who responded to the survey had no schooling at all. A similar survey of the same villages made in 1969 showed that over 50 per cent of those in the same age bracket had received primary school education.

Formerly, a village meeting held to discuss rural problems would be characterized by traditional ways of thinking. Now, a majority of participants in such a meeting will be those who possess modern ideas and a sense of self-assertion.

Thirdly, the propagation of mass communication media has greatly increased in the rural regions. According to the same 1958 survey, only a few people in the villages, 14.9 per cent of the total had access to radio. Those few radios were of a primitive type. Today, more than 80 per cent of the households in the area have radios.

This increased availability of mass communication media may stimulate a propensity among the rural populace for luxury and wasteful spending. But it enables rural residents to keep abreast of external developments; it helps them develop critical views of their problems; and it makes changes in their attitudes and sense of values. At the same time, it increases the time of family get-together for recreation, which in turn reduces a tendency of village men to engage in gambling or other unsavory pastimes.

Radios thus bring family members together at their homes and give them more time for conversation, especially between man and wife, which contributes to developing a rational home life. Also significant is that radios provide farm children with a new form of amusement and indirectly help them foster a positive attitude toward the nuclear family.

Fourthly, the social status of the female population has improved, marking yet another significant change. This phenomenon is particularly evident in those rural communities which are close to cities. The improved educational standard of rural women and the cultural influence which they receive through mass communications media or directly from their adjacent cities are responsible. But no less responsible is the increased opportunity for them to participate in economic activities such as vegetable cultivation which gives them a bigger voice in handling household problems.

Men, holding a strong reverence for their ancestors and a deep interest in their family leadership, are more or less oriented toward tradition. Women, whose chief concern is the welfare of their husband and children, to whom they are deeply attached, seem to be future-oriented, with an eye on material improvement for their families. They often reprove their husbands for inertia and waste, saying that they do so because they care about the happiness of their children. Despite the often decried urban-rural gap, the clothes worn by the pupils of an average primary school in the rural area today are about the same in quality as those worn by their counterparts in the urban areas. This is highly indicative of the strong attachment of women to their children and the growing power of women.

Fifth are the political changes in the rural communities. There are many aspects to such changes. The numerous elections exposed the rural people to a considerable amount of political experience. Their political consciousness must, therefore, have gradually increased. Also through their frequent contacts with government organizations and through the government instructions and supervision they received, the *ri* chiefs have changed their social characteristics and roles. Their influence as the old-style local dignitaries seems to have diminished.

The village-centered unity of the rural people, as promoted by the government, is believed to have reduced the influence of the previously bureaucracy-centered setup in the social life of the village. Most of the public officials at the *myŏn* level come from the same communities in which they have long lived and they have been influenced by democratic notions. This is likely to decrease their proclivity to fear the government. At any rate, it is easy to see changes that have taken place in the farmers' political awareness and behavior since the liberation.

Sixthly, there has been a notable migration of the rural populace into cities. The rural population has sharply increased since the latter part of the Yi-dynasty. However, the farm lands, the primary means of rural living, were limited and there were no other tangible means of making a living. Nor were there easy opportunities to move into cities and settle down. The resultant population pressure in the farming regions added increasingly to the rural poverty.

But as industrialization proceeded at an acceleratig pace in the past decade or so, cities began to exert a magnetic power to draw the rural population. Hence, a massive influx of population into the cities started like a rising tide. Some of those rural people who moved into the urban areas were capable of making a living as they had job experiences or vocational skills. Others may have had enough financial capability to build new lives. Yet there were a sizable number of poor people who were seeking to do whatever odd jobs they could find through their families or other connections. A good many farm youths left their homes and family members.

The migration into cities of the surplus rural population, especially the poor people, greatly relieved the rural communities of the economic pressure. As a result, such shameful terms as "the spring lean season" or "the foodless farmer," which were heard almost annually, have now disappeard. But the movement into cities of rural youths has created a manpower shortage in the farming communities.

Speaking of the human migration from villages into cities, it must be noted that geographical movement of farmers has become far easier than before. There are two reasons for that. One is that they are readily bent for such migration because of the experience they acquired in the Korean War or in their military service and the cultural stimulus they received from the cities. The other is the vast improvement of highways and transportation facilities. The door for such movement is now open not only to adults but also to youth and women.

There are other changes that are taking place in the rural communities, but it is impossible to enumerate all of them in this limited space. So, lastly, mention must be made of the psychological impact on farmers of the changes that are afoot outside of their own communities. In fact, the changes which the rural communities have undergone so far were not inspired by the communities themselves but were motivated or forced externally. The government influence is especially great. But there are many cases in which farmers themselves witnessed or experienced the changes through their direct or indirect contact with external society.

They are aware of the fact that high-rise buildings and apartments are being built in cities, that a modern expressway was constructed between *Seoul* and *Busan*, and that roads are teeming with automobiles of various types. Furthermore, they see increasing opportunities to meet with city dwellers who visit the rural communities for real estate investment and other enterprises, election campaigns, angling, hunting or other recreational activities. Thus they are bound to find themselves caught in the midst of changes and recognize the inevitable need to adapt themselves to the changes.

Problems in Community Development

We have reviewed changes that have taken place in rural communities since the 1945 liberation. Such changes were necessary for the development of rural communities. Despite such changes, however, the development of rural communities cannot be taken as an easy task to achieve.

The majority of farmers, who were not economically independent, were unable to accumulate capital for increased production. This is due to the fact that the reform in agriculture failed in removing poor peasants.

It was difficult for an average farmer to make a living by cultivating an average of less than 1 *jŏngbo* (2.45 acres) of arable land. Besides, farmers lost productive incentives because of the low grain price policy that has in effect until just recently.

Stagnation in agricultural productivity was also attributable to poor irrigation facilities and poor agricultural technology.

A great weakness of farmers was their traditional outlook. Although changes took place in their values during the past 10 years some traditional thinking still persists. All the traditional values, however, need not necessarily be eradicated in the course of modernization. Most advanced countries actually did not eradicate conservative elements in the course of their modernization. But to achieve efficiency in production and welfare, it is necessary, to some extent, to secure rational thinking, reform in technology, belief in science, a spirit of independence and equality, and systematic cooperation through which to achieve a common goal.

There are many farm villages in which a common clan predominates. Farmers of a common clan are proud of their clan and practice combined ancestor worship. Ancestor worship itself is not detrimental to modernization, but it is possible that such a conservative element may do harm in the development of democratic political activities and in the attainment of a common economic goal.

A traditional value in our farm villages is the family-centered life style. In advanced countries, the concept is somewhat prevalent among farmers but weak among city people. In Korea, such a concept is popular even among city people. The family-centered life style in our rural communities derives from the fact that

Korean farmers engaged in small-scale farming by family units and that they were under the influence of Confucianism. This family-centered life style adheres to family-centered management and makes it difficult to attain an organic unity in the economic and social activities of farmers.

As in most underdeveloped countries, important material resources in Korea are monopolized by the government which wields great power. The development of a community, therefore, is dependent upon the support of the government. The government has laid emphasis on the development of industries, and agriculture was not considered important in the first and second economic development plans. As a result, there was considerable development in industry while agriculture remained stagnant. The gap between the two became greater because newly-developed industries were not related to the development of agriculture.

But the government authorities did not neglect agriculture. The government's investment in agriculture was considerable. Unfortunately, the government's support was not suitable to realistic conditions of farming communities. For example, the government encouraged the production of sweet potatoes and mushrooms, and the raising of rabbits and pigs. But their prices actually dropped as farmers were unable to find adequate demand. This resulted in the farmers' loss of confidence in the government.

Korean farmers today are no longer illiterate. Nor are they unable to adopt new technologies or incapable of productive incentive. They merely lack capital for new projects and systematic foundations and experiences for market exploition. So far as they can secure enough capital and markets, they will be able to actively produce farming products.

The fourth problem relating to rural community development is the weakness of self-directed organizations. According to an American rural sociologist, community development is a series of activities to achieve economic development through community organizations (In this connection, the writer had an opportunity to discuss the problem, under the title of "Problems of Community Development," as part of a symposium dealing with community development activities of 1958, and the discussion was published in *Jaejŏng* (finance), December 1958, pp. 68-79). In other words, the most important thing for community development is community organizations.

The rural communities in Korea do not seem to have any community organizations which can expedite economic development. Most of the organizations the rural community has are the so-called *gye*. a private mutual financing organization, related mostly to ceremonial occasions such as marriage and funeral, but not to economic development activities. In addition, there are so-called *jonghoe* (family councils) in the rural community which are not related to any economic activities but rather impede the unity of the rural community as a whole.

Other social and political organizations are also penetrating the community but they are literally paper organizations which do not perform any economic functions in the community. If there are any economic organizations, they must be the mutual financing organization for water irrigation, the water irrgation union, the mutual financng organization for forest protection, and the agricultural cooperative union.

Why then have self-directed economic organizations not existed in the rural community? Two reasons can be advanced. First, the rural community has not been self-supporting spiritually and materially; secondly, they were under continuous government suppression to a great extent. Even the farm-land reform has not been materialized by the farmers themselves, stimulated by their internal circumstances, but imposed upon them by the government. In other words, they have never been given the chance to do self-directed activities for their community.

Since they have been too long under government control,

they entertain the tendency to distrust the government, although superficially they behave obediently. Quite recently, another unfavorable tendency has been created in the minds of the farmers: high dependency on the government. Such a tendency was caused by the government's recent favors given to the farmers.

The government's careless interference with the activities of the farmers has produced a sense of discouragement in the farmers as well as in their farming leaders. As a result, the farmers have been driven out, intentionally or unintentionally, from markets where they usually compete for better products.

The agricultural cooperative union is the most well-organized economic organization in the rural community these days. The agricultural cooperative union is, in a sense, a government-controlled organization and therefore is not a pure farmers' organization which can contribute to the improvement of their economic activities. In the union, orders usually are given by the government, not farmers, and its employees are selected and sent to the community by the government.

Another weakness the rural community has in its organization is the fact that all of the community activities are undertaken by the units of *dong* and *ri*, the two smallest administrative units in Korea, directly connected to the *myŏn* office. The community activities implemented at *dong* and *ri* levels are not appropriate for modern economic development because their scale is too small. When community activities are connected in broader units, such as cities, they can be implemented more effectively for the economic development of the community. The broader units do not necessarily mean the *myŏn* level. Rather they must include market-connected communities. In this sense, it is highly noticeable that the agricultural cooperative unions which formerly operated at the *dong-ri* level expanded their activities to a wider base a few years ago.

Conclusion

According to a survey made by the author, the living standard of the farmers has risen considerably compared with that 10 years ago. The reasons are four-fold: first, many poor rural people have left the community; secondly, they have been enlightened to some extent; thirdly, they have received various social, cultural, and economic stimuli from cities; and finally, the government's policy has been directed to some extent to improve the living standard of the rural community. In a word, the improvement of their living standard has not been achieved by the farmers themselves but influenced by external forces such as the government.

In this process, some self-improving abilities have been accumulated in the rural community, and the individual farmer's capabilities have improved significantly. We can expect the rural community, therefore, to lay a firm foundation for its own development, sustaining its dynamic connections with industry. Some appropriate measures might include:

(1) Economic projects have to be planned according to the conditions and circumstances of the rural community. The projects then must take into consideration three things: priority between agriculture and industry, financial support and technical guidance for production, and guarantee of product price and market ability.

(2) The government must avoid its direct and close guidance and supervision of the farmers and act only as a patron in order to build up the spirit of self-support and self-help among the farmers in order to allow then to solve their problems by themselves.

(3) The government must encourage the agricultural community to form many self-directing organizations. The Agricultural Cooperative Unions have to be changed so as to be organized and operated by the farmers themselves. The small village-based projects have to be expanded to wider community based ones. The

government has to find and educate many capable farm leaders and include women in the thus far men-centered projects.

It is very unpredictable what kind of results the current *Saemaŭl* Movement will bring about in the future since there has never been as strong an agricultural community movement as the current one. If this historic *Saemaŭl* Movement maintains its pace and corrects the many problems created in the process of trial and error, it is expected that the Movement will contribute to changing the rural community and constructing a modern rural community in Korea.

In conclusion, the current *Saemaŭl* Movement must include in its projects not only economic development but also the establishment of a new moral and value system as its ultimate goal.

As revealed in the author's survey findings, the farmers said that although their living standard has improved considerably, their moral fibre, such as relations between parents and children, husband and wife, and the young and the old have deteriorated to a great extent. Perhaps their judgments may be related to their old traditional value system based on the Confucian thoughts. If that is the case, their judgments are wrong.

If we believe that the construction of a new society must be based on new values, it seems needless to say that the current *Saemaŭl* Movement has to be connected directly with the construction of new values in the society.

Urbanization and Rural Development

Introduction

Water flows down from higher ground. Likewise, if there are too many people, to the extent that no means of living are available for them, or they have difficulty, they have to go somewhere else for immediate survival or a better living. This phenomenon happens in many countries which are in the initial stage of industrialization, and which have developed improved medical care resulting in a drastic increase of population. The developed countries had it in the last century or early in this century, and developing countries have had it recently.

Mass migration of rural people to the cities does not seem to have been positively accepted. The over-population in the cities brought many serious problems such as the emergence of shanty areas, unemployment, delinquent behavior, shortage of educational facilities, difficulty in transportation, water supply, and disposal of sewage, and so on.

Some criticize the inability of the city government but they are disregarding the difficulties the city really faces. First of all it has serious financial limitations. There are many poor citizens who pay no income tax at all, while expecitng to be treated equally with others.

Secondly, some people may disturb or interfere with the administration of the cities. Men in power, such as legislators, may exert unreasonable pressure, and some others may bribe the government officials in order to get special favors.

---

* Keynote speech presented at "The 4th Asian Pacific Social Development Seminar" in Seoul organized by the Cultural and Social Centre for the Asian and Pacific Region in 1978.

This is likely to cause disappointment to young intellectuals who are strongly concerned with national development as well as progress in social justice. Consequently, intensification of political instability may be worrisome, although the urbanization itself does not seem to cause serious political problems as used to be felt.

So far many countries have made energetic efforts in order to control over-population; one method is to control fertility through family planning programs, and another is to create jobs through industrial development. Governments often try to discourage the outmigration from the rural areas and sometimes even attempt to send them back to their original areas; this can hardly be successful and may not be beneficial for personal or national development. The increase of poverty in the rural areas caused by over-population without outlet may be a more serious cause for political instability.

Favorable Aspects of Urbanization

In spite of the deep-rooted notion unfavorable to the outmigration of farmers, which derives from the selfishness of urban dwellers, sentimentalism of the romantic idealists, or practical anxiety of responsible administrators, the moving out of the excess population from rural villages seems to be conducive to rural development.

Among other things, it obviously decreases the economic burden of the rural communities. Moreover, looking at the migration in Korea, those who left their villages for cities during the past one or two decades are more likely to be found either among the well-to-do or the poor people rather than the middle class. This has intensified the homogeneousness of the rural people in terms of their economic standing as well as their social consciousness which had been already improved to some extent by the land reform and compulsory education.

It is very important that people in a community are homogeneous in their economic capacity and mentality to promote the cooperative activities for betterment. If the people are heterogeneous in their knowledge and way of thinking, particularly values, effective communication is hardly achieved among the villagers, or between the leaders and the lay villagers. Consequently, it is rather difficult for them to recognize the nature of their common problems and reach a decision to solve them. Now most of the Korean rural people who are of the age to be active in economic endeavour have completed elemental education, and therefore they do not basically have any serious difficulty in communication and introduction of new knowledge and technology.

Economic heterogeneity is another important factor to impede cooperative efforts among the villagers. In the process of the *Saemaŭl* Movement in Korea, complaints have been more frequent and stronger both from the rich and the poor people rather than from those in the middle. The rich say that they are asked to donate land or money for widening or constructing roads or some development project without reasonable compensation, ignoring or devaluating more benefits they might obtain. On the other hand, the poor complain that they are asked to work free too often. Their voices of complaint are usually weaker than those of the rich, but their situation is more serious because the frequent time away from their regular job may threaten their survival.

The rural people of course recognize the necessity of any cooperative movement, as the governmental officials and intellectuals do, but because of diversity in the extent of their contributions to, and of the expected benefits from the cooperative projects, they cannot put them into practice. However, the out-migration of the rural people has decreased their heterogeneity.

The tentative migration of the individual persons to cities is also conducive to rural development. They earn money in the cities and may give some economic assistance to their families left behind. If they are boys or girls who cannot be of great help to the increase of family income through farming or other activities, then their moving out to cities may at least decrease the economic burden of their family. And also they bring new ideas to their families and help them change their traditional attitudes.

The increase of urban population results in the increasing demand for agricultural products in the urban markets, and this stimulates the farmers to produce more cash crops, or stimulates the women, who have someone who can take care of home affairs during their absence such as a daughter-in-law or grown daughter, to make money as pedlars.

If urbanization is taking place along with industrial development, which seems usually to come in a later stage of developing countries, the farmers may develop new devices in order to supply high-priced vegetables or fruit which were available only in particular limited seasons. At this stage agricultural mechanization is recognized as necessary because of labor shortage. And also the improvement of an infrastructure such as more convenient transportation facilties becomes significant for a closer relationship with markets, administrative agents, and other areas includings educational institutions.

The improvement of an infrastructure in the rural communities may be carried out by three approaches: one is individual efforts of the villagers; the second is by the cooperative efforts of the villagers as a group; the third is by the government. Needless to say, they are in fact all essential and should be combined in a proper way according to given conditions in and out of a community. Among these three approaches, however, the second would be the most important, because it is efficient and economical, and because it improves their ability to solve their own problems through *esprit de corps* on the basis of democratic principles. But this needs not only what were described above, both mental and economic homogeneity, but also financial ability to the extent that they can invest money for further development.

It can be said that the *Saemaŭl* Movement was launched when the Korean farmers were anxious to improve their infrastructure, and ready to invest money and cooperative effort to some degree, and yet the conditions were not fully met. In the late 1960s when the second five-year economic development plan was about over, many voices were often heard about the rural urban gap. The gap between the rural and urban areas, which might be largely economic, might be widening, and industrialization which was taking place in or around the urban areas might look to bring disastrous problems to the rural areas. Looking back at the situation, however, it does not seem to have been as serious as it has been worried about. The prosperity in cities caused by the industrial development has decreased the economic burden of the rural people by pulling out excessive population, and also has brought some money and other benefits to the rural areas. In addition, the psychological impact of industrial development imposed on the rural people must not be ignored.

Unfavorable Aspects of Urbanization

Urbanization, of course, has brought some undesirable results in both the short and the long run. First of all, the rushing out of young people from the villages results in drastic labor shortages. Consequently, the wage of agricultural labor has risen sharply and farm products have become expensive. Unless administrative treatments such as the agricultural mechanization program and the price adjustment of agricultural products are provided adequately and effectively, productivity will drop. Moreover, the prevailing feeling that only incompetent youngsters remain discourages them from working hard at farming.

Secondly, urbanization inevitably disseminates urban values to the rural people. What was distinctively observed in the Korean rural society during the past several decades is that people were eager to have a radio set. There is no question about the great benefits mass communication brings to the rural people. They are able to learn quickly what is happening outside, new ideas, and technological things. Moreover they can have enjoyment. Through more frequent contacts with mass communications, however, the rural people, particularly the younger generation, more or less change their traditional values, and this brings psychological and social conflicts or maladjustment among the people.

In one survey, the Korean farmers said that while the material aspects of the rural life were becoming greatly improved, the moral aspects were getting worse. It seems more serious in the areas where new towns are suddenly emerging because of industrial or other projects on a large scale. A similar phenomenon occurs where rural areas are absorbed rapidly into the fringes of newly developed cities.

It is often suggested that another undesirable effect of mass communication on the rural society, although it applies to the urban society as well, is stimulation of their desire for consumption goods beyond their economic capacity. It seems, however, that little evidence to support this hypothesis is available. Even if they are stimulated to buy more, it may still be uncertain whether that brings better or worse economic effects for their future development.

The third undesirable aspect of urbanization with regard to rural development is the maladjustment of the individual rural migrants to city life. Keen academic as well as practical attention has been paid to the delinquent behavior or maladjustment of the teenagers in the cities at large, but there seems to be little study focused on how those individuals from the rural areas adjust to the urban setting without proper guidance and protection, and how these problems are related to the anxiety of their parents and the integration of their family life.

This socio-psychological aspect is usually overlooked, partly because it is rather invisible, while material aspects show very distinct and shocking appearances, and partly because many people, native or foreigner, academicians or practitioners, who are strongly concerned with urbanization problems in the developing countries, are largely from either political or economic fields.

More Varieties in Views

So far the writer has discussed both the favorable and unfavorable aspects of urbanization bearing on rural development, which he thinks would be generally observed in the developing countries of Asia, though they are largely based on the Korean experience.

The characteristics of urbanization in modern social settings in most Asian countries are greatly different from those in many Western countries. In Western countries the development of modern cities has gone on parallel with industrial development, and people there could be relatively free from the strict political control of governments. But these characteristics can rarely be observed in many developing countries of Asia. Therefore what is found in the urbanization of the Western countries may not be relevant for Asian countries.

And also what is found in one Asian country may not necessarily be the case in other countries. Some countries were colonized by the Western powers for a long period of time, but some others were not. Some countries have ethnic varieties, while some others do not. Some countries have religious elements which might impede the family planning practice or economic development, while some others have cultural elements to encourage striving and progress.

Korea has some unique characteristics in her historical background, geopolitical setting, and socio-cultural context. She is the only country, except Taiwan, that was colonized by her oriental neighbor, not by a Western power. She was in extreme social confusion because of first, the sudden withdrawal of the colonial force and then, the Korean War. And also she is very homogeneous in terms of ethnic and cultural background. Therefore, what is observed in her urbanization process may not necessarily happen to other Asian countries.

Even in Korea, the urbanization process has very diverse and complicated facets. Its social implication in one community at one stage of social development may be changing at a later stage. During the 1950s and 60s urbanization seemed to be interpreted as caused by the economic destruction in the rural area. As rural development has been taking place recently, the discussion of urbanization has been focused on pollution, traffic difficulty, and the horrible confusion which is expected to occur with the possible invasion from the North; and the frequency of referring to rural problems seems to have decreased. And the present public concern with urbanization and rural development is to prevent over concentration of population in Seoul and to accelerate industrialization in the villages or rural communities.

Conclusion

Looking at the population and economic trends in Asia, the massive out-migration of the rural people is obviously inevitable, whether it is desirable or not either from the government or individual point of view. And it may be even necessary for decreasing the economic burden of the rural people, unless there are some developmental programs to absorb the excessive population within the rural communities. And the over concentration of population in large metropolitan areas could be the cause of disasters, although it may not necessarily cause serious political instability as it as formerly believed. Therefore it seems to be quite indispensable for the government to take strong and effective action for controlling the population increase on the one hand and for accomplishing industrialization on the other.

As far as the Korean case is concerned, the massive out-migration of the rural people seems to have brought more positive effects to rural development than negative. However, it is not certain whether it brings the same result in other countries where the social, cultural, or other characteristics are different from Korea.

At any rate, water flows and has to flow. If we want to control it and make use of it effectively, we have to know the nature of water and other environmental characteristics related to it.

Participation in the Saemaŭl Movement

Introduction

Saemaŭl Undong[1] is the nationwide community development movement in Korea which offically started in 1971 after a one-year experiment. 1971 was the year when the second five-year economic development plan terminated. A large-scale industrialization was taking place at that time as a result of the two economic plans. In this process of industrialization, the gap between the rural and urban sectors in terms of economic standing seemingly became distinct and the rural population was more rapidly flowing into cities. Consequently a voice for a balanced development between the two sectors was often heard. It was in this climate that the *Saemaŭl* Movement was first launched.

The *Saemaŭl* Movement was initiated by President Park, and has been planned and practiced under his dynamic leadership. The song for the *Saemaŭl* Movement is said to have been versified and composed by the President himself. He seems to be well informed of on-going *Saemaŭl* projects, pays keen attention to them, and gives important directions. He attends the annual convention of *Saemaŭl* leaders, which is usually held after the harvest and before the leisure season for the farmers, listens to farmers' speeches about their successful developmental activities, awards medals and citations to the successful *Saemaŭl* contributors, and gives an address which invariably includes his evaluations, targets, strategies and tactics, and future perspectives of the Movement.

During the first year of the *Saemaŭl* Movement, the government provided each rural village with 335 sacks of cement in order to let the villagers improve their environment in the slack season.

* This paper was prepared for a work shop arranged by ESCAP in 1978.

What they were encouraged to do with them was the establishment or widening of local roads and bridges, the construction of small irrigation and flood control projects, storage tanks for compost, meeting halls, and so on. In the second year, the government provided 500 sacks of cement and one ton of steel reinforcing rods. This time only villages which had made the best use of the supplies during the previous year were favored. Later the government classified the villages into three categories: basic, self reliant, and independent, and converted its policy by favoring less successful villages, thus leveling up the under-developed villages. At the same time the kinds of projects have been increased and diversified.

Up to 1976, the total amount of investment for *Saemaŭl* projects in the rural sector is estimated to have been 893 billion *won* (approximately 1 billion and 786 million U.S. dollars), of which about 44 per cent was covered by the government, and the rest by villagers themselves. The principal investment of the villagers of course, was their labor. This investment included large scale projects which involved two or more villages. If these inter-village projects had not been put into practice, what the villages had to contribute would have been five times as much as the government's subsidy.

The *Saemaŭl* Movement has indeed been a real success. This writer once carried out a comparative study of *Saemaŭl* in four villages.[2] Each two villages are located in the same area with similar characteristics in terms of population size and distance to main road or community center, but one village is more successful in the Movement, and another less. In this study he asked the heads of village households to what extent their economic situation had been improved compared to 1971. To this question, about 40 to 55 per cent of the respondents replied that it had been 'greatly improved', and 25 to 43 per cent said 'a little improved.' And they indicated *Saemaŭl* Movement was one of the most important causes, along with the introduction of new kinds of rice and the government policy to guarantee a reasonably high price of rice.

Important affairs concerning *Saemaŭl* are regularly reported to the President at the cabinet meeting. The Minister of Home Affairs, the responsible minister, presides over the Central Committee of *Saemaŭl* which is composed of the vice ministers of the related ministries and the heads of other organizations such as the Office of Rural Development and the Agricultural Cooperatives. A similar committee exists in local governments both on the provincial and city-county levels; *ŭb* (county seat) and *myŏn*(the lowest administrative district which is composed of about twenty villages) each have a Committee Promoting the *Saemaŭl* Movement.

Each village has its own Development Committee which consists of 5-15 members. These had been established before *Saemaŭl* started. Basic plans of development for a village are formulated by this committee, but the final decision of the important projects is made in the general assembly of the residents. What the general assembly does concerning *Saemaŭl* is as follows:

(1) Formulation of long term *Saemaŭl* development projects and evaluation of their results.
(2) Formulation of *Saemaŭl* projects and evaluation of their results.
(3) Arranging the acquisition, maintenance, and disposition of *Saemaŭl* common properties.
(4) Enactment of *Saemaŭl* regulations and their amendment.
(5) Election of *Saemaŭl* leaders.
(6) Other affairs concerning the common welfare of the residents.

The real responsible persons to execute the projects, however, are the *Saemaŭl* leaders. Each village has one male and one female *Saemaŭl* leader. The male *Saemaŭl* leader usually works with the *ri* (village) chief who represents the village, administratively though not a government official. The female *Saemaŭl* leader has equal status with male *Saemaŭl* leader, but she is usually less active than her male counterpart. A *Saemaŭl* leader is elected by the villagers. The desired qualifications for a *Saemaŭl* leader are as follows:

(1) Hopefully a native.
(2) One with strong interest in and aspiration for a rural development.
(3) One with agricultural education.
(4) One of good understanding, patience, sympathy and cooperative attitude.
(5) One creative in his thinking and respectful of others' opinions.
(6) One of devotion.
(7) Healthy and diligent person.
(8) One who financially independent.

No salary is paid to a *Saemaŭl* leader, but he has special privileges:

(1) An identification card is issued to him and he can use *Saemaŭl* postcards for raising questions or making recommendations to the appropriate agents.
(2) He has the highest priority in obtaining a loan for farming.
(3) He is entitled to discounted fares on train, boat, and so on, when he makes a trip in his official capacity.
(4) His children are favored in their applications for scholarships.
(5) He can be favored for employment by a government organization.

Conventional Way of Participation

Korean farmers made communal efforts in order to improve their life, or to remove or decrease various kinds of threat in the past, and they are still practicing many of them even now.

One example of these communal efforts is the religious one. To avoid disasters which were thought to be caused by the possible anger of demons or other supernatural beings, they have practiced certain religious ceremonies on a communal basis.

The second type of communal effort in the traditional rural community is for agricultural production. The rural people have cooperated in transplantation of rice, harvest, construction of dike, irrigation, housing, and other productive works. These cooperative works may be classified into three kinds: one is *dure* which is the working team of about ten or twenty persons, but it has disappeared in the modern age; another is *pumasi* which is the mutual labor exchange on an individual basis; and the last category is the various kind of cooperative work on *ad hoc* basis according to the working situation.

The third type of communal effort is cooperation on special occasions such as wedding, funeral, or 60th birthday ceremonies. This is widely practiced even now.

The fourth type is cooperation among the people belonging to a special group. One of the most distinct and important of its kind is that which kinship members of *yangban* (the noble class during the traditional society) background have. They have often established a kinship organization in order to maintain their ancestors' tombs, to hold ancester worship ceremonies, and to manage their common properties. When there is one dominant *yangban* group, it is likely to impede the cooperative group work among the villagers as a whole. When there are two different *yangban* kinship groups, they often have conflict.

The fifth type is not cooperative work but compulsory group work. During the traditional or Japanese periods the rural people were frequently forced to work together against their interests. But this has faded away since 1945, and the sixth type, which is self-initiated cooperative work on an equal basis, has become distinct.

The modern community development program based on the Western concept was introduced by the government into Korea in 1958. In the first year three counties were selected as demonstration areas, and it was planned to spread to the rest of the entire nation. But it was discontinued by the military government in 1962, and rural development was attempted through the ordinary administrative organizations including the Office of Rural Development and agricultural cooperative agencies.

The Agricultural Cooperative was formed around the same time that the community development program started. Since they did not perform a credit service, the rural people were not attracted much by a program. Later their organizations were reinforced and the credit service was also added to their functions. But their activities do not seem to have been as much appreciated by the farmers as expected.

Participation in the Saemaŭl Movement

Saemaŭl was not initiated by the rural people. It was conceived, planned, and put into practice by President Park himself, and accordingly the administrative machines of the government have been involved in its implementation. But the administrators of the *Saemaŭl* Movement seem to be a little different from those in other government organizations. Their activities in driving *Saemaŭl* are watched and evaluated by their supervisors with special attention and finally by the Blue House itself, the office of the President.

According to the suggestions made by one who is familiar to the whole process of *Saemaŭl*, many exciting stories of the amazing accomplishments of the voluntary farmers for development seem to have impressed the President to convince him of the readiness of the farmers to carry out a large-scale community development program like *Saemaŭl* successfully. In fact, in spite of loud discordant voices that the economic gap between the rural and urban sectors would be widening, the economic situations of farmers were steadily improved and their vigorous attempts for better life could be observed in any rural areas even before *Saemaŭl*.[3]

Many factors might be involved in their readiness for *Saemaŭl*. First of all, one of the most important factors seems to be their rapid educational development. Consequently they could make themselves better judges of their own situations, the nature of problems they would have, and the possible scientific solutions. Secondly, because of the wide dissemination of mass media, particularly radio, they could have more adequate information. Thirdly, they were strongly stimulated to make successful adjustment to the dizzy social changes such as the disastrous confusion after the liberation and during the Korean War, and rapid urbanization and industrialization. Fourthly, their economic situation was improving owing to the land reform, the diffusion effect of industrialization, and a close economic relationship with cities. And finally, the moving-out of both the rich and poor rural residents to cities intensified the homogeneity of the villagers in terms of economic standing as well as their social consciousness so that their interrelated group work as a whole obviously became easier.

Needless to say, the participation of the people in the development program and their cooperation in its practice is one of the most important factors in bringing a successful result to the *Saemaŭl* Movement. In the study mentioned above the writer asked the villagers which would be the most important for bringing success to *Saemaŭl* among the three factors: cooperation (which can be used interchangeably with participation) of the villagers, leadership, and support by the government. In the two more successful villages cooperation of the villagers was indicated as the most important.

Though one can hardly doubt the success of *Saemaül* now, a few rural people were sceptical at its initial stage, since they were accustomed to observe that government programs usually started with the splendid appearance of "dragon head" and eventually got reduced to "snake tail." According to the study again, about 40 or 50 per cent of the respondents said that they had been sceptical in the beginning. Considering this question was put five years after the promulgation of *Saemaül* Movement, we can well guess how greater their sceptical attitude might have been at the very beginning of the Movement.

Now, what motivated them to make a more active participation in *Saemaül*? The first thing is that the government provided every village with the material, which could be effectively used for developmental projects they had long had in mind. Secondly, the government actions, as far as *Saemaül* is concerned, have been trustworthy. The government put into practice what it had promised to the villagers.

Thirdly, the methods of the government were practical and relevant to give cement to all villages during the initial year, in the next year to give the materials, cement and steel reinforcing rods only to the villages which made better use of them in the previous year, and later to provide the under-developed villages with more support; all these steps seem to have stimulated the people in the backward villages to make a greater effort for *Saemaül*. Besides this strategy, to have an annual convention of *Saemaül* leaders, to train *Saemaül* leaders in the *Saemaül* Training Institute, to award medals, ribbons, or special Presidential grants, to make it mandatory for the fresh government officials who just passed the national examination for high ranking officials to contribute to the *Saemaül* Movement for one year also proved to be very useful methods. Fourthly, it also counted that villages were given the right to make final decisions according to their own free will in selecting the kinds of projects and basic criteria in the process of implementation, though the government gave, guidance and advice.

Fifthly, the active roles of the *Saemaŭl* leaders are definitely important. In the poor villages, they are inclined to give slightly more weight to governmental assistance than leadership, but there is no question about the importance of leadership in carrying out developmental programs, particularly in the developing countries. The striking thing about the *Saemaŭl* Movement policy, however, is that the women's participation was deeply taken into consideration; and as a result, the woman *Saemaŭl* leader has been given as much incentive as the male leader. Again according to the study, about a half of the respondents in the most successful village among the four said the women's participation was "absolutely" necessary for the successful accomplishment of *Saemaŭl*.

Problems in Participation

All villagers have neither the same understanding about the common affairs in their community, nor reach full agreement concerning the suggested solutions for their problems. Their interests may conflict with each other according to their age, sex, family size, educational level, economic standing, family background, and so on.

Those who are proud of their prestigeous *yangban* status background may think that the maintenance of the tombs of their glorious ancestors and strong solidarity in their kinship group are more important and urgent than the development of the village as a whole. Some people who have children going to school may want to construct a bridge rather than widen a road. The rich may emphasize the necessity of having electric facilities, while the poor may prefer the idea of constructing a working place for common use, and women may be anxious to have common washing facilities.

The most serious factor impeding the active participation of the rural people in the development project seems to be the heterogeneity of the villagers. In the Korean rural area, there are many villages where one or several *yangban* kinship groups exist. If the leaders of the kinship group are tradition-oriented, and are more concerned with the development of their kinship group than with the development of the village as a whole, or if one kinship group has been in conflict with another kinship group within the same village, then the leadership structure of the village is likely to be disintegrated, and the common efforts for common development can hardly be achieved.

Another heterogeneous factor impeding cooperative participation in Korea, as in other countries, is an economic one. If there are too many rich and poor people, no effective development program can be set up through democratic procedures. In the process of implementing *Saemaŭl* projects, many rich people who had to donate a small patch of land for establishing or widening a road frequently expressed their unhappiness about the unfairness or irrationality in the matter. On the other hand, the poor people have complained that the rich do not contribute as much as they do, and the labor mobilization schedule is unfair to the convenience or economic interests of the poor.

The third heterogeneous factor is the geographical variety of houses or farm lands. In many villages there are some people who are living in places relatively remote from the main residential area. In this case no community plan, such as the project introducing electricity from outside or constructing a water supply system, can be made to the satisfaction of everybody concerned.

The fourth factor, though it may be most serious in some developing countries, is educational variety. Fortunately, as mentioned earlier, there are not many illiterates in the Korean rural villages; and there are particularly few, male or female, among those who are supposed to take economic responsibilities. Almost everybody has elementary education.

Another important matter that impedes the promotion of the people's participation is the economic surplus they can invest in developmental program. Sinces most *Saemaŭl* projects are scheduled to be carried out in the slack season, labor contribution may not be a serious burden to many people; but it may be really disastrous to those who are extremely poor, or who have to be engaged in business which should be done even in winter. And also *Saemaŭl* projects are not limited to the work which can be completed with the materials the government supplies and labor they can contribute. Therefore, if there are too many poor people who cannot put in money, no substantial development project, except the traditional type of cooperative work that needs only labor, can be put into practice. Of course, even the poor people recognize the importance and necessity of cooperation and active participation as social leaders, government officials, or intellectuals advocate; but actually they are not economically in a position to practice it.

The participation may sometimes mean death to those who have no savings and have to work to earn some food for immediate survival. Fortunately, however, most Korean rural people now have some savings to invest in projects for future betterment. One farmer says that many might not have accepted the project of introducing electricity, if it had been proposed ten, or even five years ago. They know how convenient the electricity is, but since they have to spend ten times more on it than on a kerosene lamp, many rural people might not be able to afford it.

In conclusion, the people's participation in *Saemaŭl* is of great importance, right along with assistance from the government and the competent internal village leadership. We can learn from experience in *Saemaŭl* that the participation may be productive, if it is organized basically in compliance with the needs, interests, traits, and capacities of the individuals, as well as with the characteristics of the social structure of the community. And the reward can be accepted by each of the participants as reasonable, fair, and feasible. The participation must be guided by responsible, competent, industrious, and trustworthy leaders. However, the people should be motivated, encouraged, and sometimes challenged either from outside or from the top to make them more actively participate in development programs. Finally, the participation of women also seems to be very important in driving development programs.

[NOTES]

1) *"Sae"* means new, *"maŭl"* village, and *"undong"* movement. *Saemaŭl* Movement in this article is often indicated just as *Saemaŭl* in order to avoid awkward duplication.
2) The result of the study was reported recently. See Vincent S.R. Brandt and Man-gap Lee, "Community Development in the Republic of Korea," *Community Development*, ed. by R. Dore and Z. Mars, (Paris: Unesco, 1981), pp. 47-136.
3) See Man-gap Lee, *Hangug nongchon sahoe ŭi gujo wa byŏnhwa* (*The Social Structure of the Korean Village and Its Change*), (Seoul: Seoul National University Press, 1973), Chap. 8, Part. II.

III

SOCIOLOGY IN KOREA:
ASIAN PERSPECTIVES

Trend of Social Sciences in Korea after World War II

The academic activities of the Korean social scientists after World War II have been greatly handicapped by two main facts; one is the fact that Korea was ruled by the Japanese government before the War and another is the fact that Korea has suffered from successive disorders in various fields of living which resulted from the collapse of Japanese ruling system, the division of Korea and the Korean War.

Because of the former reason, Korean social scientists were not able to enjoy academic freedom and were extremely handicapped in terms of both material and spiritual conditions. Therefore, numbers were few and their achievements small. Those few social scientists who already participated in academic circles during the Japanese period and the young scholars who were trained at about the period of World War II formed the nucleus of the academic institutes which were newly established or expanded since the liberation (1945). Except for those few scholars who continued research on particular subjects initiated during the Japanese period, most of them could not concentrate their effort on any creative research work because of social instability. Thus, the period from 1945 to 1955 was characterized by academic stagnation.

As suggested just above, however, the research activity of some social scientists, of course, did not completely stop even during this hard period. Several economists studied economic problems in pre-modern Korean society and one sociologist studied the Korean family system from a historical aspect.

* Presented at the first inter-council conference of the Research Councils for East Asian Studies of China, Japan and Korea in 1960.

On the other hand, Marxist-oriented social scientists were very active in studying the social and economic features of ancient feudal and Japanese dominated Korea for several years after World War II, but, all Marxist-oriented scholarly activity had ceased by the time of the Korean War.

During the first decade after liberation, the major activities of Korean social scientists were to introduce and translate Western scholar's works. This was really necessary as the students who aspired to new knowledge were increasing and it was almost impossible to buy foreign books. Most of the books, however, which were introduced or translated in that period, were those published before 1945. Therefore, new theories, methods and techniques and results of research which were greatly developed by Western social scientists during and after World War II were rarely known to Korean social scientists.

Most Korean social scientists were eagerly but inconsistently introducing European and American achievements through their knowledge and experience which were biased by the pre-war Japanese academic circles during this period. In general, it seems that Japanese social scientists in the past were absorbed in mastering the theoretical achievements of Western social scientists, particularly those of German scholars, and consequently worked along rather speculative lines and tended to neglect the study of their own society. Korean social scientists, greatly influenced by Japanese scholars, were also speculative in their orientation and did not have much interest in a scientific empirical approach to their own society.

About the time of the Korean armistice, the United States invited a considerable number of Korean social scientists to America through exchange programs. As these programs are usually scheduled to support each scholar for one year, one must not overestimate the extent to which the programs have contributed toward changing the academic attitudes and ideas of older scholars. But it should not be overlooked that the programs have greatly stimulated Korean scholars, particularly young scholars, to the extent that they have come to understand the newer trends in the contemporary social sciences.

On the other hand, some of the students who studied in the United States and other foreign countries after World War II came back to their own country and began to participate in scholarly acitvities. Their academic attitudes and basic concepts of social sciences are very much different from those of the scholars who were educated before World War II in that they have been directly influenced by the achievements of social science in Western societies. Though they are few in number and their influence in the Korean academic society is still minor, it may be expected that they will become more influential. For the time being, the main body of Korean social scientific circles are scholars of the generation between thirty-five and forty-five years of age who are familiar with the Japanese academic mode but sensitive to the new trends and achievements of social sciences in the Western societies.

Partially because of their academic tradition and because of the fact that they have recently been absorbed in introducing the advanced academic achievement of Western countries, Korean social scientists have been rather uncreative and have not engaged in extensive scientific study of Korean society.

Let me review briefly some of the current general trends in the social sciences in Korea.

First, with respect to the science of law, the main efforts of legal scientists seem to be concentrated on explaining the theoretical basis of the new Korean laws and their applications. A few young scholars have expressed a faint interest in the historical study of legal institutions, but there has been no empirical study of legal phenomena in relation to contemporary social behavior.

In political science, the main activities of Korean scholars so far have been to introduce and translate the political theories developed in foreign countries. Only a few have approached scientifically the post-liberation political phenomena in Korea. In the past there were a few historical studies about political aspects of the end of the Yi-dynasty. One of the main reasons for so little scientific study on the political features of contemporary Korean society might be the overt or covert interference of the authorities under the Rhee regime. After the "April Uprising" (1960) there has been some evidence of new trends toward the study of political phenomena including studies of voting behavior and political attitudes by younger scholars.

In the field of economics also, the major activities have been to understand the economic theories developed in foreign countries and to translate them. However, a few economists have engaged in the study of Korean economic history and the economic structure of Korean agriculture.

Studies seeking to explain the structure and operation of the Korean economy have been rather numerous, but they are rather fragmental and speculative, and are largely based on Western economic theories. Among the Korean economists, there is no research activity which is related to Korean social or cultural factors except a few surveys to collect basic economic data.

Sociology is not yet widely understood in Korea and there are but few sociologists. Until recently, sociological investigation of Korean society has been really unproductive. In the past several years, however, a few sociologists who have been influenced by the sociological achievements in the United States and who are familiar with social research methods have become active in researching Korean society. The main objects of research have been such subjects as family life in Seoul, the rural family, the social structure of the rural village, values represented in Korean newspapers and, land reform. One of the major problems with which sociologists are confronted whenever they attack their society is the lack of materials and systematic knowledge about the historical background of the Korean society and its culture. The academic activity in the field of Korean history perhaps is the most conspicuous among the social sciences in this country, but it appears that Korean historiography has not yet reached a point where it can provide a conceptual scheme which social scientists could utilize for investigating contemporary society. In this respect, it must be emphasized that accelerated research activity in the field of Korean history is strongly desired not only by sociologists but also by other social scientists.

In terms of numbers of scholars and academic departments, psychology may be considered more well developed than sociology in Korea. Before World War II a well-equipped laboratory for psychological experimentation was established in Seoul National University, but experimental research in the laboratory has lagged since the liberation because of a lack of funds. The young psychologists are very anxious to follow up psychological theories and methods in the foreign countries and to apply them. Recently, they have been becoming active in educational psychology, especially in the field of counseling. Korean psychologists have been relatively isolated from other social scientists but the gap between them is being narrowed. Some competent young psychologists have begun to study the student uprising of last April from the aspect of social psychology.

Generally speaking, it may be concluded that in the social sciences except for the field of history, Korean scholars have not made a great effort toward a scientific approach to their own society as well as to the Orient in general. In particular, they have rarely attacked the problems of contemporary Korean society. If the speaker may be allowed to present his own opinion, the main reasons why the Korean scholars have been indifferent to or unproductive in Korean and Oriental studies might be summarized as follows:

(1) Korean social scientists have been speculative rather than scientific in their mode of study.
(2) Research work has not been properly rewarded in Korea.
(3) They have not had methodological training enough to conduct research.
(4) They have not been sufficiently supported financially so that they would be able to concentrate their efforts on academic research. Consequently, the scholars prefer easier ways to increase the income rather than through research work.
(5) The political situation discouraged them from undertaking research work on the present society.
(6) The material conditions such as laboratories, libraries, and other facilities are insufficient.

Some of those factors have been considerably improved, though some others remain as before. For example, factors such as income level of Korean scholars or the material conditions for their study have hardly been improved. Some rising scholars, however, who have come in contact with the new academic achievements and methodology which have been developed in the Western countries, are gradually coming to represent a strong aspiration for a scientific approach to social phenomena. Although the old fashion appears to be predominant among Korean social scientists, the new trend is widening its academic front. Another fact which should be mentioned is that academic freedom has been secured to a great extent as a result of recent political changes. It can be anticipated that the free political atmosphere will stimulate social science research.

In addition to these two positive factors, it would be well to consider other favorable factors which provoke a scientific investigation of society.

(1) As interest in under-developed countries increases, the necessity for scientific study of Korean and other Asian societies is becoming more strongly felt.

(2) A scientific approach in the social sciences has been encouraged by academic foundations, and certain national and international institutions.
(3) Some Korean social scientists are beginning to recognize that no application of theories or principles of social sciences developed in foreign countries can be useful unless they are related to the social and cultural traits of Korea.
(4) Some Korean social scientists are becoming aware that it would be easier to create new knowledge and contribute to the development of social sciences in the world by studying the society around themselves than by studying others.

The scientific study of Korean and other Asian societies is still in its infancy. Hopeful signs of progress, however, have begun to appear in the past half decade.

Most of the leading universities in Korea have established institutes for Korean and Oriental studies, though their activities have been largely focused on historical subjects and are still weak; the Korean Research Center, for example, is supporting research activities on Korean studies. This organization has published six volumes of research reports so far and will publish more than ten books in the near future. An organization, directed by Dr. Yi Pyung Do, publishes an academic magazine, "Social Science"; and, the Korean Council for East Asian Studies has changed its policy toward promoting research activities in the field of social sciences. Perhaps in the coming few years we may find more hopeful signs of development.

In advancing the social science in Korea, Korean scholars hope that social scientists in neighboring lands will become interested in conducting research on Korean society, and that there may be a mutually beneficial exchange of research findings.

Development of Sociology in Korea

Sociology in Organization

1. Establishment of Sociology Department

No independent department of sociology existed in Korea before World War II. Even Keijo Imperial University, the only university in Korea at that time, did not have one, but included some sociology courses in the department of philosophy as a specialized sub-field.

Therefore, no sociologists were educated in the Korean educational institutes until the liberation of Korea. There were some Korean sociologists, however, who were trained either in Japan or in the Western countries, mainly in the United States. But some of them were not active in teaching sociology.

After Korea was emancipated, what is now called Seoul National University, formerly Keijo Imperial University, established a department of sociology. In 1954, the second sociology department was established at Gyŏngbug National University. Four years later Ewha Womans University opened a department of sociology, and the newly founded small college, Seoul Woman's College, established one in 1961. In the same year the first rural sociology department was opened at Sungsil Christian College. In 1963, a sociology department was included at Korea University. In 1968, Gugmin College opened a sociology department, but it only survived for one year. The sociology departments in Sungsil and Seoul Woman's colleges were also abolished later. Now there are only four schools in Korea which have departments of sociology. This may reflect to what extent sociology has been

---

* Presented at the 1970 annual Conference of the Association for Asian Studies in San Francisco

popular in this country. This does not necessarily mean, however, that sociology is less popular or less important than other social sciences, as we will discuss more in detail.

Since many universities and colleges do not have a sociology department, the academicians who are working in sociology in the educational or research institutes are limited in number. Now the total number of qualified sociologists in Korea may be about fifty. Approximately fifteen more competent sociologists, mostly young, are in the United States in advanced training or teaching positions.

2. Korean Sociological Association

In the fall of 1956, 14 sociologists in Korea gathered in order to promote organization of a professional association of sociologists in Korea, and on the fifth of May 1957, the Korean Sociological Society (later changed to the Korean Sociological Association) was launched in the first general meeting of the Association. Since then the Association has held a general meeting every fall to elect staffs and discuss business affairs following the presentation of papers and debates. Several years later the Association decided to include a spring conference, since the number of papers for presentation were increased.

In the beginning, a lack of finances made it impossible for the Association to publish a journal. In 1964, however, with the support of foreign aid organizations and a special fund donated by the regular sociology faculty members in the various universities, the Association was able to publish the first issue of the Korean Journal of Sociology. Up to 1969 five annual issues of the Journal have been produced with much painful effort. The Association may be out of financial difficulties in publishing the Journal from now on because a Korean organization, the *Sŏng-gog* Foundation, has begun to support some social science associations, including the Korean Sociological Association.

Besides the Korean Journal of Sociology, another sociological journal of a professional sort was published in the same year by the Korean Sociological Research Association, composed exclusively of the sociology graduates of Seoul National University. This journal, called Korean Sociological Review, has been published twice so far. There was a Rural Sociological Review published but a subsequent issue did not appear after the first issue. Besides journals by the professional sociologists, two student sociological magazines have been published in the departments of sociology at Seoul National and Ewha Womans Universities, and the sociology students at Seoul Woman's College also published one issue of their own magazine.

Trend of Sociology

1. The Initial Stages

It may be convenient to divide the history of sociology in Korea into several periods according to the nature of sociological orientations in discussing the development of sociology in Korea. Once in a different paper, the writer set up four different stages as follows: (1) sociology before 1945, (2) the early establishment stage of a decade after 1945, (3) the period of new sociology up to the early 1960's, and (4) the phase of emerging self-awareness in the latter half of the 1960's.

In the first stage, some courses of sociology, most of which were of a general type, were offered in several schools and also a few sociological studies were carried out by a handful of Korean or Japanese sociologists. Sociology during this period, however, was seemingly regarded as an insignificant discipline even by the academicians in the field of social sciences and actually had no direct impact upon the discipline in the subsequent periods of rapid growth. The major characteristics in the second stage are: that Seoul National University and later, Gyŏngbug National University established departments of sociology and offered the students regular courses in sociology with many areas of specialization as the departments of sociology in the Japanese universities did before 1945; that some introductory sociological text books were published in Korean; that the major contents of the lectures or text books were largely the introduction of the Western sociological theories produced far back in 1930's or before that period (such as those of Comte, Spencer, Simmel, Tönnies, Max Weber and so on); and that social confusion after the liberation and the Korean War made the scholars inactive in academic achievement.

2. Introduction of New Sociology

The third stage started in 1956, several years after the Korean War was over and people had returned to their original stable lives and became busy in reconstruction. In that year two sociologists of Seoul National University came back from the United States after a one year exchange program and introduced up-to-date sociological theories and methods, that had been developing rapidly in the United States since the end of World War II. The curriculum was drastically changed and new courses such as social research methods and cultural anthropology were included. Another big event of the same year was that the key sociologists in Korea met together in the fall in order to make preparation for organizing a professional association of sociologists in Korea, which was formally founded the next year. These events stimulated a strong aspiration for academic endeavor with new concepts and approaches among the scholars and students who were ready to accept them. This trend was more strongly accelerated by the return of some sociologists who were trained through regular courses in the Western countries, mainly in the United States.

During this period many sociologists began to conduct empirical field research on the basis of scientific research methods. Sampling, interviewing, constructing questionnaires, content analysis, and other techniques were employed, and data processing through machine and statistical manipulation were also adopted. Funds for sociological field work were scarce in the beginning, but funding gradually started to increase. Consequently the sociologists became more active in field research. The major subjects for such research during this period were attitude toward occupations, family both in urban and rural areas, kinship organization, social structure in the rural villages, fertility in the rural area, urban residential area, industrial workers, attitudes and values, and so on. The distinct trend relating to the research activities is that the government and the private organizations such as newspaper agencies developed a strong interest in sociological investigations after the student uprising in 1960 and undertook various surveys, particularly public opinion surveys, in which sociologists were invited to participate either as research directors or technical consultants. Around this time sociology became gradually popular not only among the academicians and students in various fields but also the journalists and even some influential people in the government and private organizations as well.

3. Emergence of Self-awakening

The fourth stage may be characterized by the emergence of self-awakening in Korean sociology and an increase in the activities of sociologists as either a group or individuals, although it may be not an epoch-making change like that observed in the transition from the second to the third stage, but rather a continuation of the third stage in a broader sense.

One of the distinct developments in this stage is that the Korean sociologists began to publish their first professional magazines in 1964 as mentioned before. There are some other distinct trends in this period: In the first place, the Korean sociologists became critical of the relevance and the applicability of Western sociology in the Korean social scene and expressed a strong interest in developing sociological theories and methods relevant to the indigenous nature of Korean society. For example, in 1965, the Korean Sociological Association had a special session with a panel discussion on "the Problems and Methodology in the Analysis of Koren Social Structure," as a follow-up of their symposium on "Problems in Sociological Studies of Korean Society" which had been dealt with in the annual conference of 1963. Then, later in 1966 and 1967, the Association held symposiums on the problems of rural social research methods in Korea and on the ethical position of the academicians respectively.

Secondly, they were becoming strongly concerned with social development, modernization, and other changes in a society, and their general interests shifted gradually from the rural to the urban and industrial problems, even though the rural society remained the major topic. Thirdly, the Korean sociologists became more active in researches with connection to the research institutes such as the Council of East Asian Studies which is related to Harvard-Yenchin Institute, the Institute of East Asian Studies of Seoul National University, the Asiatic Research Center of Korea University, and the Korea Culture Research Institute of Ewha Womans University all of which were already established in the preceding period. In addition, two more significant research institutes were established in this stage: the Population and Development Studies Center at the College of Liberal Arts and Sciences of Seoul National University and the Social Science Research Institute of Korea University, which accelerated the research activities further.

Finally, Korean sociologists promoted cooperation with scholars in other fields of social sciences, extended the academic front to public discussion on the current social problems in various seminars, and became more diverse in the subjects of researches and more productive in the results than in the previous stage. The following table may show the current subjects of sociological

Classified Sociological Products: 1964~1969

Category	Papers or books published	Papers presented at KSA meetings
General (including methodology and theory)	13	5
Family, kinship, and marriage	16	12
Social structure, stratification, and mobility	18	3
Population, fertility, and migration	19	8
Rural society and its change	27	8
Urban society and urbanization	8	6
Social change, modernization and development	14	5
Mass communication and mass society	1	8
Industry	—	5
Politics	4	2
Religion	—	1
Intellectual	3	—
Deviance	3	1
Total	126	64

studies.

Factors Bearing on the Development of Sociology in Korea

1. Positive Factors

In spite of the fact that sociology was unknown to the public until recently, and that there are only a few sociology departments, it is gaining popularity and is regarded to be one of the most important disciplines among the social sciences. According to a survey which was conducted about 8 years ago in order to investigate the situations and problems of social sciences in Korea, the social scientists interviewed indicated that sociology was ranked as the second most important social science with the ability to contribute to the development of the social sciences and of the society of Korea as well. As a leading sociologist mentioned, one will find now at least one or two sociologists almost without exception in the advisory groups to the government or the seminar groups to which social scientists are invited. It seems to be generally recognized that the sociology departments have stringent entrance examinations for student applicants.

One of the major factors involved in the development of sociology might be the leadership of key figures. The founder of the department of sociology at Seoul National University and the Korean Sociological Association as well was Dr. Lee Sang Baeck. He was a man of keen and broad vision who made valuable observations not only of the academic but the world situation, and strongly encouraged his students to develop themselves. He did not press them to follow his own style of scholarship, as many old authoritarian scholars did Therefore, the young sociologists did not have any barrier in introducing the new sociology from the outside and transplanting it on Korean academic soil. Moreover, he was influential with the leading scholars in the fields of the humanities and social sciences and gave competent young sociologists opportunities to be active in academic activities.

The second factor in sociology's development in Korea might be the introduction of fresh sociological theories and the scientific social research methods from the United States. Until the end of the Korean War most of the Korean social scientists were more likely to be oriented to the speculative type of grand theories of the European Continent, as were the Japanese scholars. In this academic climate, the young sociologists could give more meaningful explanations to the current problematic social phenomena with new sociological theories on the one hand, and on the other, provide empirical data concerning social problems as the basis of the scientific approaches which other social scientists were short of.

Thirdly, the increasing cultural influence by the United States must be taken into consideration as an another important factor. After the Korean War many social scientists, old and young, had a lot of opportunities to study in the United States and many American academic materials became relatively easily available. Through this process the scholars in other fields of the social sciences seem to have been familiar with the sociological concepts, since sociology has been popular in the United States and sociological theories have been frequently referred to by other social scientists there. In addition to this, the newspapers and magazines introduced foreign ideas in which sociological concepts were occasionally involved.

What we have to note as the fourth factor, being related to the third to some extent, is the very nature of sociology—that it is a basic social science in a pure sense and it is so broad in its scope that the phenomena which other social sciences are concerned with as their original areas can be studied also from a sociological point of view, sometimes in a more meaningful way. Therefore, many works in other social sciences often have a sociological content.

The fifth is the practical usefulness of sociological knowledge for problem solving of social affairs or social and economic development. In recent years many domestic or foreign experts or advisors have often emphasized the necessity of taking into consideration the socio-cultural factors in economic as well as social planning. For example, many governmental or non-governmental programs such as community development, the family planning program, and some other development programs have usually demanded the participation of sociologists.

Finally the deep concerns of some sociologists with mass communication and their contribution to its development must also be noted to be important. The department of sociology of Seoul National University started to offer courses in mass communication in the mid 60's when the word was not widely known even among the social scientists, since the department recognized the significant functions of mass communication in the modern society. Therefore, many graduates of the department have come to have a strong interest in mass communication, mass society, and mass culture, and have since become active in that field. Now many students seem to take it that sociology may be the proper discipline to train workers for mass communication. Consequently the sociological topics or sociological interpretation of social events might be favored by the young workers in mass communication organizations.

2. Negative Factors

The fact that sociology is getting popular and is widely demanded by the society, however, does not necessarily mean either that sociology in Korea has developed to a satisfactory extent, or that it is one of the most attractive disciplines in terms of career development of a profession. It may be true that sociology in Korea has made a rapid development in a short period of time, but no sociologist can deny that the general standard of it in terms of its maturity and profoundness both in theory and methodology is still far behind the standards in the United States or advanced countries in Europe. And also, many influential social leaders in the various social sectors, including the top administrators in the universities, do not appear to recognize the usefulness of sociological knowledge as the intellectuals do.

As mentioned at the beginning of this paper, there are presently only four departments of sociology. The major reason for the abolishment of the other three departments seems to be that those colleges wanted to transfer the quota of the number of students for the sociology department to the departments of other disciplines which were seemingly more attractive than sociology from a managerial point of view. The kinds of departments and quota of students in educational institutes can not be changed without the authorization of the Korean government and usually it does not permit them to establish a new department or increase the student quota as far as the social sciences and humanities are concerned. Therefore, the educational institutes are apt to abolish less attractive departments and transfer the quota of the students allocated to the department to others. On the other hand, some universities have tried to establish sociology departments, since they recognized the importance of sociology from an academic point of view. They have failed to do so, because the government did not approve it.

There was a certain period, however, in which the government control as such was not strict. Unfortunately, many top administrators of the advanced educational institutes were not aware of the necessity of sociology. It is said that even a very influential president of a certain leading university negatively responded to the suggestion to establish a sociology department around ten years ago, saying that sociology of Simmel or Tönnies would not be useful. He did not know the current development of sociology outside at that time. Thus the ignorance of sociology among the college administrators of the top level caused the limitation of the sociology departments in number. Consequently sociology graduates have difficulty in finding a job in the advanced educational institutes. In addition, the small number of faculty members in sociology may impede the differentiation of sociological studies. This may be one of the most important reasons why sociology in Korea has been handicaped in making progress.

As far as the job availability for the sociology students is concerned, the general situation seems to have been greatly improved. As the economic development continues, sociology students can find relatively satisfactory jobs more easily than before, but the main problem is whether they can find a job in which they may be able to put sociological knowledge to practical use. Out of 437 sociology graduates of Seoul National University by the end of

1969, 114 persons are engaged in education including high school level, 64 in mass communication agencies, 45 in government or public agencies, 33 in business firms, 90 in other jobs, and another 90 are not identified. Therefore, it can be said that most of them are not working in the areas which are directly related to sociology. It is a distinct trend that the competition in the entrance examination to the sociology departments has become very severe in recent years, making it more attractive. Nevertheless, it is still another disadvantage for sociology that its proper occupational outlet is narrow.

There are some other serious problems which are not limited only to sociology such as low salary for professors, lack of research funds, and a shortage of books, materials, equipment, facilities, and office budget. Some competent scholars have to work unwillingly on various matters such as writing articles for magazines or newspapers, participating in seminars or discussions on T.V. or radio, conducting surveys which may not be directly related to their academic interest, mainly because they need additional income on the one hand and partly because they are strongly pressed on the other. Therefore, it is rather difficult for them to concentrate their efforts on work which may be academically more significant.

As to the availability of research funds, the sociologists have some difficulty, although they might be relatively in a better situation than other social scientists have been. But now it is not so serious, because the sources for research funds are increasingly available to scholars in any field. The only problems may be that the grants are small in the amount per unit of research project and that the sponsors may not necessarily support significant research. Relating to the research activities, it may be important to note two serious problems in particular; these are difficulties in using machines for data processing and in obtaining theoretical books or research materials produced in other countries.

Because of these difficulties, the analysis of most research can hardly be deep and specific, and the conceptualization in the process of making designs and the interpretation of data are usually not elaborated.

Conclusion

Sociology in Korea has made steady progress since 1956 when they introduced the new theories and methodology from the United States. They provided useful materials and concrete findings to both academic and practical sectors, and also offered meaningful interpretations and discussions to social problems. Their achievements are widely appreciated by the academic circle of social sciences and the importance of sociology is strongly recognized by many intellectuals. So far the Korean sociologists have been busy introducing and understanding Western theories and applying the methods and techniques in empirical studies, but they have not matured fully yet. In recent years, many sociologists have expressed strong interests in modernization and social change on the one hand, and have become critical of Western sociological theories and methodology on the other, in favor of a new theoretical orientation of some sort relevant to Korean society.

Even though sociology in Korea has been developed to some extent because of various reasons or conditions such as the successful introduction and application of fresh theories and methodology from the outside, good leadership, close relationship with mass communication, and so forth, it has also some serious disadvantages. The limitation on establishing more sociology departments, causing a shortage of competent sociologists, may be the most crucial one. The unreasonable salary of the professors, the shortage of materials and books, and the difficulty of using equipment for data processing must also be noted as significant conditions to impede the development of sociology in Korea, although these are not limited only to sociology.

Problems of Research in the Korean Rural Society

Introduction

The writer conducted research in six Korean rural villages in 1958 in order to understand the nature of their social structure. Again in 1969, he repeated almost the same research in the same villages in order to observe the changes during the past eleven years.

The unit chosen for the first research was the household, and the head of each household or his substitute was formally interviewed through a schedule. A sampling technique was not applied. All households in the six villages were investigated. The main reason not to employ the sampling technique came from the necessity to apply a sociometric technique in order to examine the villages' leadership structure and other structural characteristics in as much detail as possible.

In addition to the formal interview with the household heads, we also had the informal interviews with some key informants. They were the formal or informal leaders in the villages, the governmental officials, those who had relatively high education and were working in the modern functional institutions such as schools or banks, as well as a few women.

The writer strongly felt the need for informal interviews. The main reasons were: first, that it would be very helpful for reaching an understanding of the general social context of the Korean village life on which the village social structure would be based and in which its sociological implications could be relevantly inter-

---

* Presented at the 1971 Asian Regional Conference on Teaching and Research in the Rural Social Science in Manila.

preted; second, that the facts that were obtained from the formal interview through the schedule would show at most some figures about some distinct structural aspects without providing substantial information concerning the reality of the social structure, since the number of items in the schedule would be limited in the standardized interview; and third, that the rural people might not express what they actually think in the formal interview, since they have not been accustomed to expressing their frank opinions to elders or strangers.

Both the formal and informal interviews were again practiced in the second research. About two thirds of the items in the formal interviews in the second research were exactly the same with those in the first research. The only major difference between the first and second researches is probably that some households which had been the subjects of the first research moved out of the villages. Since they had already left the villages, they could not be subjects in the second research. It would have been very useful for reaching an understanding of the structural changes to examine the migration patterns.

This paper is concerned with the problems which the writer found through his experiences primarily with the two researches mentioned above. However, he may also refer to some problems that he found in other researches. The discussion in this paper deals with three stages of research activities, that is, the research design, data collection, and analysis and interpretation.

The Problems in the Stage of Research Design

There are various problems in the stage of research design. The most serious problem among others in this stage, however, seems to be how to formulate whatever we may call a conceptual scheme, or theoretical frame-work. A sociologist does not deal with all aspects of the phenomena which are related to his particular subject, but makes selective observations on the relevant facts on the basis of a certain theoretical frame-work.

Unless the research design is elaborated on the basis of the valid theoretical frame-work, he may not be sure what items should be included in the questionaire and what would be irrelevant to his topic. Even though he has found many facts, he may not be able to understand the sociological meaning of the facts and the logical relationship among the facts. What he may do is at most present a bunch of facts without any particular systematic arrangement.

When the sociologists attempt empirical research in Korea, they are inclined to rely on theoretical models developed in the Western countries. The Western sociological theories have often not been sufficiently introduced to them, because of the financial difficulty of obtaining the books, magazines, and other materials necessary for their academic study.

The Western sociological theories may be applicable to the local situations of the developing countries to the extent that they are universal generalizations. However, most of the Western sociological theories may not be so universal that they could be applicable directly to the countries in Asia. It is particularly so in applying them to the rural societies of those countries where the unique and traditional indigeneous socio-cultural elements are deeply rooted.

Let me offer one example. The concept of status would be one of the key concepts in discussing the social structure in any country. No matter how important the concept of status may be, it is not workable unless it is discussed with concrete empirical references to the indigenous status system which one is going to investigate. There was a *yangban* system in the pre-modern Korean society. *Yangban* refers to the family of a person, who was a governmental official during the Yi-dynasty which lasted for five centuries until the early period of this century in Korea.

If we do not know about this particular status system and are familiar only with the class system of the modern Western societies, then we may not be able to include any item in an interview schedule concerning the *yangban* status, which has disappeared as an institution, but still exists as a prestige system in the Korean rural society.

In the writer's own study about the Social Structure of the Korean Rural Villages, he delineated three essential factors; that is, the consanguineous system, the solidarity based on the traditional prestige system, and the modern economic stratification. He can hardly say that the Western sociological theories were not conducive to the formulation. It is apparent that the sociological mind he had, whatever it might be actually, was the mental foundation which made him able to delineate the factors. His sociological outlook in turn would have been originally formed by a comprehension of the Western sociological theories. However, he thinks that more pertinent help for formulating a workable theoretical frame-work might have been obtained from the results of the studies on the Korean society and its culture by various disciplines rather than from the Western sociological theories *per se*.

Needless to say, the sociological studies on the Korean rural society were extremely helpful for making the research design of the writer's first study, but there were only two works available when he studied. Some ethnological and anthropological studies on the Korean culture were of a great help. In addition some historical works on the Korean society were very much conducive to his study on the village structure. Particularly, the historical works on the traditional status system, the traditional administrative system, and the organizations in the past village communities were useful.

Prior work done in the field of agricultural economics were of help to his studies on the rural social structure to some extent, since the economic factors were obviously related to the social structure. But agricultural economics in general is not much concerned with the human relationships or group phenomena, and therefore, the writer could not get much help from it.

Some times the agricultural economic works misled the writer, although he was primarily responsible for the mistakes. For example, agricultural economists usually classify the economic strata of the rural farmers into the land-owner, partly land-owner and partly owner-farmer, owner-farmer, and partly tenant, tenant, and farm laborer. However, there is another category of farmer, the grave-guard (*myojig*). He is a farmer who cultivates the land specially prepared for the ancestor worship by a wealthy individual or an eminent kinship group like *yangban*. He makes a living with the farm products from the land, while maintaining the tomb of a particular ancestor of the landowner, and preparing the ancestor worship ceremony with some part of the income from the land. He is neither a tenant nor a farm-laborer in the strict sense.

I do not know why most of the agricultural economists did not include grave-guard as one of the categories in classifying the economic stratification of the Korean farmers. It might have been neglected because the number of grave-guards was not large before the land reform in 1949. From the sociological point of view, however, I think it should not be neglected, because they have been playing very important roles, particularly in relationship with the functions of the *yangban* kinship organizations. I missed the category in the schedule for my first study of the village social structure, because I did not recognize their important roles on the one hand, and the agricultural economists did not indicate the category on the other.

The writer feels that in the developing countries where useful theoretical models and materials are not sufficiently available, the pilot study is quite necessary for elaborating the conceptual scheme on the basis of which the relevant data will be collected. However, there is another important thing that should be noted.

A researcher may be so impressed by the curious facts he finds through the pilot study that he may proceed to give the peculiar details too much attention which can eventually lead to a bias. Therefore, it is desirable that one tries to understand objectively the meaning of the facts by referring to the relevant materials or by discussing it with the experts.

The Problems in the Stage of Data Collection

One of the important problems in the stage of data collection is how to train and control the interviewers. Economic surveys often attempt to infer the numerical characteristics of the universe such as the means or frequency of the particular variables on the basis of the appropriate figures obtained from the samples and therefore are very much concerned with the sampling error. Because of the different nature of much of the subject matter, the sociological surveys often pursue the attitudes, values, and opinions which are not easily subject to objective measurement. Usually the non-sampling error, particularly the errors originated in interviewing process seem to bring more serious failure to the surveys than the sampling errors.

Since the roles of the interviewers are so important, a research director must make every possible effort to improve the interview techniques. He gives the interviewers the orientation to the research, lets them perform the role-playing with the schedule, and checks the mistakes they made in the interviews for the pretest. In the experiences of the field researches, the writer often found the following problems with the student interviewers.

The first problem arises in their relation with the interviewees, the research director, and their associate interviewers. Generally speaking, the student interviewers do not seem to conduct themselves properly when interviewing with the rural people. In the relation to the research director or with their colleagues, they are likely to behave as they are used to doing on the campus. Sometimes, their urban behavior patterns may not be appreciated by the people in the rural setting.

The writer did not find this kind of undesirable conduct on the part of the students often, and no serious difficulty was caused by it in the field survey, but such behaviour may hamper rapport.

Another problem that the writer found often is that most of the interviewers are very poor in probing. Therefore, it seems to be hard to expect them to get valid, reliable, and useful responses to the questions such as those that are open-ended or are likely to induce "don't know" answers, unless the interviewers are well trained and have much experience in interviewing.

Some interviewers do not understand the real meaning of the words which the farmers use or their unique humor. For example, to the question, "do you raise any livestock?", one farmer replied that he was raising "three thousand fieldrats," and the interviewer misunderstood rat as being one of livestock. Once I myself asked one farmer about the religion in which he believed. He answered that he believed in *"daibon-gyo"* (great origin religion). I asked further who had initiated the religion. Then he smiled and said that "farming was the great origin in human life." There is such a saying in Korea. What the interviewee said in fact was that he did not have any religion but farming.

When the writer conducted the field research for a study of the social structure, he did not have any particular difficulty in controlling the interviewers, since the number of the interviewers was not large, and they were supervised by myself or my assistant. Supervision may be a serious problem, however, with a large scale sample survey such as a nation-wide opinion poll which I conducted several times. There are likely to be a few interviewers who do not carefully listen to the instructions in the orientation. Sometimes we may happen to find irresponsible interviewers who do not even conduct the interview, but leave the schedule behind asking the respondents to fill it out and then pick it up later. This does not happen with a small group of interviewers under the research leader's direct supervision.

Among the mistakes which the interviewers make frequently, we have to note wrong recording. Some interviewers do not indicate the figures clearly. It is also the case that we find inconsistent responses. This may be partly caused by the wrong expression or mistakes in the schedule, but usually this happens because the interviewers are not critical listeners. Therefore, it is quite desirable to let them check what they recorded right after interviewing and also to make editing as soon as possible in order to correct the mistakes while their memories are fresh.

The second category of the problems in the stage of data collection is the possible interference of government officials. The writer has not had any direct interference as such so far. In the latest period of Syngman Rhee's regime, the writer was once slightly disturbed by the police while conducting field research. Of course, the policeman did not intend to interfere with the academic activities, but he seemed to wonder if there could be any political implication in the survey. It might be natural, because many intellectuals were critical to Rhee's regime at that time.

The policeman asked the writer about his occupation, the objectives of the survey and the major contents of the questionaire in much detail. He even wanted to have one copy of the questionaire. Moreover, he visited the villages surveyed after the research team left, and asked the farmers various questions concerning the research activities, and reported it to the higher echelon. This did not cause any serious difficulty to the implementation of the survey. But it is true that the research team was psychologically depressed to some extent, and that the researcher found a slight suspicion about the research on the part of the villagers when he revisited the village for the follow-up study.

The writer has not experienced a repetition of this type of

incident in the decade since that time. It may be partly because the society has become politically stable, but there are some other reasons. Field research, sponsored not only by the governmental agencies but also by the academic institutes, has become very popular in this country. The public recognition that academic freedom should be secured has been increasingly enhanced. And academicians are becoming careful not to be involved in political matters.

The third category of the problems may be raised in the relationship with the rural people. It is not hard to maintain rapport in interviewing them. They are friendly to their visitors, at least on the surface. Moreover, they are inclined to respect academicians. It must be noted, however, that they tend to be covertly suspicious of strangers. And in some villages, it is not easily accepted that the male interviewers question village women, unless it is specially arranged by the village leaders.

Usually the villagers do not seem to be frank in replying to the questions, particulalry in the formal interviews, which ask their attitudes toward or opinions about the government agencies, or the basic traditional values to which many people conform. Therefore, the writer feels very strongly that the participant observation or the informal interview will be able to obtain more reliable answers to such questions than the formal interview. In recent years, however, the rural people, particularly the young, seem to be becoming more frank than before. The writer observed in his second research on the village social structure that the farmers did not much worry about possible trouble with the government officials in expressing their ideas about administration or political matters.

It has been often argued that the main difficulty in the rural surveys might come from the very nature of the mentality of the farmers and of the agricultural way of life. In a seminar on the "Utilization of the Government Statistics and the Problems in It," which was held about a month ago, one participant who presented a paper on agricultural statistics indicated the various reasons why the agricultural statistics would be inaccurate.

First, the farmers do not live according to a regular time schedule, and therefore, their concept or perception of time is not clear. Second, their concept of quantity of numerical values is also not clear cut. Third, there are many things in the rural affairs that might not be easily indicated by numbers. For example, it is very difficult to estimate the actual value of a vegetable manure heap in terms of its monitary account. Fourth, the farm management is not differentiated from the household economy. Fifth, the farmers are reluctant to show the amount of some items, (although this may not be limited only to the farmers). For example, they show easily the amount of debt, but tend to hesitate to indicate the amount of credit. Finally, many items of farm products can not be standardized in terms of size or quantity.

The writer presumes that the rural sociologists may have had exactly the same experience in finding facts concerning the economic affairs of the rural life. The writer himself asked one farmer about his monthly living expense. The first answer of the farmer was that he spent nothing except the expense for eating. Then the writer raised various questions successively. Don't you smoke cigarettes? Don't you donate money to your relatives or friends in the special occasions such as the wedding ceremony or funeral ceremony? Don't you have a child going to school? With these questions, he was astonished to realize that he had spent so much for various items other than food.

It has been also frequently heard that it is hard to obtain valid and reliable answers from the farmers, because most of them are ignorant and are not perceptive enough to articulate clearly what they have actually experienced. It may be true to some extent, and particularly so in comparison with the urban people. In the writer's personal experiences, however, he did not have the impression that they were so ignorant that it would impede the successful accomplishment of the field research.

In the first research on the village structure, the writer found many "don't know" answers to some items of the schedule. He also found the same tendancy with public opinion surveys he has conducted himself. The "don't know" answers might be partly caused by their illiteracy or ignorance. The writer speculates, however, that more important reasons might be that they did not experience or think in specific ways about the matters to which they were asked to reply.

Some items of the questionaire were probably not relevantly structured to meet their mentality or unique experiences. Or perhaps the interviewers did not have a sufficient interviewing skill to make further probing.

During the past eleven years, the illiteracy rate of the respondents—mainly the household heads—decreased from 58 per cent to 20 per cent and the proportion of the radio-owners increased from 15 per cent to 72 per cent in the villages investigated. Many of them had in the interim had organizational training in the army for several years. They have had a chance to visit the cities and be introduced to the modern ideas. From now on, then, the difficulty of interviewing with the rural people caused by their ignorance will be continuously reduced.

I have one more thing relating to the mentality of the rural people which I would like to discuss with the fellow participants in this conference.

Seven years ago, the writer tried as an experimental attempt to construct a scale to measure the attitude of the rural people toward democracy according to the Guttman scale technique. He listed eleven items which he regarded to be unidimensional. What he found after analysing the returned data was that the scalability was far lower than the expectation.

He pondered about the possible reasons for this. There seemed to be two major reasons; one was that the scale might not have been constructed well enough to secure a sufficient degree of validity and reliability, or that the selected items might not have been unidimensional; another was that there might not be a continuum in the attitude of the rural people toward democracy, since their experience with democracy was not long enough and therefore, their concept of democracy would be still arbitrary and ambiguous. The writer did not make further examination in order to know the real reason, but he has been inclined to think that the latter would be substantially responsible for the low reproducibility.

The problems in the stage of data collection are obviously not limited to the interview, but may arise in other techniques such as observation, questionaire construction, or the technique of mailing questionaires. The writer did not find any serious difficulty in observing the rural affairs. As to the technique of mailing questionaires, he once attempted it in the study on the evaluation of the pre-service training for the community development workers in which the workers dispatched to various villages were the respondents, and it was not successful.

Although this opinion might be intensified by the particular experience, the writer was originally convinced that the technique of mailing questionaires should be avoided as much as possible in the developing countries because of various reasons such as the following; the mailing system is likely not to be sufficiently developed there; the way of living at home may discourage the respondents from taking a pen and giving a reply to each item of the questionaire patiently; and many respondents are not educated enough to understand the questions.

There seems to be no particular problem in constructing questionaires directed to the rural people except in wording. It must be emphasized, the writer feels strongly, that the words in the questionaire should be easy and familiar to them.

Problems in the Stage of Analysis and Interpretation

The most serious problem many researchers in Korea encounter in the final stage of research may be a lack of equipment and facilities for data processing. Some equipment such as punching and sorting machines and small computers have become available at some universities very recently. But in the past, the researchers had to use equipment which was available in a few places outside of their own research institutes. Accordingly it was very inconvenient to use them. Moreover, the fund for using the machines was usually insufficient. Therefore, they had to be satisfied with single correlation analysis at most.

The second important problem in analyzing and interpreting the data or writing a report may be the availability of statistical data or other materials related to their research topic, although this problem may also arise in the stage of research design. The problem here is not a lack of materials, but the usefulness of the existing materials.

As pointed out by an expert at the seminar on "The Problems with the Utilization of the Government Statistics," the inaccuracy or insufficient reliability of the statistics concerning the agricultural economy may be partly caused by the mentality of the farmers and the nature of rural life. Also the interviewers who are not well qualified might be responsible for inaccuracy. It can hardly be denied, however, that the agencies or institutes responsible for the surveys are likely to carry them out in an inproper way through or sometimes even distort the statistical figures. At any rate, these inaccurate data often bring confusion to the researchers.

In this connection, there is another point that the writer would like to emphasize. That is the utilization of the research results from other Asian countries. Whenever the writer conducts research on the rural society, he regrets that these data are not easily available. It is obvious that these results may be very useful references to his own study, because many Asian countries have rural problems similar to those that Korea faces. With this regard, the writer is going to end the presentation with the recommendation that a system or organization be established through which the rural scientists will be able to utilize easily the research results produced in other countries of Asia.

Cooperation among Sociologists in Asia

The purpose of this paper is to examine possibilities for cooperation and steps that can be taken both to establish channels of communication and to found a formal academic association of Asian sociologists.

From a brief look at the problems involved in cooperation among Asian sociologists, I will proceed to discuss the possibility of establishing a separate, self-sustaining association and the initial steps that can be taken, beginning with the present conference.

Basic Problems for Cooperation

Cooperation is usually regarded as a virtue. It is the act of operating jointly with another or others, and concurring in action, effort, or effect. We at this conference may raise some basic questions about cooperation among ourselves. Why is it necessary? Under what conditions is it advisable? What meaning do cooperative efforts impart to the members involved? Cooperation provides a good opportunity to understand both one's own situation and that of the the counterpart more deeply. It stimulates one toward self-development, and it bestows long-term benefits upon all those involved.

In human history, however, we often observe that cooperation has brought pain, disaster, or even slavery to the weaker participants unless those who are to be cooperative have enough good will to guarantee fair and equal treatment for each member. It is the historical experience of many Asian countries to have suffered lengthy colonial rule under the veil of cooperation. In the past

---

* Presented at the Symposium "Sociology and Social Development in Asia" in 1973 at Tokyo.

several decades, an "intellectual conscience" that opposes any attempt of strong powers to oppress the weak has grown increasingly stronger in the world. The weak have had the wisdom with which to penetrate the disguised intentions of the strong and the will to resist threats.

Academicians are deeply concerned with the "intellectual conscience" achieved in the process of human history. They are likely to consider the standpoints of others objectively. Therefore, Asian scholars, even though they recall periods of unequal cooperation in the past, should not be overly cautious about new efforts to cooperate in the scholarly world.

Before proceeding to discuss the concrete forms and conditions for cooperation among Asian sociologists, I think it would be important for us to reach an understanding about some basic problems.

The first consideration is the objective of cooperation: why is it necessary for Asian sociologists to cooperate? The answer to this question should be obvious to everyone. Cooperation is necessary for the promotion of sociological research in every region of Asia. Efforts toward this end would contribute not only to the economic and social development of each region but also to Asia as a whole and to mankind.

The second consideration is that of membership in a cooperative body. By this I tentatively mean an Asian Sociological Association. The regular members of such a cooperative body would be sociologists who belong to any of the Asian regions. Such members would represent only academic institutions which are directly related to sociological education or research. I think this is very important, because non-academic concerns may possibly impair the success of our cooperation.

When I talk about the qualifications of the regular or ordinary members of the cooperative body, I do not intend to reject the possiblity that non-Asian sociologists could be members of or participants in this body. If it is rewarding to have certain non-

Asian sociologists as members, I think the association should invite them to join through the proper procedures.

Another remark that I would like to make regarding qualification for membership is that all Asian sociologists should enjoy equality, whatever their nationality may be. In other words, any sociologist or sociological institute should have the right to be a member or participant regardless of his nationality.

The third problem is that of ethical principle. No utterance or activity by members of the body should be blameful of any nation, or supportive of any kind of political ideology. This is one of the ethical principles developed in Western academic societies and generally accepted in international academic conferences. I believe it should be more strictly observed in our cooperative body than in other academic societies. Because there may be some countries in Asia whose political and economic situations are unstable and weak, any utterance with even only slightly unfavorable political implications may cause serious conflict within the organization.

The Possibility of Establishing an Asian Sociological Association

What we are concerned with in this session is not just cooperation among individual sociologists but also cooperation among sociologists from various regions of Asia. The most common way academicians in a certain discipline cooperate on an international scale is to establish an international academic association. Accordingly, it is quite natural for us to discuss the possibility of founding such an organization during the present conference. And I expect that many of our colleagues attending the conference may expect the evolvement of a formal association.

There is no doubt that it is very desirable to found an Asian Sociological Association as soon as possible. Most Asian countries have unique academic as well as practical problems different from those of the developed countries.

Even though Western sociologists have dealt with these problems to some extent, the focus of their studies, the formulation of conceptual schemes, the ways of collecting data, and the interpretations made on the basis of data may be more or less different from those of indigenous sociologists. This is because the motivations for study, the social standpoints, and the general cultural background of Western scholars often differ considerably from those of Eastern scholars.

Furthermore, Asian sociologists may have some handicaps in taking an active part in international sociological conferences. For example, there is a limit to the number of Asian participants since many of them have difficulty in securing financial support to attend. Also, Asian sociologists are likely to feel alienated by the more dominant Western modes of thought. The language barrier, different cultural backgrounds, and a sense of constituting a minority are factors which may discourage Asian sociologists.

There are some problems, however, in the way of establishing an Asian Sociological Association immediately. The first problem is the extent to which Asian sociologists share common academic interests and concerns on which successful communication can be based. From an ideal point of view, all sociologists, that is to say sociologists who are teaching in universities or who are engaged in research in academic institutes, are supposed to have a basic knowledge of contemporary sociological theories and methods. They are expected to keep up with the main trends in sociology. But we are not sure to what extent the real situation approximates the ideal one. Some sociologists may identify sociology with social philosophy, and others may regard it as a type of ideology. Still others might know pre-World War II sociology but not much about current developments. We, at least I, do not know what kind of activities the sociologists in the various regions of Asia have been engaged in, and what kind of acadomic and practical problems they have faced in order to attempt to coordinate activities on an international scale.

The second problem is financial. It is easy to announce the establishment of an organization, but we cannot accomplish substantial programs without a sound financial basis. There are ways to secure funds for our organization, such as dues paid by members, grants from foundations or from benevolent individuals, and money acquired through special programs sponsored by the organization. We cannot be sure, however, to what extent we will be able to secure the necessary funds.

The third problem is concerned with leadership. We need a staff which will willingly give of themselves to the purposes of the association. It may be no exaggeration to say that the success of the association depends chiefly upon their ideas and efforts. It is desirable that the they have a high academic reputation, a sense of fairness and political neutrality, the vision and capacity to develop the association, and hopefully a good enough command of foreign languages to promote international communication. I personally do not know how many sociologists with such qualifications are available at this moment.

The final problem is the determination of programs to meet the particular needs of Asian scholars. Our academic organization should have two major programs: one would be to hold periodic conferences during which members present papers, discuss important problems, and recommend necessary actions. Another program would be to publish official journals and reports. As far as these matters are concerned, I presume that all participants in this meeting would be anxious to see the implementation of these programs as soon as possible. Many Asian sociologists seem to face both academic and practical problems in the process of social development. As they confront these problems, they may want to know how problems similar to their own are dealt with by sociologists from other parts of Asia. Therefore, a useful function of the association would be a forum for the exchange of information.

No one will deny that many of the papers presented by sociologists from Asia would be interesting to sociologists from other regions of the world. But there is no guarantee that they would be as well received as expected. Let me take an extreme case, which I hope is most unrealistic. There could be the possibility that some regions may have a few sociologists who have never been engaged in research work. Their papers, based on mere speculation, might be boring to many members at the forum, and consequently the conference organized by the association might not be successful.

Initial Programs for Cooperation

Under the present circumstances, I think it is too early to establish an Asian Sociological Association. It is obvious, however, that we have not gathered here solely to confirm that it is too early to promote cooperation among Asian sociologists.

It is desirable to move toward founding an Asian Sociological Association as soon as possible. The most effective action we can take in the initial stages would be to form a preparatory committee for this purpose. The mission of such a committee would be to examine the sociological activities of each region of Asia, to draft a statement of regulations, to determine meaningful programs, to seek ways of securing funds, and to prepare for full-scale operation.

It must be strongly recommended that a conference similar to this one be held again. It does not matter whether the conference is on the same scale as the present one or smaller. As far as time is concerned, I personally think it is desirable to hold another conference three years from now. By that time, I would hope that the preparatory committee could present concrete recommendations for developing cooperative activities among Asian sociologists.

One of our most serious problems may be determining who will take a leading role in promoting and organizing another conference. It is a great project to keep up contact with Asian sociologists, to disseminate necessary informatian and to maintain communication with related organizations such as the ISA and Unesco.

Fund-raising is an even more critical factor. If it is possible, however, for participants to secure financial support from local foundations or other sources, it may not be so difficult for the host country to arrange the conference. I am not in a position to give further suggestions, since I do not know the fund-raising situation in each country. I only wish to express my hope that a conference will be held again.

Besides establishing a preparatory committee and planning another conference, we should consider the possibility of publishing a journal for Asian sociologists. Theoretically, a journal could be published prior to formal organization, but it may be difficult to undertake such a project without first establishing channels of communication. For this reason, I would suggest considering the possibility of publishing a book or a report of the names of Asian sociologists, their organizational affiliations, their topics of interest, and the trends of sociology in each region of Asia. Such information would facilitate mutual understanding among us, and would constitute the initial data necessary for establishing an Asian Sociological Association.

Finally, I would like to make one more suggestion regarding cooperation within the International Sociological Association. Because it will be difficult to establish an Asian Sociological Association in the near future, a Committee of Asian Sociologists within the ISA would be an additional channel through which progress could be made toward an independent self-sustaining organization. I sincerely hope that the preparatory committee formed during this conference could approach the ISA about this matter.

In conclusion, I would like to reiterate that cooperation among Asian sociologists is essential. Concrete forms of cooperation can be established in the foreseeable future. Problems which arise in the process are solvable if the interest manifested in this conference is genuine and sustained.

Forum for Asian Sociologists

Introduction

Asian sociologists have rarely had an opportunity to meet to discuss their common academic concerns. "The International Symposium on Social Stratification and Social Mobility in East Asian Countries," which was held in Tokyo in 1964 under the joint sponsorship of the Centre for East Asian Cultural Studies and the Japanese Commission for Unesco, was one, and "the Asian Regional Conference on Teaching and Research in the Rural Social Sciences" at the University of the Philippines in 1971 was another. However, the topics of these two conferences were specific, and participation in them was not necessarily limited to Asian sociologists, although they were dominant.

It was not until "the Symposium on Sociology and Social Development in Asia"[1] in Tokyo in 1973 that the Asian sociologists gathered together to discuss sociological matters exclusively among themselves. This conference was organized by the Japanese Sociological Society in collaboration with the Japanese National Commission for Unesco along with assistance of Unesco Headquarters in Paris, the International Sociological Association, and other foundations or cultural agencies.

In this symposium, which was also called "the Asian Regional Conference of Sociology," the participants discussed the future strategy for promoting cooperation among Asian sociologists and reached a decision to form a Preparatory Committee in order to hold the second conference, hopefully, in a few years. Though there was a continuous effort for follow-up action, it does not seem to have been rewarded as desired, presumably because of

---

* Presented at the 9th World Congress of Sociology in 1978.

financial difficulties among others. On the other hand, the Japanese Sociological Society proposed to the International Sociological Association to reserve two sessions for Asian sociologists at the 9th World Congress of Sociology, and it was accepted.

Along with this progress, there is one more thing that should be noted, with respect to widening the academic front of the Asian sociologists: that is, the establishment of the Asian Association of Social Science Research Councils, which is abbreviated as AASSREC. The idea was conceived in the "Asian Conference on Teaching and Research in Social Sciences" at Simla, India in 1973, the same year when the Asian Regional Conference of Sociology was held.

The first conference of AASSREC was held at Tehran early in 1976 with the support of Unesco in Paris, and the members adopted a constitution including objectives such as promoting teaching and research in the social sciences in Asia, generating and developing an autonomous Asian social science tradition, and identifying major areas of national, regional, and international development efforts in order to organize cross-national research in Asia. The second conference[2] was held in Seoul the next year.

AASSREC is in its infancy and it is not widely represented by Asian countries, but it may be noteworthy that its birth is evidence of the growing need of the social sciences in Asia, and of active and important roles taken by sociologists in the association as well as in the respective local social science research councils.

Some Problems of Sociology in Asia

It is not easy to give a concise, yet general description of the present status of sociology in Asia. One of the main reasons for this is the lack of information about sociological activities in many Asian countries. Another reason is that the status of sociology in one country is too different from that in other Asian countries in terms of the degree of its development to make simple generalizations about the activities of Asian sociologists. These two reasons are actually related to each other. In other words, the more developed sociology is in a country, the more information is available about it, and vice versa.

The subject matters and methods of sociology in the U.S.S.R. or the eastern European countries are known to some extent, but no information seems to be available concerning sociology in Asian communist countries; however, we do know, or may be able to know, if we so wish, more or less about the current situation of sociology in other Asian countries. Generally speaking, many universities in these countries seem to offer sociology courses. And sociology there is also likely to be an important discipline in the social sciences, and to follow law and economics in popularity as a major in most Asian countries.[3]

Japan and India probably have the largest populations of sociologists and are the most advanced countries in sociological activities in Asia. Japan in particular has a century of history since sociology was introduced from the West. In the initial stage, Japanese sociology was largely influenced by European sociology, but after World War II, it, like those in other Asian countries, has been greatly influenced by American sociology, although recently the influence of European sociology on it seems to be again on the increase.

In some respects, however, Japanese sociology is different from that of many other countries. One of its unique characteristics is that almost all Japanese sociologists were basically trained in their own country, though some of them might have received advanced training in Western countries. Another difference is the possibility that their major academic concerns are more similar to those of Western sociologists than those of other Asian sociologists. Japan is a highly industrialized society, and the problems in the society may be like those we observe in other developed countries to some extent. Therefore, it may be said that the academic interests that Japanese sociologists have would not be much different from the interests of Western sociologists. However, it seems to be irrelevant to emphasize it too much. For it must be noted that Japanese sociologists have pursued some unique problems derived from the socio-cultural elements of the Japanese society, such as "familism oriented business management."[4]

Many of the Asian sociologists seem to have been trained in the Western countries, mainly in the United States. This may be particularly so among the leading sociologists in academic circles, though a great majority of sociologists in some countries might be domestic products. Their main role is seemingly to understand Western sociology and to transmit it to their students. Further, some of them might "feel closer to colleagues in the United States than anywhere else," as said by an Asian social scientist.[5]

All Asian countries, except Japan, are poor and have so many serious problems such as over-population, unemployment, squatters, low industrial productivity, administrative inefficiency including corruption, wide income gap between social classes, traditional values to impede the introduction of new scientific and technological devices, etc. Accordingly, one of the strongest national concerns is how to bring about development.

Sociologists are naturally involved in developmental issues and try to make an academic contribution to resolving them. While they study the developmental problems in their own country, they have recognized that indigenous socio-cultural elements are very much different from those of the developed countries, and that, therefore, sociological theories and methods developed in the Western countries, mainly in the United States, are not necessarily applicable to their own societies.

It is widely accepted as a principle that theories of sociology as a science are and should be universal, and that, because of this very nature, sociology is different from history which is concerned with individual unique events. But the existing sociological theories produced so far in the advanced countries do not appear to be as universal as desired. Theories of the natural sciences can be universally applied. Even among social sciences, some disciplines have many theories which are universally applicable, while other disciplines' theories are not as generally relevant. For example, theories of economics which assume *homo economicus* may be applied in most highly modernized urban societies.

We are not going to argue about the question of long standing, that is, "Is sociology a natural science?" But it must be admitted that the sociological theories, so to speak, developed in the Western societies, have considerable limitations in their applicability to the developing societies, the historical and cultural backgrounds of which are very much different from those of the former.

For example, the social stratification system in a society is definitely an important matter for understanding social structure and its change. Suppose we know the social stratification system of American society. But we would not be able to understand the social stratification system of any Asian society, if we do not refer to its historical context, but only rely on the American class concepts. Likewise, the Indian Community structure could not be understood without knowledge of caste; the stratification system of the traditional Chinese society without knowing about the national examination system for literati-officials and gentry; the Japanese social structure without the knowledge of the relationship between lord and his subordinate or between *oyakata*(boss) and *kokata*(follower) in which ideas of *on*(favor) and *giri*(obligation) are fundamental, and the structure of the Korean rural villages with ignorance of the Korean traditional status system and coherent *yangban*(noble class) kinship solidarity.

It may be argued that these are not theories but concepts or facts. But no theory can be formulated apart from concepts and facts. And the limitation of the applicability of Western sociological theories to the Asian societies seems to be largely derived from the confusion of sociological concepts and the irrelevance of Western sociological concepts to the Asian countries.

The second problem that the Western-oriented Asian sociologists might often encounter when they conduct empirical research in their own society is the limitation in applying sociological methods developed in Western countries to their societies. One of the causes for the problem obviously comes from the limitation of applicability of Western sociological theories and concepts we just discussed. Another cause comes from the fact that some aspects of research methods or techniques which the Western sociologists have emphasized may be somewhat irrelevant to the Asian social context. Many American sociologists seem to have employed the statistical approach on the basis of scientific social research methods rather than the qualitative one, though a new trend to give more weight to the latter than before has arisen recently.

The statistical approach which usually uses questionaires or interview techniques can be successfully carried out on the assumption that the respondents can understand what is asked, and that free conversation between the interviewers and the interviewees is satisfactorily guaranteed or private matters in the responses are put in secret. But these asumptions may not be relevant in many developing countries, because of problems such as high illiteracy rates, authoritarian human relationships, or political unrest. Therefore, the qualitative approach through non-direct interviews, participant observation, or case studies may bring more fruitful results than the quantitative one in some occasions. But these approaches may not be appreciated much by Western-oriented researchers. And also over-reliance on Western sociology may sometimes impede to develope more useful measurements and other methodological devices otherwise.

The third problem is that what the Western sociologists are interested in are not necessarily important to the Asian sociologists.

For example, Western sociologists might be concerned with problems arising in the postindustrial age, while Asian sociologists are concerned with how to industrialize their countries. Even if both are interested in common subject matters, the aspects which one looks at sometimes are likely to be different from aspects the other looks at.

If one school is dominant in a certain academic circle, then everybody may be inclined to conform to that school, and in fact opposite or antagonistic views to it may be discouraged, though criticism or generosity to opposite views is accepted as an academic principle on the surface. Academicians are required to be objective and free from values in judgement, but nobody is perfect. When the effects of economic assistance are studied, a scholar from the country which provides the economic assistance may be apt to exaggerate the amount of assistance, ignoring that much of it was spent paying those dispatched from the government which provides the assistance, while a scholar in the country which received it may be biased to exaggerate great effects with tiny assistance.

The Asian sociologists have had opportunities to attend international conferences for discussing academic as well as practical problems in the Asian region. Many of them, however, are organized and also financed by Westerners or international organizations in which Westerners are dominant. Accordingly, major themes, directions of discussions, and conclusions or recommendations in the conferences are inclined to be flavored by values or ideas which are popular in Western societies and to neglect urgent needs in the Asian countries.

The Necessity of Forum for Asian Sociologists

What we aimed at in the previous discussion is not solely to point to the disadvantages that Asian sociologists might have under the overinfluence of Western sociology, much less to deny the necessity for them to study it. On the contrary, it is desirable for them to know more about Western sociology. What we wanted to suggest in the discussion is the necessity of establishing an autonomous forum for Asian sociologists in order to enable them to discuss relevant sociological problems which they feel urgent and significant, and to exchange their ideas for sociological as well as national development in each of the Asian countries.

There are many urgent topics that can be dealt with at the forum: How can economic as well as social development be accomplished? What are the indigenous elements impeding development? Is it possible and desirable for the Asian countries to modernize their countries in the same way as the Western countries did? What are serious problems arising in the process of modernization of the Asian countries? To what extent should the traditional elements be preserved, and in what way? What would be the role of Asian sociologists in meeting national needs and attaining goals such as the peace of the world and the welfare of mankind, and how should their cooperative activities be organized? These are examples of possible major topics to be discussed in the forum.

Among the social sciences, sociology is one of the disciplines that urgently needs an international forum in Asia. We say this based on the strong confidence that sociologist would be able to make an indispensable and very valuable contribution to national development. It seems generally believed that both technology and economics are the most essential fields for national development, and it may be true to some degree if the material aspects of national development are stressed.

Even for the sake of economic development, however, it would not be reasonable to emphasize the importance of those two fields too much. For, the actual economic behavior of human beings is not the behavior of *homo economicus*, but the bahavior of real persons who are living with others, giving emotional reactions to stimulus, and making value judgements in the social situations they are involved in. If a society has social values to hinder industrious efforts for economic betterment, or it has social structual characteristics by which proper rewards are not given to the majority of the participants in productive activities, then technological and economic innovation can be hardly achieved. That is why many scholars and experts who are concerned with progress have emphasized the importance of socio-cultural elements for economic development.

K. Marx, who recognized the importance of the economic factor in analyzing social structure, stated that social change would be caused by class struggle. What we are concerned with is not whether his theory is valid or not, but whether or not class struggle is primarily a sociological subject. Max Weber noted the relationship between the spirit of capitalism and the Protestant ethic. This theory was not formulated on the basis of an economic frame of reference alone. Everett E. Hagen, an economist who once served in one of the Asian countries as an economic advisor, suggested the psycho-analytical factor as one of the important factors for economic growth.[6] And an American historian who is very familiar with Japanese culture and society noted that the successful accomplishment of modernization by Japanese might have been caused by her feudalistic experience, in contrast to Chinese historical characteristics.[7]

Now, we observe that economic development is rapidly taking place in some Asian countries, while it is not going as fast in other countries. Is it merely because there were outstanding economists and effective economic policies of the governments in the former, while not in the latter? One economist, who tried to find the main causal factors for the rapid economic growth in South Korea, emphasized that "human capital formation and socio-cultural-institutional changes are more crucial in determining the speed of industrialization than physical capital accumulation."[8]

As Wilbert E. Moore[9] said, many factors are involved in the modernization or industrialization of a nation. It seems to the writer that socio-cultural factors, particularly the characteristics of social structure and social values of the society, as Max Weber noted, are extremely important. When socio-cultural conditions have matured for modernization, then appropriate government policies for economic development may well be effectively carried out.

Economic policies may produce many non-economic effects in the process of their implementation or after. Some effects appear immediately, and some others far later. Some may be anticipated, and some others not. Some may be favorable to the following economic situation, but some others may be unfavorable. Under these circumstances, if sociological considerations are properly involved in economic policy making, then many undesirable side effects can be avoided or controlled in advance.

Economic development plans should not be limited to the national level. They must also take into account the economic situations of large or small business firms as well as individual homes both in rural and urban communities. Even on the level of the national economy, many socio-cultural factors are involved, but they may be more so on the level of business management, and still far more so on the level of home economy, particularly in rural communities in which traditional elements are deeply rooted.

So far we have said that sociology can make very important contributions to economic development. Moreover, national development is not limited to economic development, but includes social development as well. Some may argue that economic development should go together with social development at the same time, but some others may maintain that the former should have higher priority than the latter.

Western scholars often advise us not to copy Western-type modernization, because it has resulted in many undesirable effects which destroy human nature and the environment. If it is the case, then, is it possible for the backward countries to accomplish modernization to secure not only the material quality but also the non-material quality of human life? These questions would surely be better answered by cooperative efforts of scholars in various disciplines, in which the active participation of sociologists must be essential.

First, sociology is the basic science studying social phenomena. Without sociological knowledge, no one may be able to understand the nature of society in a proper way. Second, social change has been one of the most important subject areas of sociology since its birth. Therefore, sociology is in a better position to provide useful knowledge for bringing dovelopment than other social sciences. Third, sociology has developed methods, techniques, and tools for empirical research concerning social phenomena. Fourth, sociology is equally concerned with formal as well as informal, rational as well as irrational, and latent as well as manifest aspects of human behavior.[10] Fifth, sociology has close relationships both with anthropology and psychology, which are also essential for understanding human behavior.

In addition to these advantages, sociology pays keen attention to every sector of society. In the past when a great majority of people were alienated from power and wealth, political and economic events centering on a few people in political or economic power were distinct and important. At that time it was easy to mobilize, to manipulate, and even to oppress the majority of people. Now, that time is gone, and a new age of welfare state has been coming, in which everybody has basically equal rights, and everybody has to participate willingly in development programs for his own betterment. Then, sociology, which pays attention not only to those in power but to the poor, the young, and women at the grass roots of society, can give a clearer picture of a society than any other social sciences. This is another advantage of sociology by which it can give very useful advice for the development of the Asian countries where so many poor and powerless people are living.

Establishment of Forum for Asian Sociologists

Asian countries are making strenuous efforts for national development, and gradually playing important roles on the stage of world history, where the Western powers dominated during the past several centuries. In this process, it is evident that Asian sociologists are required to make great contributions through promoting cooperative activities.

In this connection, it should be noted that the Asian Regional Conference of Sociology in 1973, which was organized by the Japanese Sociological Society, has given the momentum for stimulating the cooperative development of sociology in Asia. It is also great encouragement to see that the International Sociological Society paid attention to the previous Asian Regional Conference of Sociology, and has accepted the proposal of the Japanese Sociological Society to establish special sessions in the present World Congress of Sociology on the one hand, and that Unesco in Paris has supported the cooperative activities of the Asian sociologists on the other.

In spite of these favorable trends, the path on which the Asian sociologists have to march together is neither flat nor wide. One of the difficulties in promoting the cooperation among them is obviously a lack of funds. No international organization can justify providing a financial support to a particular group of one discipline in one region, even though it recognizes the great benefits sociology would bring. The governments of the Asian countries, like those of the advanced countries, can hardly provide any academic association with financial assistance, unless it has a program which is directly connected with national interests. And non-governmental agencies, which have the capacity to give financial aid to international academic activities, are rare in the Asian countries. Of course, it is desirable for sociological associations in each country to make financial contributions for international cooperation among Asian sociologists, but it is obviously unrealistic to expect it of many sociological associations in Asia.

Another problem may be difficulties in communication between sociological associations in the Asian region. The communication difficulty seems to be partly caused by the fact that sociological associations in some countries may not function properly.

Looking at these unfavorable conditions, it may be still too early to establish an international organization such as an Asian Sociological Association which we have particularly desired since the Asian Regional Conference in 1973. Some different approaches, however, can be carried out for the cooperative activities of Asian sociologists, though some of them have been already put in practice to some extent.

The first suggestion is to make our foothold in ISA stronger and to further develop programs for Asian sociologists within the World Congress of Sociology. At the same time, it is desirable that we try continuously to seek an opportunity to hold a second Asian Regional Conference of Sociology sometime in the near future.

The second is to publish a bibliography of sociological books, articles, and other materials produced in Asia. In addition to this, we have to recommend strongly the publishing of a sociological journal.

The third is that the sociologists in each country in Asia actively participate in local social science research councils or similar organizations which are affiliated with the Asian Association of Social Science Research Councils, through which the Asian sociologists can promote mutual understanding and cooperation with the academicians in other fields of social sciences within their own countries, and with sociologists in other Asian countries as well.

The final suggestion is that sociological associations in each nation in Asia should develop programs to invite Asian sociologists either to their annual conferences or to their occasional meetings. And also it is hoped that departments of sociology or sociological research institutes make more opportunities to have colloquiums with guest sociologists from other parts of Asia.

[NOTES]

1) The proceedings of this symposium were published in a book form. See T. Fukutake and K. Morinaga (ed.), *Sociology and Social Development in Asia*, (Tokyo: University of Tokyo Press, 1974).
2) The general background of the Asian Association of Social Science Research Councils is indicated in "Asian Social Scientist," *Newsletter* No. 1, The Secretariat Office of AASSREC, c/o Korean National Commission for Unesco, Seoul, 1977.
3) See "Social Sciences in Asia, I," SS/Ch/32, *Unesco*, the Unesco Press, 1976.
4) See Shogo Koyano, "Trends in Japanese Sociological Studies with Particular Reference to the Present State of Affairs," in *Sociology and Social Development in Asia*, op. cit., pp. 343-365.
5) L.A. Sherwani, "Pakistan," in *Social Sciences in Asia*, I, op. cit., p. 47.
6) Everett E. Hagen, *On the Theory of Social Change*, (Homewood, Ill.: the Darsey Press, Inc., 1962).
7) Edwin O. Reischauer, "Modernization in Nineteenth Century China and Japan," *Japan-America Forum*, Vol. 9, No. 11, 1963.
8) Yong-il Lim, *Sources of Economic Growth in Korea*, Seminar Series SS-77-10, Korea International Economic Institute, Seoul, 1977, p. 31.
9) Wilbert E. Moore, *Social Change*, (New Jersey: Prentice-Hall, 1963).
10) T. Parsons and B. Barber, "Sociology, 1941~46," *American Journal of Sociology*, Vol. 53, 1948, pp. 245ff.

Problems and Needs of Communication Education in Asia

Some Definitions

Before discussing problems and needs of communication education in Asia, it seems necessary to clarify the meaning of communication itself. The meaning of communication is very broad, so is its education. The words "journalism," "communication" and "mass communication" are used more or less interchangeably. I notice the names of the organizations representing this conference are varied: institute(or department/school) of mass communication, journalism, communication, communication arts, agricultural communication, communication and journalism, and so on. Judging from these, I think the word "communication" here seems to be an embracing term that represents the various aspects of the communication field. Therefore, my discussion on communication education will take account in relatively great measure under the general term of communication.

Also the word "education" has more than one meaning. For example, a training of professional personnel on the job might differ from a formal education in college and university. The term "communication education" here might denote both teaching in college and training of professionals. However, I would restrict my discussion only to the formal education in college and university in Asia because I work in an university. I hope other members of this panel would cover the professional training.

---

* Presented at the Conference of Communication Research Organizations in Asia and North America which was held at East-West Center in 1974.

Having clarified some of the terms, I would like to point out some problems and needs of communication education in Asia. In so doing, let me apply Lasswell's formula to communication education with a slight modification as follows: (1) *Who*(institutes and teachers) teach (2) *What* (content) (3) to *Whom* (students) (4) through *Which methods* (5) with *What effect* (evaluation). And let us look at the problems and needs according to each of these elements in communication education.

Problems and Needs on "Who" (Educators)

1. Lack of Philosophy of Communication Education

One of the big problems of communication education in Asian countries may be the lack of its philosophy in general. Without recognizing the real needs and aims of communication education in Asia, many educational institutes of communication have been set up merely because European countries and the United States have such institutes. Even some institutes in Asian countries have copied down the aims and purposes of communication education in Western countries. These are sorts of non-sense.

As J. Galen Saylor and William Alexander pointed out, "The school is an agency established by a social group to serve a group purpose. The society has certain ends-in-view for the development of the individual. These ends-in-view become the basic factor in the determination of the aims of education. The whole structure and character of the educational program of the school will be determined by the dominant social forces at work in a society at any given time" [1] It is important to keep in mind that communication education in Asia should be related to national priorities and regional needs and should have some relevance to the societies in the region. That is, the communication education in Asian countries should adequately meet existing national needs. Therefore, communication educators in Asian countries should establish their own philosophy and aims of communication education to fully meet their national and or regional needs such as developmental tasks.

2. Short of Competent Teachers

The next problem of communication education faced by most of the Asian countries is the shortage of competent teachers and trainers for various courses and programs in teaching of communication. There is also shortage of communication teachers in number. I do not have any accurate statistics on the qualification and number of teachers in whole Asia. But in Korea, for example, there are about 1,000 communication major students in college. There is, however, only 37 professors. The ratio between the students and professors is 34 to 1. Among 37 professors, doctoral degree holders are 9, master degree holders are 10, and the rest of them are B.A. holders. These mean that there should be more qualified teachers.

There are needs to improve and update professional competence and skills of teaching of the teachers of communication. While some people argue that teaching skills cannot be taught but merely acquired by trial and error, it seems strange that society accepts unquestioningly the need for training school-teachers but not higher academics. I strongly feel that Asian communication education would be improved by giving new instructors even short courses in teaching techniques. The AMIC's refresher course held in Singapore last year proved that some things can be taught, and therefore, I hope such a course would be continued.

I know there are more problems and needs than those I just suggested above. But I think the two problems and the consequent needs are most urgent to be solved and to be met in the near future so far as the "Who" element of communication education is concerned.

Problems and Needs "What" (Content)

1. Inadequacy of Communication Curricula

Teaching content or curriculum should reflect the aims of a teaching program. In general, however, the lack of philosophy and aims of communication education in many Asian countries has made the educators unable to develop adequate curricula which could meet Asian societies' needs. Therefore, there is a need for development of suitable academic curricula and training program relevant to the national and regional situation in Asian countries.

There is a tendency for Asian communication educators, especially those who have been trained in the Western countries, to introduce courses and programs they have got from the Western countries without any modification and criticism into their curricula. In other words, they include some courses to their own curricula merely because they took them when they studied in the United States, England or Germany and so on. If the communication education in Asia were to fully meet the society's needs, such a blind follow of Western academic curricula should be ceased and, instead, the communication educators and administrators should work together to develop suitable academic curricula relevant to Asian situations.

2. Curricula Unbalance

It is hard to set up the proportion between background courses and proportional courses, or depending upon the character of an institution and the total length of the program, the proportion could be varied. However, there is no doubt that there should be a desired balance between a liberal and professional education, not unblanced curricula.

From my random observations, I noticed that quite a few institutions in Asian countries have unbalanced curricula without any pre-set proportion of courses. They tend to merely add or drop some courses regardless keeping in mind the curricula balance.

Depending upon the character of an institution and the degree program, the proportion of courses might be varied. Also, some contemporary professors of communication argue that we should perceive training in communication not as an artistic artifact, but rather as a science. By the rule of thumb, however, the proportion between background courses, theoretical courses and practical courses should be 30, 40 and 30 per cent in an undergraduate program. Besides, the prospective students should be introduced to research methods, and to the scope and area of communication research.

Having discussed the problems and needs on "What" (content) element, let's move to the next element, that is, "To Whom" (students).

Problems and Needs on "To Whom" (Students)

As AMIC's Regional Conference held in Seoul, Korea, in 1972 suggested, communication schools and departments in Asian countries should develop entrance requirements, screening tests and exploratory introductory courses which will aid in determining the aptitudes and abilities of prospective students. By doingso, the consumers of communication education could be identified and thus the purpose of communication education can be best defined to be fulfilled.

There is few of educational research on communication, specially on communication students. Students are a determinant of the curriculum of communication. An adequate, comprehensive curriculum for communication students can be planned only by taking fully into account of students. Therefore, there should be many researches on students of communication.

Problems and Needs on "Teaching Methods"

1. Too Much Lectures

Of course, depending upon the nature and level (basic, intermediate and advanced) of courses, the right type of teaching methods and techniques might be varied. For example, "lecture" type of method will be better than "seminar" for a basic level course in the theoretical field. In general, however, there seem to be too much lectures in class-room of Asian countries. Professors feed up students with heavy factual knowledge through one-way type of the communicative teaching methods while the students are busy in writing down whatever the professors speak out. This sort of the traditional method of teaching should be changed.

2. Lack of Textbooks and Reading Material

I just blamed the "lecture" type of teaching method. But I do use such a method even in advanced graduate courses. I found students complaining that they could not prepare seminar papers because necessary reading materials are not available. Especially, there are lack of reading materials which are of direct relevance to Asian conditions. Therefore, I feel that perhaps the primary need is to keep textbooks and other necessary reading material for students as well as for teachers, insofar as communication teaching in Asia is concerned. I know AMIC is putting its efforts to the solution of this problem now. We should support AMIC for this mission.

3. Needs for Equipment, Training Aides and Facilities

There are also needs for necessary support in such things as equipment, training aides, library facilities, etc. in order to upgrade communication education in Asia. To improve teaching standard there should be not only a dearth of well qualified personnel but also of resources. Adequate teaching aids and laboratory equipment should be procured to keep abreast of modern techniques of communication. To meet these needs of resource-support Asian governments, media organizations and philanthropic bodies should be approached to actively finance teaching in communication.

Problems and Needs on " Effects" (Evaluation)

Finally let us look at the problems and needs on "Effects" or evaluation in brief. There always remains much needed feedback to educators or teachers as an essential component of teaching itself. Communication teachers in Asia should develop evaluation techniques to analyze their own teaching programs and to evaluate students which will aid in reorientating and adjusting their teaching program and methods. Teaching could not be improved unless there are enough feedback and accurate evaluation of teaching program, teaching method and students themselves.

Conclusion

Asian communication educators have faced many problems to solve. Merely identifying the problems and needs just like I do here is one thing and solving them is another. It is said that "talking is easy and doing is difficult." Therefore, the most fundamental problems are who will solve these problems in what way.

[NOTES]

1) *Curriculum Planning*, (New York, Holt: Rinehart and Winston, 1966), p. 84.

Index

A

Academic freedom 261, 266, 289
Academic research 266
Achievement...........................113
Achievement-oriented action 77
Administrative
    ∼control 129
    ∼democracy 102
    ∼efficiency..........................110
Affective-neutrality 77, 112
Affective orientation 19
Affectivity 112
Agricultural Bank.....................182
Agricultural Cooperative Union
    ....188, 233-235
Agricultural management 189
Agricultural mechanization..240-241
Agricultural statistics................290
Agricultural technology 231
Agriculture Cooperation Association
   152
Agriculture Cooperative ...138, 155,
    188, 191, 198, 248, 251
    ∼agency 251
    ∼project 149
Agriculture extension station......135
Ajŏn 143
Allexander, William 318
Allied Forces (Powers) 63, 96
AMIC......................319, 321-322
Anarchism 62

Ancestor-centered attitude 76
Ancestor worship 11, 35, 38, 40,
    59, 74, 122, 138
    ∼ceremoney 39, 142, 174, 179,
    184, 231, 250, 285
Animism 13
Annexation 6, 33, 45-46,
    49-50, 56, 61
Anti-communism 14, 77-78
Anti-communist attitude 66, 78-
    97, 105
Anti-communist sentiment......84-85
Anti-democratic 96
Anti-Japanese (anti-Japanism)
    ....60, 64, 77-78, 84-85, 104
Aoi, K................................28, 93
April Uprising 9, 17, 72, 101,
    151, 211, 264
Aristocrat 138
Ascription 113, 203
Asian Association of Social
    Science Research Council
    (AASSREC) 304, 315-316
Asian Sociological Association
    ....296-298, 300-301, 315
Asian Sociologist...295, 296, 298-301
    303, 305, 309-310;
    see Sociologist in Asia
Aspiration for
    ∼better life 108, 112
    ∼consumption,...................15, 17
    ∼for education 79-80;

325

see educational aspiration
Assemblyman 169
Association of Independence 8;
　see Independence Association
Auh, Chun-Suk 92-93
Austerity 72
Autocracy................................44
　Goodwilled~........................202
Axis countries 60, 63

B

Ban chief 150
Barber, B. 316
Barringer, Herbert R. 115, 218
Biernatzki, William E.,.............115
Boy preference attitude 109
Braibanti, Ralph 113, 192
Brandt, Vincent S.R. 257
Brown, Arthur J. 90
Brunner, E. S. de, ...53, 91, 93, 191
Buddhism 13, 41, 87, 107
Buddhist monestery 185
Burag 137
Bureaucracy 131
Bureaucratic
　~hierarchy 122
　~organization 110, 112
Byŏngja Korea-China War 34

C

Capitalism 45, 62
Capitalistic country
　........................3, 15, 29, 39, 175
Catalyst 60
Census 134
Centralized
　~government 34

~political system 33
Centre for East Asian
　Culture Study 303
Charejesa 120
Chemical industry 48, 49, 55
Chief of ri 199;
　see ri chief
Chinese naturalism 39
Choe, Je-wu 42
Choe, Yong-ho 28
Chŏnmin ...5, 7, 34, 130-132, 143-144
Chong, Hong-jin 191
Christian church 156
　~missionary 59-60
Christianity......12, 41, 59, 87, 93, 107
Chu Hsi..............................38, 86
Chung, Bom-mo 115
Chung, Hyok 205
Class Struggle 63
Colonial
　~control 96, 104
　~domination 46, 96
　~governing force 67
　~governing system 59
　~rule 29, 220, 224-225
　~ruler 56
Committee of Asian Sociologists
　.......................................301
Commoner 6, 28, 34, 39-41, 120,
　　　　　　　　　143, 175-176,
　　　　　　　　　186, 193, 198
Communal tie 39
Communication 124
　~education 317-320, 322
　~research 321
　~system 82, 163

~teaching 322
Communism 62, 97
Communist 14, 62-63, 70, 102
　　　　　　　　　105, 108, 111-112
~control 76
~guerrilla 69
~ideology 62-63
~leadership 78
~rule 203
~system 67
Community development ...13, 152,
　　　　　　　　　　　181, 219-222,
　　　　　　　　　　　232-233, 251, 257
~movement 236
~organization 224, 232-333
~orientation........................160
~solidarity 188
Competing reference 104
Compulsory education ..110-111, 239
Compulsory educational system
　　　　..........................75, 98, 105, 185
Comte, A. 271
Concentration of population ...244;
　　see population
Conceptual scheme 298
Conceptualization 280
Concubine 35-36, 110, 141, 143
Confucian 60, 131, 148, 174,
　　　　　　　　　　　184-185, 222
~doctrine 37
~ethic 148, 224
~ideology 40
~norm 37
~scripture 38
~value 39, 60
Confucianism 5, 11-13, 38, 40, 59,
　　　　　　　　　　86, 111, 174, 183-184,
　　　　　　　　　　　195, 198, 223, 232
Conjugal system 76
Consanguineous association
　　　　..........122-123, 125, 128, 141, 142
Consanguineous group 119, 121,
　　　　　　　123-128,130-132,137-143,145,
　　　　　　　148, 157-158, 160, 166, 173, 203
Consanguineous kin group
　　　　..............................139, 140, 154
Consanguineous union...............179
Consanguinity 158, 160
Constructing questionnaire 271
Content analysis 271
Cooperative union 187
~movement 181
Council of East Asian Study ...273
Counseling..............................265
Cultural
~anthropology.....................271
~confusion 202
~organization........................61
~policy 62

D

Daedong-hoe 153
Daibon-gyo 287
Data processing 272, 280
Debt 53-54, 223, 225
Decentralizaton of power 22
Democracy 64, 78-79, 81, 98
Democratic ideal 59
Democratic party.........151, 181, 221
Democratic political system 167
Democratization 4, 44, 68, 101
Development Committee 248

Diffuseness 113
Discontment of the middle class ..100
Discrimination 110, 129-130,
　　　　　　　　　　　　　145, 177
Disorganization 63-64
Diversification 105
Dognibhyŏb-hoe 8, 114, 176
Dognib Sinmun 15, 43, 91, 204
Donga-ilbo 51
Donghag-dang 8, 41-43, 175
Don't know answer............287, 291
Dore, R.P. 257
Dual system 110
Dure 250
Dysfunction................81, 110, 168

[E]

East Learning 41, 175
　　～Party 8
Economic heterogeneity 239, 241
Economic stagnation...............5, 82
Economic status 139-140, 146
Educational
　　～aspiration..................16-17, 49
　　～opportunity 212
　　～system 80-81
Egalitarian 67
Electric power station 51
Electrical industry 48, 55
Elite 100
Empirical field research............271
Empirical reference.................283
Empirical research 313
Enterepreneur 57-58, 70-71,
　　　　　　　　　　　103-104, 189, 191
Exchange program 262

Experimental research 265
Exploitation 40, 42, 45, 50-51,
　　　　　　　　　　　68, 83, 85, 174
　　　　　　　　　　　224-226, 232

[F]

Faction 64-65
Factional conflict (struggle, strife)
　　......................6, 23, 37, 82, 169
Factionalism 37
Familism 13, 19, 109, 306
Family
　　～centered 231
　　～lineage 108, 110
　　～orientation 89, 166
　　～planning..................76, 93, 238
　　～solidarity 109
　　～structure.......................75, 77
　　～system 74, 261
Farm laborer.....................147, 150
Favoritism 81
Festinger, L. 91
Feudalistic...............................3
　　～lord 33, 173
Field research 291
Filial piety 11, 38, 74
Fire-field cultivation 53
Five Year Economic
　　Development Plan 73, 111
4-H Club 154-155, 196, 220
Free enterprise system ...44, 83, 103
Fukutake, T. 316
Functional organization 73
Funeral ceremony 145, 160, 196
Future-life orientation 79
Future-oriented attitude 76

G

Gab-o Reform 45, 83
Gemeinshaft 219
Genealogical
　~book 144
　~order 141
　~record 122
Genealogy 109
Generation 120-123, 125,
　　　　　　　　　　128, 139, 145
Geomancy 39
Geomantic belief 146
Gijesa 120
Gobineau, J.A. de, ...90
Grajdenzev, Andrew J. 90, 114
Guerrillas 65, 69
　~force 61
Guttman scaling 169, 291
Gwagŏ 37
Gye 108, 154-155, 188, 224, 233

H

Hagen, Everett E. 27, 311, 316
Hamhŭng 51
Hangŭl 59, 223
Hanmun..................................223
Harvard-Yenchin Institute 273
Hatata, T. 191
Herb medicine market 70
Hill, Reuben 119
Himeno, Minoru 91, 113
Homo ecomicus 95, 307, 310
Hoselitz, Bert F. 27, 95, 112, 192
Hyangban 5, 7-8, 34-35, 43,
　　　　　　　　67, 82, 86, 132, 143
Hyang-gyo 60, 156, 174, 185
Hyangyag........................13, 220

I

Illiteracy 16, 83, 190, 199,
　　　　　　　　　　226, 291, 308
Illiterate.....................186, 232, 255
Imjin Korea-Japan war 34
Im, Luke Jin-Chang 115
Imperialism 62
　Japanese ~ 99
Independence Association
　...................43, 44, 59, 61, 114, 176
Independence Movement
　.....................9, 46, 62, 64, 70, 78
Independence Press
　.........15, 43, 44, 58, 61, 81, 91, 204;
　see Dognib Simmun
Industrialism..........................115
Industrialization
　...... 4, 13, 16, 18, 22-23, 24, 94-95,
　　　　　104, 112, 115, 175, 219, 229,
　　　　　　　237, 241, 244-246, 252
Inflation 101
Infrastructure 240-241
Inheritance 80
Institute of East Asian Study
　..273
Institutional
　~avenue 105
　~constraint..........................84
Intellectual...15, 21, 62, 68, 72, 78, 81,
　　　　　　83, 97, 99-100, 102-103,
　　　　　　110, 112, 177-178, 187
　　　　　　　238-239, 245, 274
　~conscience 296

Intelligentsia 115
Interest group 177, 181
Intermarriage 144
Internal social tension 112
Interview 286

J

Japanese colonialism 12, 175
Japanese imperialism 67, 83
Japanese Sociological Society
  .... 303-304, 314
Jesil 125-126, 138, 142, 167
Jiyŏg-sahoe gaebal 219
Jŏbju 8
Jŏn, Bong-jun 42
Jong-ga 142
Jonghoe 122-123, 140-141
Jongjung 123, 140-141
Josŏn-ilbo 51
Journalism 16, 17, 177
Journalist, ... 72, 84, 99, 100
Judicial system, ... 65
Jumag 138
Jung-in ... 5, 7, 8, 34, 37, 132, 143, 176

K

Keijo Imperial University 57
Kennan, George 29
Kim, Kyong-dong 115
Kim, Kyu-whan 27
Kim, Taik-Kyoo 133, 192
Kim, Yong-mo 28
Kinship
  ~group 20, 35, 193-194, 255
  ~organization 75, 98, 140
  ~solidarity 17

~status 143
~unity 38
Koh, Whang-gyŏng 171, 192
Kokata(follower) 307
König, Rene 119
Korea Culture Research Institute
  273
Korean Council for East
  Asian Study 267
Korean historiography 265
Korean Journal of Sociology
  269-270
Korean Research Center 267
Korean Sociological Association
  .... 269, 273, 275
Korean Sociological Research
  Association 270
Korean Sociological Review 270
Korean War 7, 8, 65, 70, 75-76,
              80, 97, 111, 145,
              182, 230, 262, 271
Koryo-dynasty 107
Koyano, Shogo 316

L

Labor dispute 56
Labor movement 56
Laborer 179
Landlord ..... 69, 147; see landowner
Landowner .. 46, 52, 57, 68-69, 79, 83,
            85, 86, 97, 100, 111, 129,
            140, 147-148, 175-178,
            193, 224
Land reform 68-69, 75, 77-78, 84-
            86, 97-98, 114, 125,
            147-148, 178, 214,

                                  226, 239, 264
~law 69
Land survey 45
Land Survey Project 6
Lasswell, H. 318
Leadership.........65, 97-98, 157-158,
                              160-161, 171
~structure 157
Lee, Gag-jong 93
Lee, Gi-baeg 92
Lee, Gwang-rin 93
Lee, Hyo-jae 115
Lee, Man-gap 26-28, 91, 93, 114-
                            115, 170-172, 191-
                            192, 203-204, 257
Lee, Sang Baeck 275
Leftist movement 166
Letwin, William 26
Liberal Party 98, 101, 150-151,
                            153, 156, 162-163
                            165, 181, 221
Liberalism 60, 103
Liberation.........70-71, 78-80, 83, 88,
                            96-97, 99, 106, 108,
                            111, 129, 173
Lim, Yong-il............................316
Lineage......127; see family lineage
Literati-official 38
Local
    ~assembly 132, 168-169, 181
    ~autonomy 167-168, 204
    ~congress 180
    ~council 200
    ~self-government 180
Lower class ...6, 10, 17, 20, 107, 131,
                            139, 144, 148, 166

Lowest class 143
Lyu, Hyeog-in 114

M

Machine industry 55
Manager of mill 149
Manufacturing company 54
    ~factory 48
    ~industry 57
Market 24-25, 70, 94, 164-165,
                            168, 181, 191, 194-195,
                            198, 232, 235, 240
Mars, Z. 257
Marx, K. 311
Marxian theory 62
Marxist-oriented 262
Mass communication ..16, 81, 88, 227
                            -228, 242, 273,
                            276-277, 317
Mass media..............................76
Mass migration ..205; see migration
Mass society 274
Masuda, K. 28, 93
Material comfort 87
Materialism 111
Maŭl 137, 145
Merton, Robert K. 91, 115
Metal working industry 55
Methodology 218, 277
Middle class...8-10, 12, 16-17, 19-23,
                            26, 66, 71-72, 81-84,
                            86, 88, 90, 97, 99-100,
                            102, 115, 203, 238
    Discontent of ~......................71
    Frustration of~......................71
    ~mentality 72, 99

Migration......206-208, 210-213, 215-218, 229-230, 237-238
Military
　~government 73, 97, 101
　~occupation 15
　~organization 100, 104
　~related industry 58
　~revolution 221
　~revolutionary committee 101
　~service 72, 99
　~treat 78
Min, Anselm K. 115
Ministry of Education 100
Miracle of the Han River 73
Mitsubishi 51
Mobility ...4-5, 8-9, 12, 66, 70, 83, 274
　Downward vertical~ 96
　Geographical~ 66
　Social~ 66, 303
　Upward~ 66, 70
Modern capitalist system 63
Modern school system...............175
Modernization 2-4, 11, 13, 15-16, 18, 21-26, 28-29, 31, 37, 39, 44, 50, 52, 68, 73-74, 77, 79, 81-82, 86-91, 98, 113, 115, 140, 173, 176-177, 179, 183-194, 186
Moore, Wilbert E. 4, 26, 28, 95, 113-114, 192, 316
Morinaga, K. 316
Motivational factor 212
Munjung.........123-124, 127, 140-141
Mutual
　~assistance.....................13, 154
~labor exchange..................250
~security 147
Myojig 142

N

National Assembly......131, 162, 165, 167, 169, 180, 202
National character 21, 87
National consciousness...............61
National construction project......182
National construction work 221
National democracy..................102
National Movement Headquater
　..221
National security 85
Nationalism...............13, 61, 77, 81, 84-85, 104, 156
Nationalist 63
Natural village..................137-138
Naturalism 39
Naturalistic idea.......................13
Necromancer 132
Necromancy 185
New Civil Law 75
Nuclearization.........................75

O

Office of Economic Coordinator
　(OEC)..............................220
Office of Rural Development
　..................................248, 251
Open-ended question 287
Opinion leader 163
Oriental Development Corporation
　..52
Out-migration 238-239, 244-245;

see migration
Over-population 237-238, 306;
    see population
Oyakata (boss) 307

P

Paige, Glenn D. 171
Parent-Teacher Association...80, 110
Parsons, T. 95, 112-113, 316
Particularism............19, 77, 109, 113
Particularistic orientation............19
Patriarchal control..........19, 177, 193
Patriarchal system 74-75
Patriarchy 75
Pattern variable.........................95
Pauperization 179
Peddler 150
Political
    ～confusion 102
    ～consciousness......................180
    ～instability 238, 245
    ～power 157
    ～stability...22-23, 84, 101-102, 238
Politics 91, 100, 134, 149-150,
                154-156, 163-164, 170
                179-181, 200, 274
    Local～ 156, 169
    Rural～ 100
    Village～ 149-150, 155,
                                158, 171
Population ...10, 31, 34, 41, 46, 50, 53,
            57-59, 67, 74-75, 83, 96,
            135-136, 147, 183, 227,
            238-239, 241, 244, 247
    ～in Seoul 81
    ～of Korea...........................110

Concentration of～ 244
Farm～ 113
Rural～ 229, 246
Urban～ 50, 205
Population and Development
    Study Center........................273
Population increase 201
Population pressure 84, 112, 182
Potential conflict........................90
Power structure 200
Power struggle 169
Pragmatic attitude 106
Pre-modern
    ～age 119
    ～characteristic 126, 132
    ～Korea 39, 361
    ～stage 3
    ～value system 86
Prestige 13, 36, 41, 87, 105, 122,
            127, 129, 131, 140, 143-
            144, 149, 166, 284
Pretest 286
Primary industry 58
Principles of organization 73
Printing typography 31
Protest 152
Proto-capitalist country 42
Pro-Western attitude..................78
Public opinion survey...............291
Pulling factor 205-206, 208,
                                213-216
Pumasi 188, 250
Pungsu theory 122, 184, 185
Pushing factor............205-206, 208,
                                213-216

Q

Quasi-yangban ...6, 121, 139-140, 157
Questionaire 283, 288, 308
　　~construction 292
　　Mailing~ 292

R

Racial self-determination............61
Radio-amplification facility.........182
Railroad system 47
Rational thinking 59
Reading Academy 142
Reference 104
Reference group 85
Reischauer, Edwin O.
　　.........................33, 90, 191, 316
Relative deprivation 99
Religion 87, 107
Representative government system
　　..201
Reproducibility 169, 292
Republican Party.....................151
Research
　　~design..............................282
　　~method 321
Ri chief (head of ri).........136-137,
　　　　　150-151, 152-153, 157
　　　　　-158, 194, 196, 228
Role of women 75, 107-108
Rostow, W.W. 28
Ruling class 8, 35-36, 39,
　　　　　　　　　66, 123, 193
Rural community ...93, 98, 137, 138,
　　　　173, 180, 182-183, 227-228,
　　　　230, 233-234, 240, 250
Rural Sociological Review.........270
Russo-Japanese War 45

S

Saemaŭl
　　~leader 246, 248-249, 253-254
　　~Movement......221-222, 236, 239,
　　　　　　　241, 246-248, 251-254
　　~project.................247-248, 256
　　~Training Institute 253
　　~Undong 246
Sample survey 287
Sampling 209
　　~error 286
　　~procedure 218
　　~technique 281
Sangmin 5, 7, 13, 34, 120-121, 129
　　　　　-130, 132, 143, 144-145,
　　　　　149, 158, 160, 223-224
Sanjig 142
Sarang 163
Saŭm 177
Saylor, J. Galen 318
Schedule.........209, 282, 285, 287, 291
Scholar-official 119, 173
Scientific research method
　　.............................271, 275, 308
Seclusionism 42, 45
Secondary industry 58
Self-governing administration ...167
Seo, Jai-pil 43
Seongyo 41
Shamanism 13, 39
Shanty area 237
Sherwan, L.A. 316
Shikata, Hiroshi 27

Shin, Yong-ha 91, 93, 114
Shinto shrines...........................60
Sidae-ilbo.................................51
Sihyangje 120, 126
Simmel, G. 271, 278
Slack season 246
Social change 71, 83, 87, 107, 113
Social confusion 82, 97, 111, 244
Social contract 175
Social control 85
Social disintegration 17, 101, 185
Social disorder.................63, 75, 79
Social disturbance 97
Social identity 137
Social institution ...4, 18, 41, 64, 85,
 110-111, 112
Social integration 84, 177
Social justice 60, 71, 84, 100, 103
Social organization...4, 11, 13, 18, 65,
 68, 73-74, 77, 88-
 89, 93, 96, 109, 115,
 138, 149, 154-156,
 166, 181, 224
Social protest 90
Social research method 264, 271
Social science research 266, 273
Social security 188
Social status 4, 11, 16, 20, 41, 83,
 121-122, 128, 130,
 139, 143, 227
Social stratification 191, 303
∼system.............................307
Social structure......27, 29, 67-68, 70,
 83, 91, 93-94, 114-115,
 138-139, 144, 167, 171-
 172, 192, 204, 222, 256-
 257, 272-273, 281-282,
 284, 287, 289, 307, 311
Social unrest 16, 72, 80, 87-88,
 105, 111
Social value.....................86, 90, 94
Socialism 62
Socialist movement 62
Socialization process 74
Sociologist in Asia 314
Sociology in Korea 254, 278
Sociopolitical structure 134
Sŏdang 42
Sŏng-gog Foundation 269
Sŏ-ŏl 5, 7-8, 34-36, 67,
 82, 86, 132, 143
Sŏwŏn 127, 138, 142-143,
 156, 167, 174, 185
Specificity 113
Spencer, H. 271
Spengler, Joseph J. 113, 192
Squatter 306
Standardized interview 282
Status 85, 128, 139, 166, 184
∼discrimination 5
∼group 6, 34, 42, 132, 157, 166
∼inconsistency.....................102
∼orientation......................13, 87
∼oriented 12, 21, 73
∼seeking attitude 109
∼situation 71
∼symbol 87, 109
∼system.............5, 45, 175, 193,
 283, 307
Stratification 4, 7-8, 274, 285
Structural change 3-5, 26, 52,
 91-92, 111, 113

Structural feature 95-96
Syngman Rhee 9, 65, 71, 74, 81-
82, 101, 151, 195, 197,
199, 203, 264, 288
System of residence registration
....209

[T]

Tanaka, Tokutaro 27, 91, 170
Taoism 40-41
Taoistic
~belief 184
~theory...............................122
Technocrat 34, 143
Technology 231-232
Temperate zone 30-31
Tenancy........................53, 55, 147
~dispute 176
Tenant 53, 67-69, 113-114,
126, 132, 147, 150, 175,
178-179, 225-226
Tenant rent level 68
Territorial conflict 167
Tertiary industry 58
Toban..................5, 7-8, 34-35, 43,
67, 82, 86, 132, 143
Tokugawa dynastry 34
Tönnies, F. 271, 278
Totalitarian.............................78
~control 60
~system 97
Totalitarianism 14, 203
Toynbee, A.J. 30, 90, 112
Traditional
~institution 45, 77
~restraint 80

~status 80
~system 85, 140
~value............79, 89, 89, 110, 242
~value system....................236
Tradition-oriented 69
Tribute 120

[U]

Unemployment...................101, 306
Unidimensional 292
~continuum 169
Unification of Korea...................72
Universalism..................77, 95, 112
Upper class ...7, 9-10, 21-22, 36, 40,
71, 83, 90, 97, 99, 106,
111, 115, 138, 166, 203
Urban intelligentsia 61
Urbanization 6, 50-51, 175, 219,
237-238, 240-244, 252, 274
Urban-rural gap 222

[V]

Value 4, 11, 14, 16, 27, 60, 65-66,
74, 78, 81, 89, 91, 93, 106,
183, 192, 226, 231,
236, 241, 264, 272
Value-orientation 10, 109
Value system 161, 198, 206
Village broadcasting center 82
Village leadership 245
Voluntary organization 196

[W]

Wage 56, 112
Low~ 57
Weber, M. 311
Welfare 5, 47, 85, 103, 165,

                            222, 228, 310
Western academic society 297
Western capitalist power 83
Western civilization 8, 43, 59
                             79, 134
Western democracy.............9, 14, 60
Western Learning......................41
Western missionary 14, 59, 78
Western sociological theory
    (sociology).........271-272, 280, 283
                  -284, 307-308, 310
Western sociologist 306, 309
Western theory................ .264, 280
Western value..................76, 86-87
Westernization 3-4
Wilkinson, T.O. 205
Wito 125-127, 142, 148
Woman's participation 254

                    X

Xenophilia 15
Xenophobia 15

                    Y

Yangban.........4, 7, 10-13, 19, 21, 34-
            37, 39, 40-43, 46, 59-60,
            79, 85-86, 98, 106-108,
            111, 119-122, 129-132,
            138-141, 143-145, 148-
            149, 157-158, 160, 173-
            177, 179, 183, 193, 198,
            220-224, 250, 254-255
Yang, Jae-mo 93, 115
Yi-dynasty 5-8, 11-14, 20-21,
            28-29, 32, 34-35, 37-
            38, 43-44, 50, 58, 66,
            79, 81-84, 86-88, 106,
            122-123, 129, 143-
            144, 148, 173, 176,
            186, 195, 208, 210,
            220-224, 226, 229
Yi, Pyung Do 267
Yoo, Jai-chun 192
Yoon, Chŏn-joo 192
Yoon, Chong-ju 205
Youth Club 154-155
Yuji...............150, 153-154, 163, 167
Yusa 124, 126, 141

                    Z

Zensho, E. 132